INTERNATIONAL RELATIONS AND THE GREAT POWERS

General Editor: **John Gooch**
Professor of International History, University of Leeds

Titles in the International Relations and the Great Powers series:

Britain and the World in the Twentieth Century
by John W. Young

Japan and the World since 1868
by Michael A. Barnhart

Russia and the World 1917–1991
by Caroline Kennedy-Pipe

Forthcoming

France and the World in the Twentieth Century
by J.F.V. Keiger

The United States and the World in the Twentieth Century
by Michael Dunne

RUSSIA

AND THE WORLD
1917–1991

Caroline Kennedy-Pipe

Reader in Politics
University of Durham

A member of the Hodder Headline Group
LONDON • NEW YORK • SYDNEY • AUCKLAND

First published in Great Britain in 1998 by
Arnold, a member of the Hodder Headline Group,
338 Euston Road, London NW1 3BH

http://www.arnoldpublishers.com

Co-published in the United States of America by
Oxford University Press Inc.,
198 Madison Avenue, New York, NY 10016

© 1998 Caroline Kennedy-Pipe

The advice and information in this book are believed to be true and
accurate at the date of going to press, but neither the author nor the publisher
can accept any responsibility or liability for any errors or omissions.

British Library Cataloguing in Publication Data
A catalogue record for this book is available from the British Library

Library of Congress Cataloging-in-Publication Data
Kennedy-Pipe, Caroline, 1961–
    Russia and the world, 1917–1991/Caroline Kennedy-Pipe.
      p.   cm.—(International relations and the great powers)
    Includes bibliographical references and index.
    ISBN 0–340–65204–7 (hc.). — ISBN 0–340–65205–5 (pbk.)
    1. Soviet Union—Foreign relations. I. Title. II. Series.
DK266.45.K46 1998
327.47—dc21   98–19853
                                            CIP

ISBN 0 340 65205 5 (pb)
ISBN 0 340 65204 7 (hb)

1 2 3 4 5 6 7 8 9 10

Production Editor: Liz Gooster
Production Controller: Priya Gohil
Cover Design: Andy McColm

Typeset in 11/12½pt Bembo by Phoenix Photosetting, Chatham, Kent
Printed and bound in Great Britain by MPG Books, Bodmin, Cornwall

What do you think about this book? Or any other Arnold title?
Please send your comments to feedback.arnold@hodder.co.uk

Contents

List of Abbreviations

ABM	Anti-Ballistic Missile
CIA	Central Intelligence Agency
CC	Central Committee
CDSP	Current Digest of the Soviet Press
Comecon	Council of Economic Mutual Assistance (formed 1949)
Cominform	Communist Information Bureau (formed 1947)
Comintern	Communist International (1919–43)
CPSU	Communist Party of the Soviet Union (KPSS in Russian)
CSCE	Conference on Security and Co-operation in Europe
DRV	Democratic Republic of Vietnam
EAC	European Advisory Commission
EAM	Greek Communist Party
EDC	European Defence Community
ELF	Eritrean Liberation Front
EPLF	Eritrean People's Liberation Front
FNLA	National Front for the Liberation of Angola
FRG	Federal Republic of Germany (West Germany)
GDR	German Democratic Republic (East Germany: DDR)
ICBM	Intercontinental Ballistic Missile
IMF	International Monetary Fund
INF	Intermediate-range Nuclear Forces
IRBM	Intermediate-Range Ballistic Missile
KGB	Committee of State Security (after 1954)
MFN	Most Favoured Nation
MIRV	Multiple Independently Targeted Re-entry Vehicle
MPLA	Popular Movement for the Liberation of Angola
MRBM	Medium Range Ballistic Missile
NATO	North Atlantic Treaty Organisation (founded 1949)
NEP	New Economic Policy (1921–8)
NKVD	State Security Police (1934–54)
NPT	Non-Proliferation Treaty

OAU	Organisation of African Unity
PDPA	People's Democratic Party of Afghanistan
SALT	Strategic Arms Limitation Talks
SDI	Strategic Defence Initiative
SED	Socialist Unity Party (East Germany, formed 1949)
SLBM	Submarine Launched Ballistic Missile
SPD	Social Democratic Party (West Germany)
START	Strategic Arms Reduction Talks
TASS	Telegraph Agency of the Soviet Union
UNITA	National Union for the Total Independence of Angola
UNRRA	United Nations Relief and Rehabilitation Administration
USSR	Union of Soviet Socialist Republics
WEU	West European Union
WTO	Warsaw Treaty Organisation
YAR	Yemen Arab Republic

General editor's preface

Great Powers stand at the centre of modern international relations. The history of their inter-relationships once rested entirely on the formal record of diplomacy, and focused exclusively on the statesmen, diplomats and ambassadors who shaped and conducted foreign policy. Today, international historians, while still acknowledging the importance of diplomacy, cast their nets more widely. Power rests on many foundations, both tangible and intangible. National wealth is one ingredient of power, but so are ideology and national politics. Personalities have their influence on policies, so that there must always be a place for the individual in the history of international relations; but so, too, do the collective institutional forces of modern bureaucracies, the military and naval establishments, big business and industry. Together, in varying combinations at different times, these forces and factors find their expression in external policy.

The policies of Great Powers are shaped by their unique amalgams of internal ingredients; but they also have to act and react in a particular but changing international environment. Their choices of policy are affected by the shifting balance between them, and by contingent events: wars and revolutions sometimes offer them opportunities but at other times represent setbacks to a preferred course. The aim of this series is therefore to present the histories of the Great Powers in the twentieth century from these two broad perspectives and to show how individual powers, trying to achieve their own priorities in the regional and global arenas of world politics, have sought to balance the actions and reactions of their rivals against the imperatives of domestic policies.

In 1917, the Russian Revolution created a state which was new not merely in configuration but in nature. The existence of that state – and its aims and actions – has affected the international system in the most profound ways for most of the twentieth century. An overtly ideological power which rested on intellectual foundations that were infinitely more sophisticated than those underpinning National Socialist Germany or Fascist Italy, the Soviet Union's relationship with the liberal democratic powers was one of contest and competition. The rhetoric of competition changed over the decades: from the 1920s up to his death in 1953, Stalin repeatedly declared that war between the USSR and the West was inevitable – but would not happen in the immediate future – whereas Khrushchev and Brezhnev pitched their challenges in different but no less menacing ways by supporting 'wars of national liberation' and building up the Soviet nuclear arsenal to parity with the United States, thereby contributing to the institutionalisation of what Albert Wohlstetter called 'the delicate balance of terror.' However, a domestic regime characterised by unparalleled brutality reinforced the picture of a power which, after 1945, was regarded by many as both hostile and dangerous.

As Caroline Kennedy-Pipe demonstrates – aided both by distance and by archival sources whose availability is one of the consequences of the collapse of the power she studies – the reality was rather more complex and the Soviet Union's behaviour more varied. The regime depended upon its leaders, and they in turn legitimated their power by demonstrating that Soviet ideology was in essentials sound. Both failed. In some part, that failure was due to the inability of Soviet Russia to match the industrial output of the West. Russia attempted to 'catch up' in three pulses at thirty year intervals: in and immediately after 1927/8, 1957 and 1987. The final pulse destroyed a system which was barely 70 years old. The 'Red Empire' which Stalin won at the close of the Second World War was more a source of weakness than of strength, and the violent repression of dissent in the Soviet satellite states in 1953, 1956 and 1968 masked the fragility of Soviet control. Of equal importance were the international problems which faced the Kremlin and which it failed to manage. The rise of the People's Republic of China after 1949 produced not merely a third 'pole' in the international system, but an ideological rival which the Kremlin could neither suppress nor defeat and which greatly complicated its contest with the United States.

'Great Power status is lost as it is won, by violence,' Martin Wight once remarked. 'A Great Power does not die in its bed.' The Soviet Union has proved the exception to that rule. Explanations of its life and death – of the nature and course of Soviet policy in the years between 1917 and 1991 – occupy contested ground. Presently, it is fashionable to claim that the collapse of the Soviet Union represents the triumph of capitalism, not of democracy. While there may be some truth in such generalisations, a large part of the explanation for both the rise and the fall of the USSR resides in the story of its successes and failure in managing its relations with the outside world which this book relates.

John Gooch
August 1998

Acknowledgements

In writing this book I have incurred many debts. My first is to Christopher Wheeler and Elena Seymenliyska at Arnold Publishers, who over the last few years have been patient, helpful and unfailingly professional. Christina Malkowska Zaba has been exceptionally helpful in correcting and improving the text. My second debt is to John Gooch, the editor of this series, for providing me with the opportunity to think and write about Russia and the world. For his gentle encouragement and perceptive observations I am grateful. I should also like to thank those colleagues who have contributed generously with ideas and comments on the text: Neil Melvin, Clive Jones, Geoff Roberts and Nick Rengger have all provided invaluable help. John Gooding and Archie Brown have been generous in allowing me to incorporate their ideas into my manuscript. To all the above I am grateful; any faults or errors in the text are mine.

Introduction
Russia and the World

Could we conceive of a past without confrontation between Russia and the external world? One of the questions that has always intrigued those studying Russia and its foreign relations has been the tension between Moscow and the outside world. In part this was rooted in a deep Western suspicion of Russia, dating back several centuries and with its roots in Russia's Byzantine heritage and perceived 'oriental' character.[1] By the mid-nineteenth century this was made manifest for many in the West by the view that Russia was outside the European sphere. In 1839, on his return from Moscow, the Marquis de Custine had described the Russians as 'Chinese masquerading as Europeans'.[2] Churchill, in a similar vein, famously referred to the Soviet Union as 'an enigma wrapped in a mystery'; and when in 1946 the former British Prime Minister spoke of an 'iron curtain' between East and West, it was in the tradition of the *cordon sanitaire* with which Lord Curzon had earlier hoped to isolate Western civilisation from the Communists.[3] To many Western minds Russia was at once too remote and different to be a comfortable European power as well as also, quite literally, too close to be ignored. Remoteness from the European mainstream was a product of geography; but it was also the consequence of lack of development within Russia.[4] Difference from Western Europe was also emphasised after 1917 by the Bolshevik commitment to spreading the creed of Communism. Yet the Western powers could not ignore the formidable challenge posed both by Russian ideology and its sheer geopolitical presence on the edge of the West.

Mutual suspicions and hostilities were not helped by the fact that Russia itself was not consistent in its attitude towards the West. Throughout the nineteenth century, the Russian destiny was debated between Westernisers and Slavophiles. The former regarded the future of Russia as dependent on closer ties with European civilisation and a modernising path; the Slavophiles, on the other hand, argued that Moscow should defend Russian traditions and value its positioning between East and West.[5] This tension was never fully resolved, and even now it may be seen in the many debates about the nature of the relationship with Western Europe which take place within the post-Communist Russian leadership. At various stages of history Russian leaders have trodden a path of deliberate isolationism; but also, because of the keen awareness of the West's technological advantages, they have sought co-operation and a form of mutually beneficial coexistence in key stages of Russia's development. This book argues that the story of 'Russia and the World' is one to be understood as an evolution in Russian thinking, from wishing to reinvent the West and regions of the developing world in a Marxist–Leninist image, to an acceptance of the strength of other types of political systems, most notably those of liberalism and capitalism.[6]

If the story of Russian history may be told in terms of ambivalence about and competition with the outside world, analysts have been divided over what framework best explains the making and motivations of its foreign poli-cies.[7] In analysing its foreign policy behaviour, scholars have tended to work within one of two competing frameworks, dividing quite neatly into the clas-sic domains of *innenpolitik* and *aussenpolitik*. The first concentrates on the unique nature of the Soviet political system as it developed after 1917, and emphasises the nature of authoritarianism. In this, the preoccupation of the elite and its ideological tools are seen as keys to understanding external behaviour.[8] Advocates of the second, by contrast, have preferred to look at Russian actions as influenced by the workings of the external international environment, in particular the prevailing balance of power and the specific threats posed by the other great powers.[9]

According to the first framework, Russian behaviour in the twentieth century is depicted as an outcome of ideological hostility towards a capitalist West, consistent in its implacable opposition to the Western world.[10] However, those who advocate the second framework see foreign policy as mainly reactive to the events in an outside world and the Kremlin as flexible and able to adapt to the vagaries of global events. This book accepts that both approaches have virtues. It is important, of course, to understand the evolu-tion of the political system within Russia, not least the peculiar and particu-lar nature of the Stalinist system and its constant modification from 1953 onwards, in order to understand the dynamics which shaped foreign policy. Ideology in the shape of Marxist–Leninist thinking had a profound effect upon both the nature of the regime and the perceptions and preoccupation of Russian leaders, justifying the rule of the Communist Party and the main-taining of an elite to lead society. This legitimating function meant that any modifications in ideological thinking could – and did – exercise a profound impact upon the domestic political system. More pertinently for this partic-ular project, Marxism–Leninism also shaped the way in which the elite viewed the outside world, and therefore the manner in which responses were formed to external events.[11] The belief to be found within the Soviet elite that socialism could triumph globally led to a whole series of foreign-policy initiatives, from the sponsoring of foreign Communist parties and trade unions in the 1920s to the belief in the 1970s that socialism could take root throughout the Third World.

However, it is also worth just remarking that both internal and external theses need to pay attention to a more 'deep-structure' aspect of Russian foreign policy. Without in any way adopting a determinist view of history or society, it is at least plausible to suggest, with Aristotle, that the 'regime' that governs a society shapes not just the formal institutions and practices of politics and decision-making, but aspects of the general *mentalité* of the ruling elite and generalised assumptions of rule itself. In the Russian case, this 'regime' was shaped not just by the character of the Soviet system – as the *innenpolitik* school would argue – but at least as much by the imprint of Russian history on its practice of government. Russia was, as it had been for centuries, a 'fragile regime' held together by political will and force in the teeth of external hostility and domestic passivity or unrest. It is remarkable how close imperial and Soviet Russian practice were. Perhaps part of the explanation lies in the character of the Russian regime, imposed on it by history and geography. Perhaps, in the words of Robert Kaplan, geography is destiny.[12]

All these sets of explanations, internal and external, are embedded throughout this text. Domestic pressures and preoccupations are apparent throughout the period from 1917 to 1989. At the very least, the survival and formulation of the post-Revolution regime permitted certain types of external behaviour to find a breathing space after the traumas of civil war. Equally, the consistent inability of the Soviet economy to reach the levels of technological production found in the West also mandated at least a degree of cooperation with the West, if only to gain necessary imports. This trend was apparent in various periods of Soviet foreign policy: the later Brezhnev period, for example, was characterised by the belief that closer economic and technological links with the West, most notably with the United States, would transform the state of the Soviet economy. The book argues that it was the failure of the economic reforms attempted under Andropov in the early 1980s which led to the most fundamental reappraisal yet attempted of the Soviet economic system. The Soviet elite recognised that, in an increasingly interdependent world, some form of economic integration with the institutions of the West was inevitable.

All of these internal considerations, however, had to be matched to the pressures imposed on the leadership by the outside world. Not least, it becomes apparent in any study of Soviet Russia that it reacted – and reacted sharply – to changes in the European balance of power after 1918. Isolated by the Versailles system, it was forced into alliance with Germany to avoid complete estrangement from contact with the West. After 1945 the condition of bipolarity and the emergence of a powerful bloc under the leadership of the United States evoked a different set of responses from the Kremlin, most notably that of the formation of a competing political–military alliance in the East. However, whilst a bipolar world was convenient, at least in theory, and clearly demarcated the Communist from the non-Communist world, the global position was complicated from the 1950s onwards by the emergence of China as a significant third force in global politics.

It is not possible to overestimate the impact that the emergence of Communist China had on the leadership in the Kremlin. First Khrushchev and then Brezhnev had to come to terms with the emergence of a giant rival in the East. This development mandated not only a massive military build-up along the Sino-Soviet border, but also the targeting of Soviet nuclear weapons against a fellow Communist power. Even more problematic for the leadership in the Kremlin was the threat that China might come to be seen as the standard-bearer of global Communism. In particular, the Kremlin feared that other states might leave the Soviet orbit and follow Beijing's new lead: not unreasonably, given the constant state of unrest within Eastern Europe and its periodic rebellions against Soviet tutelage. For most of the Cold War period, a primary concern for the leadership in Moscow was how to maintain control over allies. In the Third World, in particular, it was often the case that friends proved unreliable.

Both domestic and international influences, then, shaped foreign-policy behaviour. The same is probably true for many states. Yet the Soviet Russian case was rather different, specifically because it did set itself up as a maverick state with a messianic ideology premised on Marxism–Leninism which was intent upon the revision of the political and territorial status quo. In practice, however – and somewhat ironically – the Kremlin set about sustaining and extending an empire which entrapped and subjugated peoples. Much of the historical debate over the conduct of Soviet foreign policy has centred around the question of how far Russia was motivated by ideological impulses and how far by *Realpolitik* and the search for secure borders.

It is now accepted that the first years of the Bolshevik leadership under Lenin were years of an intense clash between the demands of ideology and that of the survival of the state. As Chapter 1 demonstrates, this occurred in an open and changing international environment, as Bolshevik leaders struggled through European war, civil war, famine and the establishment of Communism in Russia. Gradually, however, over time overt ideological demands gave way to an uneven but inevitable retreat away from open competition with the West to an accommodation with it.

The first signs of the attempts to compromise with the West occurred relatively early in the 1920s, as the Bolshevik leaders recognised that the need to survive was predicated, at the very least, on the non-intervention of the Western powers in the affairs of the nascent Soviet state. It also coincided with the recognition of the failure of the Revolution to gain a grip on the European continent. Bolshevik retreats and humiliations engendered a reappraisal of Russian behaviour, and the later years of the 1920s saw a period of internal restructuring, regime-building and – as a result – relative quiet on the revolutionary front. Russian behaviour was predicated on the need to build internally and secure the state.[13] This was followed almost immediately, as Chapter 2 argues, by a recognition in the 1930s that Germany and Japan posed a double threat to Soviet security. Foreign policy became a search for alliances of many and different varieties to ward off emerging threats. Historians still debate whether the Soviet search for collective security arrangements with the West was a genuine one or not;[14] but whatever the debates, the policy in general terms was clear – to find allies, of whatever ideological hue. In 1939 the Nazi–Soviet Pact was signed.[15]

As might be expected, the beginning of the Second World War and the German betrayal of Stalin in August 1941 left an indelible legacy on the Russian state. Survival and victory over Hitler was bought at tremendous human and economic cost to the Soviet people and society. However, savage as its human toll may have been, the war produced for Stalin the opportunity to secure the Western borders of the USSR through the occupation of Eastern Europe. The story of how Stalin forged an alliance with both Britain and the United States and then used the Soviet Army to exercise influence throughout Europe is told in Chapter 3. From late 1943 onwards Soviet troops were used to demarcate lines of influence throughout Europe. Military means were the insurance policy used by Stalin in his negotiations with his Western Allies to exert influence over the future of European security arrangements: none the less, Russian demands contributed to the destruction of the Grand Alliance very shortly after victory in Europe had been achieved. Russian behaviour in 1944–6 was governed by the perception not of strength, but of weakness and fear of the future, as George Kennan (amongst others) presciently saw[16]. Stalin feared not only a revival of German power, but a growth in Western hostility at a time when the economic and technological backwardness of the USSR was becoming increasingly apparent; yet Russian actions contributed to the very end product that Stalin so feared – isolation from an increasingly hostile and nuclear Western alliance. As Chapter 4 explains, the Cold War from 1945 on saw a Stalinist leadership on the defensive, inclined to seek a measure of co-operation with the West but incapable of finding the necessary mechanisms to do so. How Russia should or could deal with the external world engendered a huge debate in the Kremlin.[17] Caution dictated pragmatism until the American nuclear monopoly had been rectified,[18] yet a series of Soviet actions – not least the Berlin blockade of 1948 and the active encouragement of the North Koreans to invade South Korea in the summer of 1950 – was calculated to increase tensions. Once again, however, we now know that Mao's China was a powerful influence on Soviet actions on the Korean peninsula.

The death of Stalin in March 1953 was a watershed in many ways. Dictatorship was replaced by collective leadership. As Chapter 5 shows, after a period of initial internal wrangling the Khrushchev–Malenkov leadership tried to dispel at least some of the tensions with Western powers. There was an end to the Korean War and a resolution at the Geneva Summit of 1955 of the Austrian question. Khrushchev also attempted to patch up the differences which had arisen with Tito, the leader of Yugoslavia. But, despite attempts by the Kremlin to prohibit further defence integration in the West, it proceeded apace, and in 1955 the Soviet leadership was dismayed to find West Germany fully incorporated into the NATO (North Atlantic Treaty Organisation) alliance. The subsequent creation in 1955 of an Eastern military alliance, the Warsaw Treaty Organisation (WTO), formalised the division of Europe and left little doubt that the peoples of Eastern Europe had been abandoned to Communism. Yet, increasingly aware of its technological inferiority and the burdens of the nuclear arms race, and frightened by the challenges of Mao's China, the USSR still sought to revise its stance *vis-à-vis* the West. Khrushchev's pronouncements of 1956 which redrew the lines of ideological battle with the West was an attempt to make peaceful coexistence the new order of the day; but his style of leadership resulted in one of the major scares of the post-1945 period, that of the Cuban missile crisis in 1962.[19] The humiliating end to this crisis led not only to the downfall of the Soviet leader, but a reappraisal of foreign-policy behaviour.

Soviet leaders drew two lessons from the débâcle in Cuba. The first was that Moscow could not afford to operate from a position of strategic inferiority, which necessitated an increase in nuclear capabilities. The second was that greater stability was needed in the central strategic relationship with the United States to mitigate against such near-disasters. Chapter 6, which examines the decade of the 1960s, shows that the period was spent in an attempt to equal the American strategic arsenal. Other less provocative methods were tried too. The establishment of the 'hotline' and the pursuit of arms-control agreements for some categories of nuclear weapons were indicative of the Soviet disinclination to take risks, as evidenced in the period of the disastrous American involvement in Vietnam, when Brezhnev was torn between wishing to see the Americans humiliated and defeated in South East Asia and recognising that facilitating a settlement could aid prospects for trade with a grateful American administration. The extent to which the Soviet leadership could exert pressure on its allies in North Vietnam, however, remained an open question. Soviet foreign policy in this period was therefore full of contradictions: pushing for a détente with the West, but also seeking to defeat the forces of imperialism in the Third World. Whilst the movement towards a *rapprochement* with the United States foundered briefly after the intervention in Czechoslovakia in 1968, the subsequent period of détente with both the West European powers and the

United States marked another phase in Russia's relationship with the external world.

By 1969–70 Russia could claim with justification to equal American nuclear strength.[20] This appeared to have satisfied the post-Cuban-missile-crisis desire to assuage weakness. But this book will argue, in Chapter 7, that Russia's claims to operate from a position of strength were increasingly at odds with its fragile economic base. The Brezhnev leadership, like its predecessors, recognised keenly the rather ironic situation that the import of Western technologies and foodstuffs held the key to the future survival of the Communist system.[21] They were also aware that partly what had cost Khrushchev his position as leader was the inability to 'deliver the goods' to the consumers of the USSR.[22] East European rebellions, most notably that of Czechoslovakia in 1968, also pointed to serious traumas in the control of the bloc, not the least of which was the inability of Soviet-style economies to produce consumer goods of the quality desired. Russian leaders therefore sought some form of *rapprochement* with Washington, in order both to accrue economic advantages through positive moves such as acquiring credits, and, rather more negatively, to avoid yet another round of the increasingly expensive nuclear arms race.

Such pragmatism did not, however, completely negate the demands of ideology. During the years 1970–2 both East and West agreed that Germany would remain divided, and the status of Berlin was clarified through the Quadripartite Protocol of June 1972. At least one hot spot of the Cold War era seemed to have been resolved. This stabilisation in Europe and the opening of the détente with Washington, however, renewed Moscow's zest for influence in the Third World. As Chapter 7 relates, Russia's agenda in the Third World in the 1970s stemmed at least in part from the challenges posed by China, but was also part and parcel of the belief that the time was ripe for the export of Soviet socialism into the Third World. Whilst Moscow did fear an alliance between President Nixon and the leadership in Beijing (Henry Kissinger's so-called China card), it was also concerned about Mao's desire to make China the premier carrier of the Communist ideology to areas such as the Horn of Africa. It was therefore decided by at least some parts of the Brezhnev leadership to compete actively against both the Soviet Union's global rivals in the Third World. The former American National Security Adviser Zbigniew Brzezinski's comment that SALT (Strategic Arms Limitation Talks) was buried in the sands of the Ogaden desert[23] reflected Washington's increasing belief that Moscow was betraying the spirit if not the letter of détente. The Soviet invasion of Afghanistan in 1979 left little doubt that Moscow's strategy of détente had failed. Yet Moscow's increasing involvement in the Third World from Angola to Afghanistan was not simply the product of a desire to undermine the fragile *rapprochement* with the United States, but the result of a far more complex set of calculations, outlined above.

Despite these global ambitions, or indeed because of them, the view from the Kremlin was an almost universally dismal one by 1980. As Chapter 8 argues, the first part of the decade saw Russia as much on the defensive as it had been in the 1920s. This time, however, the problem was not invasion, but nationalist implosion and economic expiry. An increasingly frail and ageing Russian leadership had run out of ideas as to how to make the system work. Economic ills beset an anxious population, whilst the politics of the first Reagan administration, not least the announcement in 1983 of the Strategic Defence Initiative, provided Soviet leaders with much to contemplate. In addition, Andropov's experiments to make the economic system work were a widespread failure, and by 1985 the Kremlin had decided to risk another limited reform programme under the auspices of the General Secretary Mikhail Gorbachev.[24] As Chapter 9 argues, this new leader was a man of pro-Western tendencies, a 'reforming tsar' almost in the manner of Peter the Great, as many suggested. Gorbachev set about the reinvigoration of the Soviet system through a series of bold and imaginative moves. In the foreign sphere the changes were breathtaking. Russia set about reordering its relationships with the external world. The American strategy of exerting leverage over Soviet behaviour by tying trade deals to Moscow's behaviour abroad, in particular to Communist activities in the Third World – a strategy called 'linkage' – was accepted and arms control was embraced. The Intermediate Nuclear Force (INF) agreement of 1987, although inconsequential in actual numbers, represented the first-ever attempt to eradicate a whole class of weapons. More importantly, Gorbachev increasingly adopted a number of Western political and legal concepts, such as the introduction of multi-candidate elections, in an attempt to recast the Soviet system.

Accommodation with the West on this scale, however, undermined the very legitimacy of the Soviet system. The abolition of the Communist Party and the one-party system called into question the very *raison d'être* of the Soviet Union itself. The partial opening of the archives in Moscow proved what many within the Communist world had long believed: that Eastern Europe and the non-Russian parts of the USSR had been forced and then coerced into the empire. Gorbachev's attempts, dogged by the ill luck of the Chernobyl nuclear disaster of 1986 and the Armenian earthquake of 1988, failed to hold the Soviet show on the road; and, in darkly ironic symmetry, Russia was left in a position similar to that of 1917 – isolated, internally incoherent and fearful of external intervention. By 1991, even if the West had not 'won' the competition between East and West in the terms claimed by some analysts, there is little doubt that Russia had lost. It was transformed and humbled not only by its own weakness but by its contacts with the world which, from 1917 onward, it had sought to recreate in its own image.

Notes

1 For discussions of this see the final chapter of George Ostrogorsky's classic *A History of the Byzantine State* [1940] (Oxford: Blackwell, 1968).

2 Quoted in Gabriel Gorodetsky (ed.), *Soviet Foreign Policy 1917–1991: A Retrospective* (London: Frank Cass, 1994), p. 1.

3 Gorodetsky, *Soviet Foreign Policy*.

4 See Louis Fischer, *The Soviets in World Affairs; A History of the Relations Between the Soviet Union and the Rest of the World, 1917–1929* (2 vols., New York: 1930), p. 1.

5 See Edwina Moreton and Gerald Segal, *Soviet Strategy Toward Western Europe* (London: George Allen and Unwin, 1984), p. 21.

6 Francis Fukuyama, *The End of History and the Last Man* (London: Hamish Hamilton, 1992).

7 See Morton Schwartz, *The Foreign Policy of the USSR: Domestic Factors* (Encino, Calif.: Dickenson, 1975), pp. 1–5.

8 See e.g. Bertram D. Wolfe, 'Communist Ideology and Soviet Foreign Policy', in William Peterson (ed.), *The Realities of World Communism* (Englewood Cliffs, NJ: Prentice Hall, 1963) p. 25. See also Anthony D'Agnostino, *Soviet Succession Struggles, Kremlinology and the Russian Question from Lenin to Gorbachev* (London: Allen & Unwin, 1988), Gabriel D. Ra'anon, *International Policy Formation in the USSR: Factional Debates During the Zhdanovshine* (Hamden, Conn.; Archon, 1983), and George Kennan, *Russia and the West under Lenin and Stalin* (Boston: Little, Brown, 1961).

9 Inis L. Claude, Jr., *Power and International Relations* (New York: Random House, 1962).

10 'x' 'The Sources and Conduct of Soviet Foreign Policy', *Foreign Affairs* (1947), pp. 566–82.

11 Elliot R. Goodman, *The Soviet Design for a World State* (New York: Columbia University Press, 1960).

12 R. Kaplan, *The Ends of the Earth: A Journey at the Dawn of the Twenty First Century* (London: Macmillan, 1996).

13 Kaplan, *The Ends of the Earth*.

14 Jonathan Haslam, *The Soviet Union and the Struggle for Collective Security in Europe 1933–1939* (New York: St Martin's, 1984). See also Geoffrey Roberts, *The Soviet Union and the Origins of the Second World War: Russo-German Relations and the Road to War, 1933–1941* (London: Macmillan, 1995).

15 The Protocols for the Nazi-Soviet pact were published *in Vesnik MID SSSR*, 4 (1990).

16 'x', 'The Sources of Soviet Conduct', *Foreign Affairs* (1947).

17 Francesca Gori and Silvio Pons (eds), *The Soviet Union and Europe in the Cold War, 1943–53* (London: Macmillan, 1996).

18 D. A. Holloway, *Stalin and the Bomb* (New Haven: Yale University Press, 1994).

19 Raymond L. Garthoff, 'Cuban Missile Crisis: The Soviet Story', *Foreign Policy*, 72 (Fall, 1988). Raymond L. Garthoff, *Reflections on the Cuban Missile Crisis* (Washington, DC: Brookings, 1989).

20 D. A. Holloway, *The Soviet Union and the Arms Race* (New Haven: Yale University Press, 1983).

21 G. M. Korniyenko, '*A Missed Opportunity*': *Carter, Brezhnev, SALT II, And The Vance Mission to Moscow, November 1976–1977* in *Cold War Crises: Cold War*

International History Project (Woodrow Wilson International Center for Scholars, Washington, DC).

22 This phrase was coined in this context by the Sovietologist T. H. Rigby.

23 Quoted in Fred Halliday, *The Making of The Second Cold War* (2nd edn, London: Verso, 1986), p. 223.

24 Archie Brown, 'Gorbachev: New Man in the Kremlin', *Problems of Communism* (May–June, 1985), pp. 1–23.

1

Revolution and the Origins of Soviet Foreign Policy 1917–1932

Russia is not sulking, but collecting itself.
A. M. Gorchakov, Foreign Minister to Tsar Aleksander II

Throughout the nineteenth century Russia was a partner, albeit often an ambiguous, troubled and troublesome one, in what A. J. P. Taylor has called 'the perpetual quadrille of the balance of power in Europe'[1] and, increasingly, beyond it.[2] For all that, Russia was often seen by other European powers as an enigma, albeit a familiar one playing an accepted if sometimes clumsy role.

In 1917, at least on the surface, all that changed. The establishment of the Soviet state was a landmark in world history. A radical and revolutionary regime was established on the European landmass with an explicit mission to overturn the state system and eradicate class barriers. Not since 1789 had so explicit a challenge been laid down to the norms and procedures of the international system and the expectations and hierarchies of European domestic politics.

The new Bolshevik leadership in Moscow believed that all state boundaries could be eradicated, and the official line was that such eradication would be followed quickly by the withering away of the institution of the state as such. Revolutionary fervour abroad was quickly revealed to be less effective than the Bolsheviks had expected, however, and although the Revolution profoundly affected the internal dynamic of Russia it failed either to execute a similar influence over the external landscape of international politics (at least initially) or to abolish the state as such. As this chapter demonstrates in its examination of the first phase of the Soviet experience, the failure of revolution abroad forced the new Soviet leadership into a series of pragmatic compromises with Western states in order to preserve the Revolution at home. The decade after the seizure of power by the Bolsheviks was one in which the leadership constructed a new Soviet state and sought to protect it from both internal and external enemies.

In the years after 1917 we see several key developments which would profoundly affect the conduct of Soviet foreign policy. The first, as outlined above, was the failure of the revolution abroad: a failure which threw the new leadership back into a concentration on the Revolution within the Soviet state. But the second was the fact that the Bolshevik vision of global politics was a disputed one, not just abroad, but also at home within Russia. The civil war which broke out in 1918 was fought precisely over what future Russia should take, leaving a legacy of suspicion and bloodshed which coloured future political developments. In this battle over the future the Communists' use of military force eradicted any vestiges of political opposition, and the Communist Party was the only political party to emerge from the years of revolution and civil war. However, although by 1921 they had no rivals of any substance, they still feared the emergence of opponents within the new state. This, at least in part, led to authoritarianism in all political structures and a concentration of power within the Communist party elite. Within that group itself the early years of the Soviet state were rife with factionalism, especially in the years immediately after the death of Lenin in 1924. His successors had to struggle for power as well as struggling over the course of internal and external strategies.

Two points in particular are worth emphasising. First, far from dramatically changing the character of the previous Russian state, the Soviet experience in the first 10 years after the Revolution appears, ironically, to have exacerbated certain aspects of it. These aspects, I argue, made the Soviet Union a fragile regime, creating legacies that were to last as long as the Soviet experiment itself.

Second, the impact of the Russian Revolution on Russian foreign policy is one of the great test cases of the possibility of revolutionary change in the international system. There are many who see revolutions as a major, if often ignored, factor in international relations and one which, at least potentially, has the capacity to change the character of international politics as such.[3] The contrary view, eloquently expressed most recently by Stephen Walt, is that revolutions sometimes in fact have little real impact on foreign policy, since the structure of the international system and the costs of ignoring it enforce 'business as usual'.[4] Significantly, neither view is entirely borne out in the Russian case. Without taking sides in this debate, it can safely be asserted that the Revolution is a central event for understanding both Russia and the twentieth century. Eric Hobsbawm has even suggested that 'it proved to be the saviour of Liberal Capitalism, both by enabling the West to win the Second World War ... and by providing the incentive for Capitalism to reform itself.' How, then did this protean event occur, and why in Russia?

Traditions

It is not, of course, the task of this book to look in detail at Tsarism or the Revolution; this would take us too far afield. But we cannot avoid its legacy.

Robert Service has argued, 'No Imperial power before the First World War was more reviled in Europe than the Russian Empire.'[5] Generations of democrats both inside and outside Russia hated the ruling Romanov dynasty. Nicholas II was notorious in his repression of Russian parties, trade unions and dissidents. Trouble had broken out in January 1904 which threatened to engulf the entire country, as the result of widespread discontent within practically all classes, from peasants and ethnic minorities to professionals. All protested against the nature of the regime. A strike at the Pehlov metallurgical plant at the end of 1904 spread rapidly to communities elsewhere, and in January 1905 a group of striking workers decided to take their grievances to the Winter Palace to present a petition to the Tsar. The demands of the workers included the recognition of some civil liberties and the promulgation of an assembly. However, as the column approached the palace soldiers opened fire. This incident, on this particular 'Bloody Sunday' in Russia, began a general uprising. In the following weeks the government did attempt to open up a dialogue with the workers, but it failed when the Tsar did not accede to the more radical of their demands.

Over the course of the troubles which followed 'Bloody Sunday' 100 leading officials were assassinated. A general strike ensued, which sections of the professional classes and the armed forces joined. In June the crew of the battleship *Potemkin* mutinied in the Black Sea. Under this pressure Nicholas actually conceded a Parliament (*duma*), but by this stage it was no longer enough, and on 17 October he was forced to sign what became known as the October Manifesto. This granted a modicum of civil rights; but its main effect was to divide the revolutionary forces. Once the October Manifesto became public knowledge many of the more moderate unions were inclined to accept its terms and return to work; others, however, most notably the Russian Social Democrats, considered its concessions to be the beginning of a process of democratisation, and sought greater reforms. Imperial Russia thus began the new century split on many issues from top to bottom and with a series of problems in its management of external strategies. Indeed, part of what had inspired the domestic troubles of 1904–5 had been the poor showing by the forces of the Tsar against Japan in the war of those years. Unrest at home was thus compounded by failure abroad.

In general the Tsars had operated a foreign policy which recognised the limitations imposed by the geopolitical location of Russia. In particular, its gigantic landmass was unprotected by natural barriers, such as mountain ranges; Russia was unique in its inability to deter would-be invaders. Its tradition of invasion had a history stretching back to the Mongols. The length of borders and flatness of terrain made it an appealing target for Napoleon's armies during the Crimean War. Invading enemies had actually proved difficult to expel; in 1854–6 the Russian Army had failed to drive Anglo-French forces out of the Crimea, and, although the Russians had defeated the Turks in the war of 1877, this was not a notable accomplishment as the Ottoman Empire was already in terminal decline.

In part the Tsarist response to Russian vulnerability had been to see security in terms of 'space'. This view demanded a strategy of annexation and the control of territory contiguous to the homeland, one which had been apparent during the reign of Peter the Great, when Russia for the first time became a factor of some significance within the European state system. Peter's victory in the Great Northern War, and especially the victory over the Swedes and their Ukranian allies in 1709 at Poltava, made Russia a Baltic power and provided it with a 'window' onto the Baltic. Equally, the nineteenth-century partition of Poland and the subjugation of the Ukraine and the Transcaucasus went some way to satisfying Russian desire to control the approaches to Russia. Hand in hand with what might be termed defensive urges, however, another trend was discernible throughout the nineteenth century – that of an imperial desire to engage with the other great powers through the acquisition of naval strength and warm-water ports. Peter the Great's victories provided Russia with a unique position in the Baltic from which to play the European balance of power. The continued growth of Russian power at the end of the century was demonstrated in an active foreign policy that was not just confined to Europe but also had ambitions in Asia. This was most notable in the Russo-Japanese war of 1904–5, in which Moscow received a bloody nose, lost the Russian stronghold of Port Arthur and left Japan as a considerable adversary in the East. As we saw earlier, the failure in the war against the Japanese also had particular ramifications at home.

At the beginning of the twentieth century, however, two powers in particular were of concern to the Romanovs: Germany and Austria–Hungary. Moscow was concerned that Germany would take advantage of the weakness of the Ottoman Empire and expand to the South and East. Not for the first time in European history and, tragically, not for the last either, the Balkans were proving to be the 'cockpit of Europe'. In 1912 Bulgaria, Serbia and Greece declared war on the Ottoman Empire, and Serbia moved into Macedonia. Europe was teetering on the brink of catastrophe.

War

On 28 June 1914 it fell over the brink. The assassination of the heir to the Habsburg throne, Archduke Franz Ferdinand, by Gavrilo Princip, a Serbian nationalist in Sarejevo, began a seemingly irreversible slide into war. Austria demanded humiliating concessions which Serbia refused. In support of its south Slav ally, Russia announced a general mobilisation of its armies. Russia's relations worsened with Austria–Hungary and Germany, whose

Chancellor, Theodor von Bethmann Hollweg, agreed to support Austria's claims on Serbia even though Serbia had not been acting at Russia's instigation. Germany declared war on Russia and France and, after a short interval and as a consequence of the German invasion of Belgium, Britain declared war on Germany and Austria. Europe was at war for the first time in 100 years.

Nicholas II was counting upon the fact that a short, victorious war might bind Imperial society more closely together. However, the war turned out to be a disaster for Russia. The initial public response to the outbreak of war, as Nicholas had envisaged, was an increase in patriotic fervour, especially among the upper classes; but by the end of 1915 a million Russians were dead and another million held prisoner. It has often been asked why the Russians did not do well in the war, given their huge numbers and considerable resources.[6] Part of the answer lies in the economic and technological backwardness which characterised Russia at this point. In part the war revealed the technological and economic backwardness of the state: when it actually broke out the Russian armaments industry was not up to its demands. Five months after the outbreak of war supplies were running out: there were no bullets for rifles, and no shells. There was also a problem of leadership. When war broke out the Tsar's uncle, Grand Duke Nikolai, became Commander-in-Chief. As the war began to go badly for Russia, the mismanagement of the war effort helped the opponents of the monarchy. Grand Duke Nikolai was quickly revealed to be incompetent both politically and militarily, imposing harsh regimes in areas occupied by the Russian forces and dissipating any sympathies which local populations had had for the Russian struggle against Germany. In particular, his treatment of Jews had the potential to cause problems with Russia's allies. Because of these problems Tsar Nicholas transferred his uncle to the Caucasian front and took over as Commander-in-Chief in 1915.

Another problem was that of the unrealistic geopolitical ambitions entertained by the Russian elite. In line with Russian history, Nicholas was determined to gain the greatest possible territorial advantages from the war. Russia demanded for example that the Straits of the Dardenelles should be incorporated into the Russian Empire. To that effect, secret treaties giving control of the straits to Moscow were signed with both Britain and France. Yet, despite, or perhaps because of, these ambitions, the war continued to impose massive strains upon the Russian economy and society. Mobilisation for war had at first provided the rationale for an increase in government control of all public affairs. Censorship was imposed, the Bolsheviks arrested and recalcitrant workers drawn into the Army. However, by August 1915 a broad spectrum of liberal deputies in the Duma formed a progressive bloc and called upon Nicholas to appoint a government which enjoyed the confidence of the people. The Tsar rejected the demands, and by the end of 1915 workers had reverted to the strike weapon despite the war. Worker power was enhanced at this stage by the fact that during the war and the effort to mobilise the population for it, millions of peasants had been drawn into a closer contact with national politics, and had begun to form what Edward Acton has described as a 'concentrated pool of peasant discontent'.[7] In early 1917 the number of strikes increased and a series of demonstrations over food shortages took place. The authorities failed to regain control of the situation, and on 2 March military leaders, encouraged in part by an anxious West determined to keep Russia in the war, recommended to Nicholas that he abdicate. It was advice that the Tsar took, and he was replaced by a liberal provisional government. To paraphrase Hobsbawn in an acidic comment, four spontaneous and leaderless days on the street put an end to an Empire.

Revolution and civil war

What enabled the Bolsheviks under Lenin to seize power? A key reason was that, as discussed above, by 1917 the Tsarist state lacked the support of any social class: the peasants, the workers and the intellectuals had all rejected its rule. The Tsar was unable to adjust to the demands placed upon the state. Because under the strain of war the support had disintegrated of those institutions which acted as the mechanisms of control and repression – most notably the police and the army – the Tsarist regime had few defenders by 1917. In addition, the foreign allies which might have provided economic and political aid to save the Russian regime from revolution were focused on the struggle with Germany and were unable to help. The abdication of the Tsar marked a watershed in Russia's internal and external development, and the dramatic events of February 1917 changed the politics of Russia irrevocably. The authority of the monarchy had collapsed in the face of popular demonstrations and the withdrawal of support for the regime.

However, with the establishment of the Provisional Government things seemed likely to stabilise. Moreover, at the time of the February Revolution all the leading Bolsheviks were either in emigration abroad or in exile. The Marxist deputies to the Duma, including the Mensheviks and the Bolsheviks, had been arrested after the outbreak of war in November 1914 because they had argued that the military defeat of Russia would be in the interests of the Revolution. After February 1917 leading Bolsheviks began to return to Russia. Stalin and Molotov had quickly returned from exile in Siberia, though Lenin had found it more difficult to return from Switzerland, being finally aided by the Germans and returning to Petrograd with German assistance in early April. In his absence though the Bolsheviks had already begun to reorganise.

The Russian Social Democratic Party had been founded in 1898 at the Minsk Congress, but in 1903 had split into two wings, the Bolsheviks (which meant 'majority'), led by Lenin, and the Mensheviks led by Martov. Attempts were made in subsequent years to reunite the competing factions, but they continued to lead more or less separate existences. Since he dominated the early years of the Soviet state, it is perhaps worth pausing at this point to consider Lenin's character and personality. Vladimir Ilich Ulianov ('Lenin' was a pseudonym assumed years after he became a political activist) was born in 1879 in Simbirsk on the Volga river. In 1887 his eldest brother, Alexander, was executed for trying to assassinate Tsar Alexander III. This, at least in part, seems to have spurred Lenin on to revolutionary activities. At the University of Kazan he was expelled because of his political activities and transferred to the University in St Petersburg, where he read for an external law degree. He became a member of a secret movement known as 'The Elders', and devoted himself to writing and publishing revolutionary works. Arrested in 1895, after a period of incarceration he went into exile to Siberia and then on to Switzerland.[8]

On Lenin's return to Russia, famously to the Finland Station, he faced a still-chaotic but potentially stabilising situation which did not necessarily bode well for the more radical elements, still slowly legalising themselves. The new Provisional Government was set up to represent the elite revolution of liberal politicians, the propertied and professional classes and the officer class, while the people, the working classes and the non-officer class, would be represented by the Petrograd Soviet. This sharing of power, it was envisaged, would be a source of enormous strength. However, very quickly the illusion of 'dual power', as it was termed, was shattered. The two bodies were camped in the same building, the Tavide Palace, home of the Duma. The government took the right wing and the Soviet the left wing. While the Provisional Government became more conservative, concerned with the defence of property and issues of law and order, the Petrograd Soviet became more radical under the influence of Lenin and the Bolsheviks.

The Provisional Government had little chance of exerting authority. It was in no sense representative of the nation as a whole, with few links with either the peasantry or the working class, and its policy of continuing the war and postponing the implementation of radical social change until after a settlement with Germany aggravated the armed forces. By contrast, Lenin and the Bolsheviks were openly hostile to the war's continuation.

On his return from exile Lenin had argued that no support should be given to the Provisional Government, as the bourgeoisie had to be overthrown by the proletariat. In what became known as the April theses, he argued that the Soviets under revolutionary leadership were the key organs in securing power for the proletariat, and coined the slogan 'Peace, Land and Bread', arguing that Russia had to be withdrawn from the war and land had to be redistributed amongst the people.

Throughout the summer of 1917 the Bolsheviks began to assume a more radical position, and although they remained a minority support for them was growing, particularly in the factories and big towns. In mid-June A. F. Kerensky, the Provisional Government's War Minister (later Prime Minister), oversaw a major offensive by the Russian Army on the Galician Front. This was the first major military offensive since the Revolution in February, and the Russian High Command had until this point ignored the pleas of its allies to engage the Germans. But the offensive proved a disaster for the Russians. The Germans mounted a counter-offensive, and the Russians lost 20,000 men. In the wake of this disaster troops began to desert the armed forces. The Provisional Government was discredited, and in July street violence broke out in Petrograd, as St Petersburg was now called. Those engaged on the streets included sailors from the Krontsdat naval base and workers from the Petrograd factories. The slogan 'all power to the Soviets' became a popular one.

Lenin and the Bolsheviks appear to have been caught off-guard by this development, and although it strengthened their position with respect to the Provisional Government they now faced a crackdown. The Bolshevik Party was banned, and Lenin was forced into hiding in Finland while, in the meantime the Provisional Government was under threat from the right. General Kornilov attempted to restore law and order using the military. He dispatched troops from the front to impose law and order in Petrograd and impose authority. On the eve of this dispatch of troops the Germans captured Riga. It was an offensive which proved effectively to be the last straw. From the summer onwards, revolution simmered below the surface, and the Bolsheviks found their membership and influence growing. On 25 October 1917 the Bolsheviks seized the Winter Palace, and on 26 October the Government of People's Commissars was established, with the explicit goal of the creation of a Communist society. By November, when the moment finally came, as Hobsbawm puts it: 'Power had not so much to be seized as picked up ... the Provisional Government, with no-one left to defend it, merely dissolved into thin air.'[9]

Ideology

A word is probably necessary at this point about the Bolsheviks' basic assumptions. The ideals of Marx and Lenin underwrote the ideology of the new regime. While it would clearly be false to say that Soviet foreign policy in the twentieth century was wholly dictated by ideological considerations, it would be equally misleading to be as dismissive of the ideology of the Soviet state as some realists tend to be. Thus, in order to understand the manner in which its ideological underpinnings shaped Soviet foreign policy, we should start by underlining some of the more salient aspects of that ideology.

Specifically, the Bolsheviks believed that it would be possible to develop a 'utopia', embedding socialist principles, throughout Europe. The utopia consisted of the establishment of revolutionary socialism. At the core of this was the need to abolish private property, because the product of private property was profit, and the means of realising the profit was the market – which also, therefore, had to be abolished. It was envisaged that all this would come about through class struggle.

Marx had believed that Europe was the natural home of the socialist revolution, not only because it was an economic system close to collapse but because the European proletariat were the most suited to build a new social order. He had not, however, envisaged that Russia could be the home of socialism. But Lenin disagreed, believing that Russia could be the core of revolutionary change in Europe. There were two key aspects of this belief. In the first place, Lenin, unlike Marx – and, indeed, unlike most Social Democracts of his time – believed that a society did not necessarily need to move through all the stages of history to reach socialism. In particular, he believed that the transition from feudalism to capitalism to socialism could be greatly speeded up through the intervention of dedicated individuals working with the grain of history. It was this belief that led him to combine Marxism with a particularly Russian form of revolutionary activism, in the process creating the idea of the vanguard party as the 'shock troops' of revolution. The second idea was that revolution in one place necessarily meant revolution elsewhere, for capitalist powers would seek to crush the revolution wherever it occurred, and only by accomplishing global revolution could the Russian Revolution be secured. In his *Imperalism: The Highest Stages of Capitalism*, Lenin argued that it was the Revolution in Russia which had dealt a blow to capitalism in Europe, shocking those who had invested in Russia and providing an example for other peoples, and that the task of the proletariat in Russia was to 'complete the bourgeois democratic revolution in Russia in order to kindle the socialist revolution in Europe as a whole'.[10]

Initial moves in foreign policy

Of course, these expectations had enormous ramifications for the conduct of future foreign policy – not least the propagation of the notion that traditional diplomacy was redundant. The Decree on Peace of 26 October 1917 abolished all secret diplomacy, announced that all annexations were void, declared an armistice and called for all workers to support the peace after the war.

Here it is worth considering the position of Leon Trotsky in the formulation of foreign policy. Lev Davidovich Bronstein ('Trotsky' was a pseudonym) was born in October 1879 in the Ukraine to Jewish parents. He had become a Marxist in 1897 and in 1898 he was arrested and exiled to Siberia. His exile lasted until 1902, when he escaped and fled from the country. On his return in 1903 he favoured the Mensheviks more than the Bolsheviks and was exiled again after the events of 1905. He had joined the Bolsheviks in 1917, and after May 1917 had become a close supporter of Lenin, being involved in the Revolution of October.

At this point, as the Commissar for Foreign Affairs, Trotsky perceived his function to be 'to issue a few revolutionary proclamations to the peoples of the world and then shut up shop'.[11] In line with this belief, after the toppling of the Provisional Government in December 1917, he appealed to the 'peoples' of those states at war with Russia to rebel against their governments and join the Revolution. The Bolsheviks characterised the First World War as a war of imperalists, pinning their hopes on an outbreak of revolution in Germany which would fundamentally alter the complexion of European politics. One of Lenin's central propositions was that revolution in Germany was necessary if socialism was to survive, and the Bolshevik leadership fully expected that the German people would rise up against the Kaiser. However, the uprising failed to materialise and the German army advanced deep into Russian territory. Dispirited Bolshevik forces put up little resistance and anyway had been seriously weakened by the desertion of the *muzhiks* rushing home to share in the break-up of the estates. Despite an earlier Bolshevik commitment that the war would only be ended when a new and revolutionary group was in power in Berlin, they were forced into a humiliating armistice, in late 1917, signing an agreement on 2 December which was to last until 1 January 1918. Peace talks at Brest-Litovsk began shortly after with Berlin determined to exact the maximum reparations from Russia. Not least, German conditions demanded a huge annexation of Russian territories.

The nature of the settlement with Berlin provoked huge controversy among the Bolshevik leadership. Lenin argued that, in the short term, a pragmatic course should be adopted. He believed that, if necessary, peace would have to be accepted on German terms, so that at least the Revolution in Russia itself could survive. Stalin reasoned that the German people at home were not going to support revolutionary aims, and that war was weakening the Bolshevik position, arguing that there was no revolutionary movement in the West, that there was no evidence for one, and that they could not base themselves on a mere potentiality.[12] In this view he was supported by Maxim Litvinov; neither man actually held out hopes for revolution in the western parts of Europe. A group led by Nikolai Bukharin, however, argued that the Revolution could only be continued through war, and that peace with Imperial Germany would be an utter humiliation.[13]

Trotsky also disagreed with Lenin. He had been the representative at the peace talks with Germany, and he prolonged the discussions in the erroneous but optimistic belief that the German proletariat could still rise against the Kaiser. Much to his chagrin, however, the working classes did not rise, and German power proved irresistible. On 3 March 1918 G. F. Sokolnikov, the head of the Soviet delegation, signed the treaty of armistice – the Treaty of Brest-Litovsk. Sokolnikov signed the treaty because other leading Bolsheviks refused to attach their names to the document. Lenin intended to repudiate this agreement at the earliest opportunity. It was at this point that Russia's capital was moved from Petrograd to Moscow, as the Bolsheviks feared that Germany would renew hostilities.[14] The Treaty represented a considerable defeat. Russia lost a third of its population and conceded 32 per cent of its cultivable land, 27 per cent of its railways, 54 per cent of industry and 89 per cent of its coal mines.[15] All the Baltic provinces, the Ukraine, Finland and territories on the Russo-Turkish border were to be ceded.[16] Trotsky resigned in protest.

The new government moved from Petrograd to Moscow in mid-March, and the Bolsheviks adopted a new name – the Communist Party. (In 1952 it would change its name again to the Communist Party of the Soviet Union, or CPSU.) This change of name was meant to distinguish it from the Social Democrats of Western Europe. The Communists became the ruling party in Russia and began the task of leading society towards Communism. Initially power was shared with the Socialist Revolutionary Party, but the agreement at Brest-Litovsk had sparked a fragmentation of the ruling coalition in Russia. The left-wing Socialist Revolutionaries resigned from the government and encouraged uprisings against the Bolsheviks. To counter rebellion, as early as December 1917 a group known as the All-Russian Extraordinary Commission for the Suppression of Counter-Revolution, Sabotage and Profiteering (Cheka) had been established under a Pole, Feliks Dzierzyński, to deal with internal 'enemies'. This organisation was necessary in part to combat looting and black-market activity, but also because opposition began to gather against the Bolsheviks after the abolition of the Constituent Assembly which had had a Socialist-Revolutionary majority in January.

Despite this in-fighting, on 10 July the Russian Soviet Federated Socialist Republic (RSFSR) was created, but the Socialist Revolutionaries attempted to oust the Communists through insurrection. The assassination of the German Ambassador, Mirbach, brought about a crisis, and Lenin himself was injured by a would-be assassin. By the summer of 1918 a civil war was raging which was to last until 1921, the period known as 'war Communism', during most of which the Bolsheviks only ruled fragments of Russian territory. As far as possible they tried to set up an economic and political system that was centralised. This process was aided by mechanisms which had been implemented by the Tsar to provide for the war effort. However, much of the process of centralisation was hampered both by the dislocations of the First World War and by civil war. These years were dominated by the Bolsheviks' struggle for power with the so-called White Armies.

Lenin responded to the threat of opposition by outlawing both the Socialist Revolutionaries and the Mensheviks, and engaged in a ruthless campaign to eliminate them. Indeed, the activities of the Socialist Revolutionaries provided the stimulus for the launching of a mass terror, the so-called 'Red Terror' in which the Cheka was extensively used. It established its headquarters in the offices of a former insurance company in Lubyanka Street in Moscow. At these premises thousands of victims of the terror were executed, and by 1918 the Cheka had detachments in all the areas under Bolshevik control. It was here that we see the origins of the 'police state'. The new Communist state was thus created in a climate of 'spymania', in which enemies of the Bolsheviks were eliminated and ordinary people were enlisted in the search for people of doubtful political allegiances. Russia had splintered between the forces of the Bolsheviks (the Reds) and the Whites.

The new state was also one that placed a premium on 'force of arms'. In early 1918 Trotsky, who had become Commissar for War, established the Red Army, constructing it upon pro-Bolshevik units from the old Imperial Army and fleet. Voluntary recruitment accounted for additional numbers, but from the summer of 1918 conscription provided a high proportion of combat troops. By the end of the civil war period the Red Army was a massive entity, with over 5 million men under arms, consisting mainly of peasant conscripts. However, only a small percentage under arms were fighting troops, most being used for administrative and supply work.

The Red Army actually took over most key administrative tasks for the new leadership. From the first it was organised on regular army lines, with the soldiers subject to military discipline and the officers being appointed rather than elected. There was a shortage of trained military professionals, and Trotsky appointed officers from the old Tsarist Army. By the end of the civil war the Red Army had over 50,000 former Tsarist officers in its employ, most of them having been conscripted. (Stalin actually disliked the practice of employing former Imperial Army officers, and objected to their use.) To ensure these officers remained loyal they were paired with political commissars who were usually Communists. In the first instance the new Red Army had to face not an external threat but the Whites. The situation was complicated by the activities of so-called 'Green Armies', that is, the peasant and Cossack bands which operated indepedently of either the Whites or the Reds in the more far-flung parts of the nascent state.

Both the Reds and the Whites were guilty during the civil war of numerous atrocities. As more has been learnt about Lenin and the Russian civil war, it has become apparent that the Red Army was used in the battle again 'internal enemies'. Richard Pipes, for example, has recently argued that Lenin himself authorised pogroms against Jews. Indeed, Lenin appeared to have few scruples in sanctioning violence against those who opposed his rule. The longer-term significance for the Soviet regime of this open acceptance by the Bolsheviks that terror was an effective instrument of power has been widely debated.[17] As a result of this acceptance and the ideological isolation in which

Soviet Russia developed, military defence was institutionalised within the regime to a far greater extent than elsewhere.

Civil war

Admiral Kolchak, a former Tsarist admiral and one of the leaders of the White armies, proclaimed himself ruler of Russia upon taking power in Omsk on 18 November 1918, a claim which was actually recognised by the Allied Control Council in Paris.[18] The White forces were encouraged to a certain extent by the American, British, French and Japanese forces which intervened onto Russian soil during the years of civil war. British troops even landed at Murmansk in 1918. However, in a fine illustration of the ambiguity and confusion of the war, this action was actually taken at the invitation of the city's Soviet, although in later Communist literature the invitation was described as a local aberration. Newly published documents show that Lenin and Stalin actually approved of the British landing, as it prevented the Germans from taking the port and the motive at this point was to prevent a German occupation. (Somewhat ironically, however, in 1940 Stalin allowed German forces to establish a U-boat base in a nearby port. It never became operational, because the British sank the two U-boats destined for operation from the new base.) The British force in Murmansk did come into conflict with the Bolsheviks later on, but the original intention was not to intervene in the civil war. Thus the notion that there was a large-scale intrusion by European powers at this point in the civil war is not a correct one, although it is true that French troops occupied Odessa while the British navy assisted White commanders in the Bay of Finland. Even less impressive than these efforts, though, was the American 'intervention' in the Russian Far East, where US troops were only once – and then briefly – in action against the Bolshevik forces. There were some in the West, most notably Winston Churchill, who did argue for a Western intervention to assist in the overthrow of the Bolshevik regime; but, overall, it cannot be argued that it amounted to a massive attempt. As George Kennan later explained, there was no 'intention that these forces should be employed with a view to unseating the Soviet government'.[19]

Not that they seemed to be needed in any case, initially at least. By the autumn, White forces had practically reached both Moscow and St Petersburg. After a year of vicious fighting, however, the Red forces managed to repel them, and the Red Army under Trotsky claimed victory. The main consequence of the civil war was that the Communist Party was the only political party to emerge from it, with no rivals for power. By September 1918, for example, the Red Terror (to which reference has already been made) was officially inaugurated, with widespread killing of opponents, both real and created, of the Bolsheviks. Alexander Yakovlev, one of the forces behind the policy of *glasnost* in the 1980s, has estimated that in the period from 1918 to 1922 there were 8 million victims of the civil war and the terror, and that these casualties were drawn, in the main, from the peasant classes.

The eradication of opponents meant that, almost from the beginning, the Soviet political regime was a one-party system. But it was also important that Bolshevik behaviour was formed in the midst of a civil war. The civil war had been fought against the White armies, who had the support of a number of Russia's former allies from the First World War and who numbered many ex-officers from Imperial Russia among their ranks as well as conscripted soldiers. The Bolsheviks depicted this struggle as a class war in both domestic and international terms, arguing that the Russian proletariat had overthrown the bourgeoisie, and that this revolution meant that the subsequent international revolution would threaten international capitalism. It was always expected that the forces of international capitalism would attempt at a later stage to subdue Soviet Russia.

The civil war itself polarised society, destroyed the economy and in some regions smashed local industrial production, creating sizeable refugee communities in such far-flung areas as Manchuria. It was in this context that the Bolsheviks had their first taste of ruling. It is worth noting, as Sheila Fitzgerald has pointed out, that of all the members of the Bolshevik party in 1927, 33 per cent had joined during the years 1917–20, while only 1 per cent joined before 1917. The experience of many Party members was that of a party at war. This, it could be argued, led to a heritage that included a reliance upon coercion, the centralisation of administration and the widespread use of summary justice for those who opposed the party.

Exporting the revolution

In March 1919 the Comintern (the Third Communist International) was established in Moscow to assist the spread of revolution abroad. But hopes of revolution proved illusory. In 1919 preparations had already been made to break though to Romania in order to aid Bela Kula in Hungary in his bid to establish a Hungarian Soviet republic. But by the end of the year the government which he led had collapsed.[20] In 1920 Lenin's view was that 'the revolution in Italy should be spurred on immediately, and ... to this end Hungary should be Sovietized and perhaps also Czechia and Romania'. Even more optimistically, Lenin foresaw a revolution in England, and in September 1920 he took the view that the Bolsheviks could 'and had the obligation to exploit the military situation to launch an offensive war'.

Despite his pragmatism at Brest-Litovsk, then, Lenin remained commited to the extension of the Revolution into Western Europe. During the years immediately after Brest-Litovsk, the Bolsheviks attempted to make good on this ambition, and sought to inspire revolution in Poland. However, Piłsudski, the Polish leader, decided that offence was the best defence, and launched an invasion of Ukraine in an attempt to recapture territory which had been ruled over by the Poles before the nineteenth-century partitions. The Poles actually captured Kiev before Bolshevik forces managed to repel the attack and with the encouragement of Lenin proceeded to follow the retreating soldiers back on to Polish soil. As the Red Army marched to Warsaw, the Bolsheviks confidently refused to consider an armistice proposed by the British based on the so-called Curzon line.[21] In Moscow, a provisional Polish revolutionary committee, headed by the Social Democrat Marchlewski, awaited the call to take up power in Warsaw, while Stalin began to plan for the creation of a Bolshevik super-federation. Yet again, these dreams came to nothing when the Poles inflicted a humiliating defeat on the Red Army and forced the Bolsheviks back. The Treaty of Riga, agreed in 1921 between the Russians and Poles, actually established the border well to the east of the Curzon line. Poland was given control of territories that included large numbers of Belorussian and Ukranian peoples, which would later form the basis for Soviet claims for a new European settlement.

In the meantime the early years of the Soviet regime posed an interesting question. Given that revolution had failed to transform the external world, what was and could be the nature of the relationship between the only socialist state and the rest of the world? By 1921 it was apparent to the leadership in Moscow that an accommodation had to be found with the numerous capitalist states surounding them. Four years after the October Revolution some of the Bolshevik leadership called for a truce with the capitalist world. This required a major revision of the 'truths' and the view which had sustained the initial vision of global revolutionary change, in particular the proposition that war was inevitable between states. Initially Lenin had asserted that as long as capitalism existed wars were inevitable. In his report to the Eighth Party Congress in 1919 he enunciated his view that 'the existence of the Soviet Republic side by side with imperialist states for a long time is unthinkable'. Yet by the first years of the 1920s he had modified his line to such an extent that he began to envisage a long period of peace between East and West. In his closing speech to the Tenth All-Russia Party Congress in late May 1921, Lenin held that a rough 'equilibrium' prevailed between Russia and the capitalist world. He did not speak at this stage of a coexistence with the capitalist world, but of a cohabitation (*sozhitel'stvo*).[22] This later developed into the extensively used notion of a coexistence with the West. The origins and intent of the idea of peaceful coexistence have been extensively debated, but in essence it was a further reinforcement of the principles established by Lenin at Brest-Litovsk: in the shorter term, revolution had to take second place to survival. However, Lenin did not, it should be said, abandon his basic assumptions. Revolution in one place still meant revolution elsewhere – it just meant that the revolution would have to come more slowly. This belief remained central for the Soviet elite. The various vicissitudes consequent on this assumption throughout the century are examined in the chapters that follow.

Lenin and some of the Bolshevik elite hoped that a proclamation of coexistence would reassure the Western states that Russia was essentially peaceful, and so would stave off immediate conflict.[23] The desire to 'normalise' relations with the outside world was inspired by the economic demands of Russia, if nothing else. In 1921 Moscow launched its New Economic Policy (NEP), formulated after the Tenth Party Congress in March. Destined to last until 1927, it offered concessions to attract foreign capital into Russia to facilitate its development after the ravages both of the civil war and a horrific famine in 1921, in which up to 4 million people perished. It was hoped that a period of peace would enable Russia to acquire Western aid and technical assistance. These attempts at normalisation with the external world bore some fruit when, in March 1921, the Anglo-Soviet trade agreement was signed. In addition to these pragmatic reasons, Lenin also hoped to derive personal political benefits from an increased collaboration with the outside world, believing that the forging of personal relationships with leading statesmen would help in his battles with political rivals.[24] Normalisation was a hotly contested policy amongst the policy elite specifically because such a strategy sat uneasily with the commitment to proletarian revolution.

Yet the Revolution was not abandoned. Even as the NEP was formulated, the Bolshevik leadership attempted to incite the Communists in Germany during what became known as Red March. Lenin supported this tactic despite his apparently more moderate stance with respect to the Western states. Unrest in Germany in 1923 also created strong expectations of change, and there was direct support from Moscow for a rebellion in Hamburg in October 1923. All of this sat uneasily with the notion of the creation of a 'breathing space' with the West, and in Russian foreign policy it left a two-pronged policy of both coexistence with the major Western powers and the encouragement of revolutionary activities abroad whenever possible.[25] It did little to inspire confidence amongst the Western powers that the Bolshevik leadership was sincere in its declarations of peaceful coexistence – a distrust which was apparent at the Genoa conference in 1922.

Genoa

In one respect at least the Genoa Conference, convened by the Supreme Allied Conference, marked an attempt to try and re-establish the basis on which the West could live with the new Soviet state and ties between Russia and the West.[26] On 7 January the Soviet Government received its invitation. The conference, which lasted six weeks, was attended by 34 states, but ultimately no agreement was reached. Despite the fact that, in March 1921, the Anglo-Soviet trade agreement had been signed which had appeared to indicate a new era in relations between the two states, at Genoa harsh terms were presented by British Prime Minister, Lloyd George, to the Russian delegation, including recognition of all Tsarist debts and compensation to property owners. There was no mention of loans or, indeed, of the possibility of recognition for the new Soviet state. In response, the Russians demanded recompense for the Allied intervention during the civil war. Little was achieved, despite the rhetoric of coexistence. One analyst has phrased it thus: 'Both sides while talking of "appeasement" and "coexistence" still heard the sound of the other's gunfire and referred continually to their recent military and ideological battles.'[27]

Although Lenin had been originally scheduled to lead the Soviet delegation to Genoa, the Soviet group was led by Georgi Chicherin (who had replaced Trotsky as Commissar for Foreign Affairs) and Maxim Litvinov, who in 1921 had been appointed Deputy Commissar for Foreign Affairs. The delegation had hoped for trade, loans and general agreements on disarmament. The most important issue for the Soviet leadership, however, was that of recognition. This was part and parcel of the attempt to achieve a 'breathing-space' for the Soviet economy and government. There was also the hope for Lenin that he could enhance his own position as Soviet leader though a strategy of selective personal contacts with Western leaders. Intriguingly, there exist snippets of information that indicate that Lenin and the other Bolsheviks who attended the conference were nervous of the impression that they might make at Genoa. It was the first occasion on which they met diplomats from other states in a formal setting, and they made a point of dressing formally in striped trousers and long coats to meet their counterparts. Litvinov reveals in his memoirs that the Soviet delegation was aware that rumours were rife in the Western press that the Bolsheviks would arrive wearing red shirts and black waistbands, boots and tall fur hats!

If the Bolshevik leadership drew one chief lesson from the conference at Genoa, it was that multilateral agreements with the West were difficult if not impossible to achieve, but that some bilateral agreements were possible and profitable. Although no formal diplomatic arrangements could be made with Britain and France, the new Soviet leadership did find one power willing to negotiate with it – the other pariah of the European state system, Germany. On the Easter Sunday of the Genoa conference, 16 April, the Germans and the Russians had signed a treaty at Rapallo. Both sides mutually repudiated debts and claims and provided for longer-term economic assistance. In a subsequent and secret protocol it was agreed that the *Reichswehr* and the Red

Army would collaborate.[28] This agreement set in motion a period of extensive economic, political and military co-operation. The Soviet–German relationship flourished throughout the 1920s: there were undoubted benefits in trade, as well as a desire on the side of both Moscow and Berlin to counter the political weight of the Franco-British axis. Both the Russians and the Germans also had a mutual enmity towards Poland which, as we saw earlier, had benefited after the First World War from the occupation of both German and Russian territory and a general opposition to the Versailles agreement. The Bolshevik leadership, despite its revolutionary ambitions, had engaged at Rapallo in diplomacy of a very traditional nature. Indeed, during 1921 the new state had concluded treaties with Turkey, Iran, Afghanistan and Mongolia, thus demonstrating a not inconsiderable interest in the Near East. As Richard Debo has written, the first few years of Soviet foreign relations were 'an amalgam of ideology and expediency, utopian expectation and realistic calculation, daring innovation and classical diplomacy'.

Perhaps, though, one of the most important features of Russian foreign policy at this juncture was the fact that the Bolshevik leadership was divided both over general policy formulation and over the future course of Soviet policy both at home and abroad.

The leadership struggle

While Lenin lived he was the obvious and acknowledged leader of the Party, in spite of the fact that the Party did not, at least officially, have a leader. The office that Lenin chose for himself after the revolution was that of Chairman of the Council of People's Commissars. The Bolsheviks were generally agreed that they had no intention of allowing one man to occupy the position of leader, in the fashion of Mussolini in Italy, say: the danger of one charismatic individual emerging to take over power was quite often discussed and warned against. This became more of a danger as Lenin's health began to deteriorate from 1921 onwards: he suffered a stroke in 1922 and a second stroke in March 1923 that left him paralysed. In this period his responsibilities were assumed by the goverment under the chairmanship of Aleksei Rykov; however, real political power lay with the Politburo, which had seven full members including Lenin himself, Trotsky, Stalin (who occupied the post of General Secretary but had originally held that of Commissar for Nationalities), and G. Zinoviev and Kamenev, who were respectively heads of the Petrograd (Leningrad) Party Organisation and the Moscow Party Organisation. Although the Politburo pledged itself to act as a collective leadership, as Lenin ailed a fierce struggle over the succession began, and continued throughout 1923, with Trotsky opposing Zinoviev, Stalin and Kamenev.

Lenin himself, in the final months of his life, watched the emerging factionalism within the Party elite and made his own assessment of the various candidates. He identified Stalin and Trotsky as the two outstanding individuals within the Politburo. Interestingly, Iosif Vissarionovich Dzhugashvili (Stalin was a name derived from the Russian word for steel that he assumed some time after 1913) was a non-Russian. He had been born in Georgia in 1879, and attended the ecclesiastical academy at Gori before moving on to the Theological Seminary in Tbilisi, where he remained until 1899. It was whilst attending the seminary that he joined a local underground political movement. At first he took the pseudonym 'Koba', after a daring outlaw of local legend. During the period of 1904–6 he led a series of strikes in the oil fields, but was imprisoned for his activities. Stalin, as he had become, played a much smaller role in the upheavals of 1917 than either Lenin or Trotsky, and it was during the civil war that he made his reputation, holding the town of Tsaritsyn on the river Volga during the upheavals. This town would later be named Stalingrad in honour of his achievements.

As he ailed, though, Lenin attempted to prevent Stalin from becoming leader, arguing that he had accrued too much personal and political power. Indeed, Lenin's criticisms of Stalin were read out to delegates as they arrived for the Thirteenth Congress in May 1924. Stalin, however, confessed all his faults and promised to correct them.

Stalin's battle with Trotsky over the leadership came to a head in the winter and spring of 1923–4, and it was actually at the Thirteenth Congress that Stalin managed to defeat him. As the various accounts show, several factors were involved. Not the least of these was Stalin's ability to propagate Lenin's heritage. With Lenin's death in January 1924, at the age of 53, Stalin played a major role in developing a cult of Lenin. On 16 January all the leaders, except for Trotsky who was in the south of the country, paid public homage to Lenin. All of them, except Stalin, expressed their appreciation of Lenin in the standard Marxist terms which had been used at the funerals of other Bolsheviks: Stalin, however, expressed his tribute in terms of his ability to interpret and fulfil the Leninist legacy, depicting himself as Lenin's pupil who could carry the Party forward. Many authors have pointed to the political acumen which Stalin deployed in this oration, when he cast himself not as Lenin's equal, but as his disciple.[29] He was also greatly helped in his battle against political rivals by his position as General Secretary, which provided him with a position within the Secretariat and an organisational base from which he could gather support and operate. The Secretariat appointed the secretaries who oversaw local party organisations. These people could be dismissed if they were considered untrustworthy, and the local organisations then voted and elected the delegates who would attend the national Party congresses. The national congress then elected the members of the Politburo, the Central Committee and the Secretariat. This placed enormous power in the hands of the General Secretary, because it was possible for him to ensure that at every stage the congresses were in his favour. Through this system of patronage Stalin built a virtually impregnable position that enabled him to control advancement through the Party machinery and oversee vast numbers of Party members. The post of General Secretary was thus probably the most powerful in the Party.

After the battles of 1924 against Trotsky, Stalin moved to eliminate Zinoviev and Kamenev as potential rivals for the leadership. Their supporters were banished from the Party. Trotsky himself was expelled from the Politburo in 1927, after some street demonstrations in his favour, and in January 1928 banished to Alma-Ata in Central Asia; at this stage he was allowed to take some of his followers with him, and he remained in contact with 'allies' throughout the Soviet Union through correspondence. In January 1929 he was expelled from Soviet soil. But Stalin did not forget about his erstwhile rival for power, and Trotsky's movements were followed closely by the NKVD as he sought to expose the nature of the Stalinist regime from his exile.

The revolution abroad

It should be noted at this stage, however, that after Lenin's death there is a question-mark about the processes through which foreign policy was made. Up until Lenin became seriously ill he appears to have actually controlled the policy-making process on a day-to-day basis, as well as overseeing the work of the Foreign Commissar, Georgi Vasilievich Chicherin, who had taken up the post after Trotsky's resignation in 1918. Richard Debo has argued that we cannot be certain of who or what controlled foreign policy in the period after Lenin's death, and that it is still not clear at which point Stalin assumed control of the making of external strategies. By 1926, however, Chicherin was complaining bitterly that Stalin was interfering in the conduct of foreign policy.[30]

After Lenin's death the problem of reconciling a revolutionary ideology and the relationship with the West was eventually if not immediately inherited by Stalin. He had long been interested in foreign policy. Throughout the civil war period he had intervened in policy-making, and as a member of the Politburo he made his views clear on a range of issues. In December 1924 Stalin announced that the energies of the Soviet state would henceforth be devoted to a programme of 'Socialism in one Country'.[31] Building on ideas that Lenin had espoused,[32] he argued that Russia could achieve socialism without the help of a Western revolutionary movement. In the meantime the priority was the construction of a strong state at home. In espousing these ideas, Stalin transformed both the conception of the Soviet state and its relationship with the outside world. His worldview was predicated on the idea that the Soviet state could survive alone in a capitalist world, and he also shifted the notion of revolution away from an emphasis on the outside world to a focus on the internal, quite literally succeeding in isolating the state from the rest of the world. Trotsky had come to believe that Russia was politically and independently strong enough to re-enter into economic relations with the rest of Europe. Indeed, he had espoused an integrationist view of Europe in which he argued that contact with Europe would strengthen the economic base of Russia and further the economic development of Europe as a whole; and he put forward the idea of permanent revolution. Stalin, however, favoured an autarkist or isolationist route, which had the added appeal of appearing non-provocative and easing the threat of war, at least in the short term.[33] Trotsky and Stalin disagreed over practically every area of foreign policy. As outlined above, Trotsky believed that the Soviet Communist Party should play an international role, and he argued that they should support the Communists in China against the nationalist leader, Chiang Kai-Shek. But Stalin argued that it was premature in the 1920s to support a Communist uprising in China, and was cautious, seeking to protect the young Soviet state from foreign embroilment.

The notion of 'socialism in one country' did not directly address itself to the question of war with capitalism: on the whole, it was concerned with domestic, not revolutionary war. But Stalin did not abandon the notion of revolutionary war. Indeed, the 1920s saw two major advances in the way that the Stalinist leadership thought about the outside world: one was the 'two camps' thesis, and the other was the notion of 'capitalist encirclement'. The first held that war was inevitable between the polarised groups of capitalist and socialist states, the second that capitalism was literally encircling the Soviet state. Whilst Stalin asserted that war was inevitable, he also held that it would not occur yet, but that the Soviet Union had to operate carefully in the meantime, not least because of its own internal weaknesses.

By 1925, in line with both these assumptions, Stalin predicted the inevitability of war in Europe. Despite the Rapallo alliance he specifically pointed to the rebirth of German militarism and the potential for conflict between the capitalist states. He made clear what the position of the Soviet Union would be if such a situation arose:

> We shall have to come out, but we ought to be the last to come out. And we should come out in order to throw the decisive weight on the scales, the weight that should tilt the scales.[34]

Soviet foreign policy was premised on a belief that sufficient differences existed amongst the Western powers, particularly over economic issues, that could be carefully exploited to Moscow's advantage. The idea of capitalist encirclement was related to this idea. Stalin deliberately inflated the notion of the threat of war with the capitalist states, so providing a part-justification for the regime at home. In particular, in the late 1920s he blamed the Conservative Government in Britain (which had replaced the Labour Government which had extended recognition to Moscow) for conspiring against the Soviet state. Mutual suspicions were bad enough between London and Moscow in 1927 for Anglo-Soviet relations to be broken off. There were actually good reasons for the Soviet leadership to believe that the external environment was threatening in 1927. In addition to the fact that the British had broken off diplomatic relations, the Soviet ambassador to Poland was murdered in June and there were a series of attacks on Soviet personnel in Berlin and Beijing. Stalin himself declared this year to be one of 'maximum danger'. In the light of these events the government began preparations for future conflicts with capitalism. Already in 1926 Chief of the General Staff Tukhachevsky had commissioned a study to define what future conflicts might look like, and in 1928 some of these findings were released, naming the most likely belligerent states as Britain, France, Poland, the Baltic States and Italy.[35]

As discussed earlier, Stalin had fundamentally disagreed with Trotsky over the role of Soviet Communism abroad, believing that domestic issues came first. Throughout the 1920's he followed a policy of forced industrialisation, for which he needed a guaranteed supply of agricultural surpluses. Believing that this could only be ensured through control of the farms, Stalin imposed the collectivisation of agriculture, in which all privately owned livestock and machinery were seized for the use of large collective state-owned farms. Those peasants who resisted were exterminated or exiled to Siberia. Some estimates put the figure of those who suffered this fate at around 5 million people. The towns were supplied from the collective farms, but for the rural communities it was a human and social catastrophe. To justify the regime's actions, Stalin steadily propagated the notion of an imminent onslaught on the USSR.

Whilst there are still question marks, as indicated earlier, over how Soviet foreign policy was made in the period after Lenin's death, by 1929 it appears that Stalin was in charge. Even by 1929 it is still not clear exactly what his relationship with the Foreign Ministry was. The dismissal of Chicherin in 1928 on the ground of ill health is probably one small clue to the fact that Stalin was inexorably moving his own appointees into all aspects of Soviet governance. By the time of his fiftieth birthday, in December 1929, the 'cult of personality' was in place and his dominance in power was established, if not unchallenged, as we will see in the next chapter.

Conclusions

It is a difficult task to assess Soviet foreign policy in the turbulent years after 1917, especially as so much of the period is under historiographical revision (not least, Lenin's reputation is again being reassessed). Nevertheless, while bearing the caveat in mind that the archives will undoubtedly tell us more about Lenin, Stalin, the civil war and the NEP, we can offer some conclusions.

The Soviet state was forged in war and civil war. Bloodshed, violence and arbitrary acts of cruelty were accepted ways of life within the early days of the Soviet state. Those who dissented from the Bolshevik vision were eradicated. Lenin himself had proved relentless, for example, in his imposition of atheism on the country: the Red Army under his instruction had put to death thousands of clerics. Jews, too, had suffered from pograms instigated by the Bolshevik leadership (despite the fact that Trotsky himself was a Jew). Purges of political and religious opponents to the regime were commonplace in the early 1920s. Mikhail Gorbachev has remarked that 'cruelty was the main problem with Lenin'; but his legacy is important in that this manner of 'governance by terror' was established and given legitimacy. It was this legacy that set the stage in part for the 1930s. There were other legacies too.

The first period of Soviet foreign policy was concerned with the preservation of the revolution at home, and with gaining from other states the recognition of the new Soviet state. In particular, given the demands of the economy, credits and loans were needed to repair the ravages of war, civil war and famine. The failure to win recognition at an early stage threw the Soviet state back on to the relationship with Germany that developed at Rapallo and after. In some respects this was not a surprising turn of events, as the Soviet-German relationship was based at least in part on a joint hatred of the Versailles system and a mutual desire for the revision of Poland's borders.

In this period we also see that it was grudgingly accepted after 1924 that global revolution would not occur – not just yet. In the meantime the Comintern was established to subvert and manipulate the workings of the capitalist system. In the mid and late 1920s its activities were noticeable in Britain; but, on the whole, ideological confrontation was placed firmly on the back burner after 1924. The Chinese Communists, in particular, received little support from Moscow.

What does emerge clearly is what has been termed by Gabriel Gorodestky a 'dualism' in Soviet foreign policy. This dualism may be characterised as, first, a desire to continue the Revolution, and, second, a pragmatic acceptance that this would not occur in the short term. At the same time as pursuing revolutionary activity, however, what might be termed the usual 'mechanics' of diplomacy were put in place by the Bolshevik leadership. (This was a disputed course of action and, as discussed above, the leadership was torn apart at times by feuding over policy.) Nevertheless, under both Lenin and then Stalin, 'normal diplomacy' or intercourse with other states was sought. There was a desire for recognition, respect for the principle of non-intervention (at least in the Soviet state) and the acknowledgement that Russia had a need for reciprocal trading relations. The alacrity with which the Soviet leadership accepted the invitation to the Genoa Conference denoted a willingness to assume a traditional role in European politics. Indeed, as the 1920s progressed Moscow expanded its relations with other states, particularly on its periphery in the Far East and in the Middle East, and increasingly began to behave not as a revolutionary state but as a 'normal' state, playing the balance-of-power game. In fact, the most noticeable feature of Moscow's behaviour, aside from the foundation and activities of the Comintern, was its desire to become part of the international community or, at least, to become a member on its own terms.

Yet Russia in this period was regarded as 'different' by the other European states, and some in the West were loath to accept the new status of its regime. It was this exclusion that in many ways explains the relationship which was built up and sustained between Russia and Germany. Both Moscow and Berlin had good reason to seek a revision of the Versailles settlement, and in particular to find ways of undermining the post-1919 division of territory in the East. Poland had, after all, benefited at the expense of both. In this respect it might be argued that the new Soviet state (the USSR replaced the RSFSR in December 1922) was actually more revisionist than revolutionary. None the less, there were still certain features of the revolutionary inheritance which would remain important – not least the emphasis upon a strong leadership and the use of terror. These traits would become even more apparent in the next decade.

Notes

1 A. J. P. Taylor, *The Struggle for Mastery in Europe* (Oxford: Oxford University Press, 1954), p. XI.
2 See Peter Hopkirk's account of the long contest for supremacy between Russia and Britain, the so-called 'Great Game', in his book *The Great Game* (Oxford: Oxford University Press, 1994).
3 For example, Fred Halliday, *Rethinking International Relations* (London: Macmillan, 1994), ch. 6.
4 Stephen Walt, *Revolution and War* (Ithaca: Cornell University Press, 1996).
5 Robert Service, *A History of Russia* (London: Allen Lane, 1996), p. 1.
6 See John Gooding, *Rulers and Subjects: Government and People in Russia 1801–1991* (London: Arnold, 1996).
7 Edward Acton, *Rethinking the Russian Revolution* (London: Edward Arnold, 1990), pp. 21–3.
8 Paul Dukes, *A History of Russia c. 882–1996* (3rd edn, London: Macmillan, 1998), pp. 228–9.
9 S. Fitzpatrick, *The Russian Revolution 1917–1932* (Oxford: Oxford Paperbacks, 1982), pp. 34–7. E. Hobsbawm, *Age of Extremes*. (London: Joseph, 1994).
10 Allen Lynch, *The Soviet Theory of International Relations* (Cambridge: Cambridge University Press, 1987), p. 17.

11 L. Trotsky, *My Life* (New York: Scribner, 1930), p. 341.

12 *The Bolsheviks and the October Revolution Central Committee Minutes of the RSDLP, 1917–1918* (London: Penguin, 1966), p. 195.

13 R. Conquest, *Stalin: Breaker of Nations* (London: Weidenfeld & Nicolson, 1991), p. 75. For a depiction of Stalin's realism in this period, see D. Volkogonov, *Stalin: Triumph and Tragedy* (London, Weidenfeld & Nicolson, 1991).

14 J. N. Westwood, *Endurance and Endeavour: Russian History 1812–1986* (3rd edn, Oxford: Oxford University Press, 1987), p. 266.

15 A. Bullock, *Hitler and Stalin: Parallel Lives* (London: HarperCollins, 1991), p. 69.

16 Dmitri Volkogonov, *Stalin: Triumph and Tragedy*.

17 See Richard Pipes (ed.), *The Unknown Lenin: From the Secret Archives* (New Haven: Yale University Press, 1997). See also Robert Conquest, 'Terrorists', in *The New York Review of Books*. (March 6, 1997).

18 J. L. Gaddis, *Russia, the Soviet Union and the United States* (New York: McGraw-Hill, 1990), pp. 82–3.

19 George F. Kennan, 'The United States and the Soviet Union, 1917–1976', *Foreign Affairs* (July 1976).

20 V. Mastny, *Russia's Road to the Cold War* (New York: Columbia Press, 1979), p. 13.

21 W. Lerner, 'Attempting a Revolution from Without; Poland in 1920', in T. T. Hammond and R. Farrell, *The Anatomy of Communist Takeovers* (New Haven: Yale University Press, 1975), pp. 94–106.

22 Allen Lynch, *Soviet Theory of International Relations*, p. 17.

23 V. I. Lenin, speech delivered at a Meeting of Activists of the Moscow Organization of the RCP, *Collected Works*, vol. 31 (Moscow: Progress Publishers, 1966), pp. 438–59.

24 A. O. Chubarin, 'V. I. Lenin I Genuia', *Istoriia SSSR*, 2 (1970), pp. 39–50.

25 For an appraisal of Russian attempts to influence British politics in the 1920s, see Gabriel Gorodetsky, 'The Formulation of Soviet Foreign Policy – Ideology and Realpolitik', in Gabriel Gorodetsky (ed.), *Soviet Foreign Policy 1917–1991: A Retrospective* (London: Frank Cass, 1994).

26 For the best account of the conference, see Carole Fink, 'The NEP in Foreign Policy: The Genoa Conference and Treaty of Rapallo', in Gabriel Gorodetsky, *Soviet Foreign Policy*, pp. 11–21.

27 Fink, 'The NEP in Foreign Policy', p. 18.

28 See H. W. Gatzke, 'Russo-German Military Collaboration during the Weimar Republic', *American Historical Review*, 63 (1957–8), pp. 565–97.

29 Dukes, *History of Russia*, p. 235.

30 Richard Debo, 'G. V. Chicherin', in Gabriel Gorodetsky, *Soviet Foreign Policy*, p. 28.

31 J.V. Stalin, *Sochineniya* (Moscow: CPSU, CC Marx-Engels Institute), VI, p. 396, 399.

32 E. H. Carr, *The Bolshevik Revolution 1917–1923*, vol. 3 (New York, 1953), pp. 436–7.

33 Iver B. Neumann, *Russia and the Idea of Europe* (London: Routledge, 1996), p. 117.

34 Quoted in I. Deutscher, *Stalin* (London: Penguin, 1966), p. 405.

35 See Steven J. Main, *The Red Army and the Future War in Europe 1925–1940* (Oct. 1997, C96: Conflict Studies Research Centre, Sandhurst). See also N. S. Simonov, '"Strengthen the Defence of the Land of the Soviets": The 1927 War Alarm and its Consequences', *Europe–Asia Studies*, 48/8 (1996).

2
The Search for Security 1933–1939

The story of the 1930s is the story of the USSR under siege. During this decade the leadership were preoccupied with two key questions in foreign policy: how to restrain Fascist Germany in the West, and how to repel Japan in the East. In both cases, similar strategies were adopted. Soviet security requirements mandated alliance with other states to act as a counterweight to these threats of aggression. The 1930s were a story of the making of an intricate foreign policy as the Kremlin sought to find allies, further complicated by the fact that the Soviet leadership itself was divided over what strategy would best subdue Hitler. While Litvinov strongly favoured a pro-Western collective security arrangement, his ideas were opposed by some, most notably Molotov, who favoured a tactical rapprochement with Fascist Germany. The question of the role of key individuals in the making of Soviet foreign policy was important in this decade, not least because it was a decade in which 'elites' were ruthlessly purged as Stalin eradicated his political opponents. If the 1930s was about the very survival of the USSR, it was also a tale of individual survival.

The decade was also characterised by the expansion of Soviet foreign policy into areas such as Spain, and of a rapprochement of sorts with the United States. In 1941, as Soviet strategies failed in Europe, it was the relationship with Washington which became of critical importance. It would appear that Stalin completely jettisoned any vestiges of Marxist–Leninist thinking with his policy of alliance with capitalist states, but as will become clear, ideology was far from forgotten in Stalin's assessment of both friends and enemies.

Beginnings

Conventional wisdom tells two stories of Soviet foreign policy towards Germany in the 1930s. In the first, Moscow, fearful of the threat to security posed by Nazi expansionism, sought an anti-German alliance with Britain and France. This came to a head in 1939 with a proposal for a

Soviet–British–French triple alliance to halt Germany. Failing in this ambition, the USSR turned to a deal with Hitler as a last resort, and signed the Nazi–Soviet Non-Aggression Pact of 23 August 1939. The most famous supporter of this story is A. J. P. Taylor. He has argued, in support of this version, that 'However one spins the crystal and tries to look into the future from the point of view of 23 August 1939, it is difficult to see what other course Soviet Russia could have followed.'[1] This version of history was until recently also endorsed by Soviet historians, who claimed that this collective-security approach was pursued relentlessly by the Kremlin in a bid to defeat German aggression. The second story rejects this. Rather, this version asserts that the Kremlin's foreign-policy orientation was not towards a collective security arrangement with the Western powers at all, but one in the tradition of Rapallo, in which a pro-German strategy was followed. The logical and sought-after culmination of this strategy was the Nazi–Soviet Pact.[2] This chapter argues that neither version is entirely accurate: rather, it will suggest that the Kremlin operated elements of both strategies in the decade before the war.

With Hitler's takeover of power in Berlin, Moscow began to feel uneasy. Soviet leaders declared initially that the established Soviet–German relationship would not change. As if to prove that this was indeed the case, on 5 May 1931 Germany and the USSR ratified a protocol which prolonged the 1926 Berlin treaty of neutrality for another five years. In September 1933 Soviet military leaders declared their commitment to the Rapallo Treaty, while Tukhachevsky in November stated that the Red Army would never betray its co-operation with the *Reichswehr*. Despite these public pronouncements, however, Moscow decided to close down all German military stations in the USSR. In June 1933 fears about Hitler's intentions had grown when, at the World Economic Conference, Hugenberg, the German Economics Minister, submitted a document which Moscow perceived as a demand for 'living space' in the USSR. The Soviet leadership protested to Berlin, and Hugenberg resigned.

Despite their suspicions, however, the foreign-policy options for Moscow became more constricted when Germany left the League of Nations in October 1933. *Izvestiya* commented, 'Germany's exit from the League of Nations is for the supporters of Peace an alarming warning of the need to be on guard.'[3] In December 1933, Maxim Litvinov in a speech to the Central Executive Committee of the Congress of Soviets divided the states of Europe into two camps. Litvinov distinguished not between socialist and capitalist states, but rather divided Europe between revisionist powers such as Germany, and those who wished to maintain the status quo. The Soviet Foreign Minister emphasised Hitler's ambition, outlined in *Mein Kampf*, to 'enslave the Soviet people'. To avert this threat, he proposed that the USSR seek collaboration with other anti-revisionist states.[4] On 12 December the

Politburo passed a resolution in favour of collective security which was subsequently approved on 20 December. The Soviet leadership sought a multilateral assistance pact between the USSR, France, Poland, Belgium, Czechoslovakia, the Baltic states and Finland.

In particular, Litvinov targeted France as a possible ally against Hitler. France was not an obvious ally of the USSR. As discussed in Chapter 1, there had been a series of conflicts which had marred the Western–Soviet relationship. The Soviet Government had already proposed a non-aggression pact to the French in 1927 and early 1928, without success. Now the USSR really sought an improvement in both political and economic relations. Indeed, according to some Soviet sources Litvinov had mentioned to the French Ambassador in Moscow as early as March 1930 that his government was indeed prepared to sign a non-aggression pact with Paris. By March 1931 it appeared as if the French might be ready to look for an accommodation with Moscow. The French were shocked by the announcement of a so-called customs union between Germany and Austria, perceived in Paris as the first step towards the *Anschluss*. By April 1931 therefore it seemed as if agreement was reached to start negotiations. These discussions rambled on without much success until in 1934 Litvinov embarked upon discussions with Louis Barthou, the French Foreign Minister, on arrangements for a security agreement which would guarantee the eastern frontiers of Germany. (Barthou was later assassinated alongside King Alexander of Yugoslavia by Croatian terrorists in Paris in October 1934.) Litvinov wanted to create a framework which included the USSR, Germany, the Baltic states, Poland and Czechoslovakia. As part of the deal, Moscow would join the League of Nations, and the French would recognise the rearmament of Germany.[5] The two Foreign Ministers also agreed a separate Franco-Soviet pact under which Paris would aid Moscow in the event of an attack and, in return, Moscow would guarantee the western frontiers of Germany. It was envisaged in Moscow that both it and France should engage in a regional pact involving Eastern Europe and a mutual commitment in the event of a German attack. However, in April 1934 Soviet hopes were scuppered when the French proposed that the Germans too should be included in any such venture. Moscow went along with this idea, provided that all agreements were mutually binding. However, fierce German opposition meant the abandonment of any such scheme. It is questionable as to how seriously the French were prepared to take the arrangement, as ratification of the treaty was obstructed in Paris, and French ministers were simultaneously negotiating with Hitler. In May 1935, however, mutual assistance pacts were signed by Moscow with both France and Czechoslovakia.

That Moscow saw some utility in collective security can be seen by the development of its positive attitude towards the League of Nations. Prior to 1933, Soviet statesmen had been scathing about the organisation.

In January 1934, in an interview in *Izvestiya*, Stalin had signalled a definite change in Soviet thinking. He commented that 'despite the withdrawal of Germany and Japan from the League of Nations, or perhaps just because of this, the League may act as something of a brake to retard the outbreak of military actions or to hinder them'.[6] He reiterated this positive view in September, when the USSR was admitted to membership. He argued that

> Given the current world situation with Japan having turned Manchuria into a springboard against the Soviet Union, and with a German-Japanese rapprochement on the subject of war a fact, one does not have to rack one's brains for an answer to the question as to what prompted the Soviet Union to accept the invitation to enter the League of Nations.[7]

Stalin probably placed little faith in the willingness or ability of the West European nations to act with the Soviet Union, but he saw alliances as a possible deterrent to Hitler and therefore acted to promote them. In particular, he recognised the antagonism that the activities of the Comintern aroused with Western governments. Accordingly, it appears that Moscow instructed the Western Communists to calm their activities during this period. For example, the French Communist Party changed its aim from class warfare to one of 'Popular Fronts'. Support for this move was confirmed by Pierre Laval, the new French Foreign Minister. After a meeting with Stalin in Moscow, in May 1935 he described how encouraging the Soviet leader had been about the new programme of rearmament in France. Subsequently, at the Seventh Congress of the Comintern, which was held in Moscow during July and August 1935, it was decided that the primary function of the organisation was to defeat Fascism, through 'popular fronts' organised along national lines.

Despite the apparent willingness of Moscow to co-operate with the West European states, the British in particular were reluctant to sanction collective action. In March 1935 Anthony Eden, at this point Deputy Foreign Minister in the British Government, undertook a trip to Moscow for talks with Stalin. During these discussions the Soviet leader attempted to impress upon Eden Moscow's desire for a *rapprochement* with the West against Germany. According to Eden's memoirs, the Soviet leader urged that Hitler be made to realise that if Germany attacked any other nation it would have the rest of Europe against it.[8] Little came from the discussions and, indeed, they seemed merely to reinforce Stalin's scepticism about the possibility of British support against Hitler. Against this backdrop, in the same month as the Eden–Stalin meeting, Hitler announced that he had introduced conscription and that Germany had achieved a level of air power to match that of Britain.

By the middle of 1935 relations between Moscow and Berlin appeared to be at a low. Yet there was a complex web of contacts and communications between the two capitals which appeared to be concentrated around the figure of the Soviet trade representative in Berlin, David Kandelaki. Whilst he was later purged, in the period between 1935 and 1937, he appeared to be a conduit for much discussion over the expansion of Soviet–German trading links: a policy which encountered direct opposition from Litvinov.

There was division within the government in Moscow about the policy of searching for agreement with the Western powers. Some Soviet officials openly advocated a strategy of self-sufficiency rather than collective security. In January 1936 Molotov stated, 'We toilers of the Soviet Union must count on our own efforts in defending our affairs and above all our Red Army in the defence of our country'.[9]

On 7 March 1936 German units entered the area of the Rhineland which had been demilitarised under the Versailles agreement. Through this action Hitler fortified the Western frontiers of Germany, and Polish and Czech soil became increasingly vulnerable. Moscow hoped that this action would galvanise the Western powers into action. Litvinov, in a speech to the Council of the League of Nations called to discuss the question, expressed a willingness to join in any or all actions that the Council might take against Hitler: his bid for a collective security arrangement was premised on the belief that these Western powers, like Moscow, had a vested interest in propping up the system established at Versailles for as long as possible.

Litinov's hope that some of the Western powers would join the USSR in anti-German alliance became increasingly less likely as Hitler continued to press German territorial claims, and Britain and France showed themselves little disposed to challenge him. After the occupation of Austria in March 1938, Hitler focused his attention on the Sudeten Germans in Czechoslovakia. At the height of this crisis, on 17 March, Litvinov stressed again the willingness of his government to act with other states against Hitler. He also informed the Czechs that the USSR was prepared to go to war if the French also carried out their obligations.[10] It is difficult to tell if Stalin was serious, because he was careful to tie Soviet behaviour to that of the French. But the French did not take up the Soviet offer; indeed, during September they exerted pressure on Prague to give in to Hitler's demands. The subsequent Munich agreement, in which the Western powers agreed to Hitler's demand for the division of Czechoslovakia, has been taken by some historians as dramatically changing the course of Stalin's foreign policy towards alliance with Hitler. As Stalin's biographer Volkogonov writes, it could not have been forgotten by Stalin that at Munich, England, France, Germany and Italy 'gathered without a thought for the Soviet Union'. On 4 October, only a few days after the deal at Munich, the French Ambassador to Moscow reported, 'After the neutralisation of Czechoslovakia, Germany will open the way to the East.'[11]

Munich

The crisis of 1938 opened with a speech by Hitler in February in which he claimed the right of Germany to protect the interests of the 10 million Germans living in neighbouring states, most notably those in Austria and Czechoslovakia. The Anschluss was not a surprise in the Kremlin. As early as 1936 Kreshinsky had predicted that Germany would simply annex Austria and alleged that it was obvious that Czechoslovakia would be his next target. He was proved right when in September 1938, at the Nuremberg Rally, Hitler proclaimed unconditional support for the struggle of the Sudeten Germans in their struggle for independence from Prague.

Throughout this crisis the Soviet leadership publicly proclaimed their continued adherence to fulfilling their mutual assistance obligations to Czechoslovakia, *so long as France also met its obligations*. Despite this, on 19 September Britain and France presented the Czech leadership with proposals that the German Sudetenland be transferred to Germany. After a meeting of the League of Nations in mid-September Litvinov recorded his view that Czechoslovakia would be betrayed, and some 90 divisions from Soviet military units on the USSR's western borders were put on alert. However, at Munich on 29 and 30 September the leaders of France, Britain, Germany and Italy resolved all differences and agreed that the Sudetenland should be handed over. Neither Czechoslovakia nor the Soviet Union was even consulted. Interestingly, the key question for the Kremlin was whether Czechoslovakia would stand alone. If so, should Moscow fight alongside?

There is little doubt that the Western countries, in particular Britain, preferred not to have to fight Hitler at this juncture, and some members of the British government would have been quite satisfied if Hitler could have been turned East. The question of why the British preferred not to align with Moscow against Germany is an interesting one, with several possible explanations. The first is that ideological antagonisms arising from the Russian Revolution had not been forgotten. It did not really matter that from 1935 onwards the Comintern had changed its 'mission' to one of fighting Fascism: only 15 years earlier it had been the vanguard of Communism into Europe. In the mid-1930s in Western Europe, particularly in France, there had been waves of social upheavals with strikes and factory sit-ins. These trends appeared to some in the West to have been orchestrated by Moscow. Indeed, Moscow's involvement in the Spanish Civil War led some to the conclusion that Stalin was seeking to undermine Western Europe.

This was simply not the case. The Spanish Civil War presented Stalin with a dilemma. On the one hand he wanted to see Franco and the Nationalists defeated, not least because this fitted with his anti-Fascist policy in Europe but also because a Fascist victory would probably increase French timidity with respect to Germany. On the other hand, a revolution might split

Western Europe and make action with the USSR far less likely. Just after the Civil War in Spain had begun in the summer of 1936, the British, the French, the Soviet Union, Italy and Germany had signed a non-intervention agreement. Despite this, both the Germans and the French were heavily involved in supplying the Nationalists. Stalin did not want to antagonise either the British or the French, but the Soviet involvement in Spain was one in which he hoped to counter the support provided by Hitler and Mussolini for the Nationalists. Soviet objectives were limited and certainly, if the quality and quantity of armaments provided by Moscow are an indication of ambition, did not seem to extend to the takeover of Spain by Communists inspired by Moscow: Stalin supplied only a small number of tanks and aircraft, along with limited personnel to operate them. The Soviet priority was that the Republicans should not be defeated by the Nationalists, but when it became clear that they would be, Stalin refused to escalate Soviet involvement, especially when it was obvious that the British and the French would not restrain either Italian or German involvement in the war. Nevertheless, Soviet involvement in the Spanish Civil War did much to exacerbate the already poor relations between Moscow and the British and French.

A second explanation for British and French reluctance to avoid alliance with the USSR was the very nature of the Stalinist regime. It could be argued that the purges of 1936–8, with their show trials and plethora of executions, created an unwillingness in Western capitals to act in concert with such a regime. The purges were the equivalent of a holocaust which effectively destroyed leading opposition figures and the heart of the Communist Party itself. The purges extended beyond the Party and into all cultural, political and military spheres. It has been estimated that by 1939 as many as nine million people were held in labour camps.

All of this seems extraordinary in hindsight. The purges reached their pinnacle (or nadir) in 1937–8, which, for the USSR, must surely have been the year of maximum danger in terms of the encircling clouds of war in Europe, and it is worth asking why Stalin chose to engage in this devastating attack on Soviet society. The purges had their origin in the Seventeenth Party Congress, which met in 1934. At this meeting the Leningrad Party Chief, Sergei Kirov, was greeted with a display of enthusiasm underlining his undoubted popularity within the Party. Rumours abounded at the Congress and afterwards that, in the voting for the new Central Committee, he had actually secured more votes than Stalin himself. It appeared that many would have preferred Kirov as leader. None of this went unnoticed by Stalin: only a small percentage of those present at this Party Congress would survive until the next one. In 1956 figures announced by Khrushchev demonstrated that 70 per cent of the Central Committee members or candidate members who attended the 1934 Congress had been arrested or shot. Kirov himself was assassinated on 1 December 1934 in murky circumstances.

During July of that year the OGPU was changed into a main Administration of State Security (GUGB) and integrated into the new All Union NKVD (People's Commissariat for Internal Affairs). All the functions of the security police were thus united with those of the regular police into a body which also included the border police and internal troops, prisons and forced labour camps (Gulags), providing the mechanism for the purges which followed.

In January 1935 Lev Kamenev and Grigorii Zinoviev went on trial accused of Kirov's murder. Found guilty, they were incarcerated and in April 1936 were tried again in the first of the show trials of the so-called 'enemies of the people'.[12] Even Litvinov recalls that, in this period, he would sleep with his revolver under his pillow waiting for the 'knock in the night' for his turn to be summoned to hear his crimes against the people.

All of this was intended to root out the opponents of Stalin and the Stalinist system. A series of purges destroyed whole categories of Soviet citizens. Millions were purged and no aspect of Soviet society was left untouched. A machinery of repression was put into place which included the use of informers to report on the behaviour of ordinary people. This Soviet holocaust was a terrifying testament to both the power of the state and its weakness, in that it so feared its own citizens. No-one was free from fear: Litvinov was not alone in awaiting the 'knock in the night' which heralded the arrival of the secret police, the accusation of crimes against the state and then, perhaps, the long train ride to the gulag. In 1937–8, during the so-called Great Purge, almost the entire political establishment was destroyed, including Stalin's own military command. The purge of the military included the arrest of Marshal M. N. Tukhachevsky and other military leaders who were charged with treason and who were dead by the middle of the year. In November 1938 Commissar K. E. Voroshilov reported, 'In the course of purging the Red Army in 1937–1938, we got rid of more than 40,000 men ... in 10 months in 1938, more than 100,000 new officers were created.'[13]

As well as provoking distaste in Western capitals, the purge of the officer corps meant that the British and the French now doubted the military ability of the Red Army to carry out Soviet promises of support. With the devastating purges of the High Command, Stalin had effectively wiped out his senior and experienced officer corps. Men such as Marshal Tukhachevsky, who had fought in the civil war and had been responsible for the modernisation of the Soviet military throughout the 1930s, had been replaced by inexperienced junior officers. Whilst Nikolai Yezhov (who himself was shot in 1940) and Molotov actually drew up the lists of those to be purged, there is little doubt that the overall responsibility for the purges rested directly with Stalin. Indeed, in 1940 Stalin appears to have succeeded in eradicating one of his major opponents and critics. On 20 August on Stalin's orders Trotsky was murdered at his home in Mexico, where he had settled to find protection, by an agent of the NKVD who wielded an ice-pick and smashed his skull.

The British and French appeasement of Hitler at Munich effectively ended the Soviet bid to formulate collective security alliances with the West European states. Deutscher writes, 'It must have been shortly after Munich that the idea of a new attempt at *rapprochement* with Germany took shape in Stalin's mind.' But, as we have seen, an approach to Germany had always been a possibility. At the Eighteenth Party Congress on the 10 March 1939, Stalin declared that the British and French had given Germany parts of Czechoslovakia in payment for Hitler to go to war with the Soviet Union. This became the official Soviet justification for the conclusion of the subsequent Nazi–Soviet pact. Soviet spokesmen claimed that the British and the French had not actually wanted to deal with the Soviet Union. As Gromyko records in his memoirs:

> For its part, the Soviet Union has shown with the utmost clarity that the pact was the result of the policy of a number of Western powers which did not wish to join the USSR in blocking Hitler's path to aggression and the unleashing of war.[14]

Early in 1939 Hitler invaded Bohemia-Moravia, a predominantly Czech territory, but with an ethnic German minority. The British and French performed a considerable volte-face and began to seek alliances to stop Hitler. Again, the British preferred not to rely on the Soviet Union, but rather sought to form a coalition with Poland. The British guarantee to Poland was extended on 31 March, and consisted of a promise that the British and French would act if Polish interests were threatened. Litvinov read this as meaning that any prospect of 'Anglo-Soviet co-operation had been summarily dropped'. It was generally expected in Moscow that with this final rejection of a collective security arrangement, Litvinov as the architect of the strategy would be dismissed from his post in the Foreign Ministry as Stalin adapted foreign policy to fit the only option left – alliance with Hitler.

The Nazi–Soviet Pact

Litvinov indeed was dismissed as Soviet Foreign Minister on 3 May 1939, an act which has been pointed to as a public signal for the opening of negotiations for a Nazi–Soviet pact. Litvinov was not only of Jewish origin (he also had a British wife), but had been closely identified with the policies of collective security and was generally regarded as a pro-Westerner. He records in his memoirs that, prior to his dismissal, he had been for some time aware that power was gradually being taken from him. After the 18th Party Congress, following Stalin's instructions, Potemkin published foreign policy articles in the journal *Bolshevik* and other mass media. Litvinov had learned about these only after they actually appeared in print. He also learnt that not all Soviet ambassadors were sending him crucial important information. Many of them were actually sending their reports straight to Molotov, bypassing the Foreign Minister. Litvinov appears to have been the victim not only of the shift to a more pro-German line but also of some high-level feuding: the circular sent out to embassies abroad on his dismissal referred explicitly to 'the serious conflict between the Chairman of the People's Council of Commissars, Comrade Molotov, and the People's Commissar for Foreign Affairs, Comrade Litvinov'. Molotov appears to have played a central role in the dismissal of Litvinov from his post at a critical time, and he was the prime advocate of a *rapprochement* with Germany. Much of this can be attributed to genuine differences over policy; but, in a vignette which introduces a lighter tone into the story of elite feuding over Soviet foreign policy, the British historian Jonathan Haslam relates a story culled from Russian sources in which, many years after Litvinov's dismissal, he and Molotov, while sitting in the back of a car, had a heated row over German policy in 1939 and 1940. The car itself was 'driven by the hapless Gromyko'.[15]

The Soviet–German Non-Aggression Pact was duly signed on 23 August 1939 (with a secret protocol signed on 28 September). It stated that 'in the case of a territorial political transformation in the area of the Baltic states (Finland, Estonia, Latvia, Lithuania) the northern frontier of Lithuania will form at the same time the boundary of the spheres of interest of Germany and the USSR' and 'In the event of a territorial and political rearrangement of the area belonging to the Polish state the spheres of influence of Germany and the USSR shall be bounded approximately by the lines of the rivers Narew, Vistula and San'.[16] In a speech to the Supreme Soviet, Molotov spelt out that the Pact meant that 'the two largest states of Europe have agreed to put an end to the enmity between them, to eliminate the menace of war and to live at peace'. In short, despite the rhetoric, a promise of Soviet neutrality was made if and when Hitler and the Western powers went to war over Poland. Through this deal Stalin seemed to have achieved his primary goal – the deflection of Hitler's aggression. He had also gained territorially. In contrast to the failed attempt of 1934–5 to achieve an Eastern security pact, Stalin had managed to obtain the German dictator's recognition of Moscow's predominant influence in Finland, Estonia, Latvia and Bessarabia, and a large part of ethnic Poland. These gains provided Stalin with greater space on the periphery to use as a militarily defensive buffer, should it become necessary.

Intriguingly, the so-called 'secret protocols' were never really secret. Very soon after their signature the American Government was notified of their existence from a German source,[17] information which was subsequently relayed by Washington to the British. (The information did not enter the public domain during the war years, because the British and the Americans feared damaging the alliance and the Soviet leadership itself remained chary of raising the issue. Soviet officials included the secret protocols and the agreements of 1939 in the list of forbidden topics they did not want raised at the later Nuremberg trials.)

With the signing of the Nazi–Soviet pact, the Soviet leadership finally abandoned any pretence that it sought a policy of collective security. Yet, as Geoffrey Roberts has pointed out, Soviet foreign policy remained remarkably fluid even so. A series of difficult questions ensued in the wake of the signing of the agreement with Germany. To an uncertain Soviet leadership there were still many questions. Would Hitler actually now attack Poland? If so, would the Poles fight and for how long? What then would Britain and France do? Would another 'Munich' ensue? In the light of these issues, the Kremlin adopted a policy of 'wait and see'. Indeed, there were a number of ambiguities in the Soviet stance. A newspaper article on 27 August by Marshal Voroshilov stated that the Soviet Union might yet supply Poland with the raw materials and military equipment necessary for defence against Germany.

This rather vague notion was quickly quashed, however. On 5 September Molotov turned down a Polish request for the urgent supply of war materials. There is still controversy over whether in fact the USSR was a reluctant 'partner' in the partition of Poland. Specifically, it could be argued that what motivated the Kremlin in this dangerous period was a fear that if the Red Army itself did not move into the Eastern parts of Poland, this might not only damage the Nazi–Soviet relationship, but might also lead to a German occupation of the whole of Poland, and that therefore Stalin prevaricated in his dealings with Berlin.

When Stalin was given the news on the night of 31 August that Polish troops had apparently broken into a German radio station in Upper Silesia, killing German troops, the dictator knew that it was war, estimating that within a week or so Hitler's troops would be close to the Soviet border; but the astonishing speed of the German *Blitzkrieg* and the rapidity with which Polish armed resistance collapsed was still a nasty surprise in Moscow, as well as in London and Paris. On 5 September Ribbentrop started to press the Kremlin to invade Poland. On 9 September Molotov telephoned the Germans to congratulate them on taking Warsaw. Now, the Red Army had to be dispatched to prevent Hitler reneging on the deal over Poland. On 17 September the Red Army crossed the border into Poland. By 25 September Soviet troops had driven 250 to 350 kilometres into Poland and had secured enough territory to create the new Ukrainian and Belorussian Soviet Socialist Republics. The Soviet–German partition of Poland had actually provided the Kremlin with a zone of occupation which corresponded to the Curzon line agreed between Poland and Russia at Versailles in 1919. Within this territory there were thousands of Belorussians and Ukrainians, whom

Stalin termed his 'blood brethren': an 'amalgamation' of territories which could at least be politically justified in terms of the nationalities question. In accordance with this type of thinking, a few days after the Soviet invasion of Poland Stalin held a meeting with the German Ambassador and suggested a change in the arrangements made under the Nazi–Soviet pact. Originally it had been agreed that Moscow would 'receive' a large piece of 'ethnic' Poland, the Lublin Province and some of the territory in the Warsaw Provinces, and that the Germans were to get Lithuania. Stalin suggested a swap, so that Moscow would control Lithuania, and this was duly agreed.

One of the most atrocious episodes of the Soviet invasion and occupation of Poland occurred in the spring of 1940, with the massacre of 15,000 interned Polish army officers at Katyn, who were prisoners of war from the 1939 campaign. The motive for this was unclear. (It was only in 1990 that the Soviet leadership stopped pretending that Hitler had been culpable and admitted responsibility for the massacre.) In 1940, though, there was Nazi grumbling that Polish officers were harboured by the Soviet military for ulterior reasons. Was the massacre of the Polish officers an attempt by Stalin to ingratiate himself with Hitler? This might have been the case as in the same period as the massacre at Katyn, the USSR was supplying Germany with vast amounts of oil, grain and cotton to sustain its war effort.

Finland

In the meantime, Stalin also had security concerns over territory to the north, in Finland. Khrushchev writes in his memoirs that the dictator had always intended to annex Finland.[18] On 30 November 1939, after a 30-minute artillery bombardment, the Red Army crossed the Soviet–Finnish frontier on the Karelian isthmus. If Stalin controlled the eastern parts of Finland, that is, the area of Karelia, he would have achieved much greater protection over the approaches to Leningrad in the event of war. Yet this was not the full story. It is true that the Soviet decision to take large-scale military action against Finland was an irrevocable break with the image that Litvinov had sought to create of a genuine commitment to non-aggression. But it was also the case that military action was a last resort. Prior to the intervention, Stalin attempted through a series of intense negotiations with the representative of the Finnish delegation, J. J. Paasikivi, to reach a non-military solution to the issue of protection on the northern approaches to the USSR. From 10 October to 13 November there were three visits by a Finnish delegation to Moscow to discuss Soviet security requirements *vis-à-vis* Helsinki. The negotiations with the Finnish emphasised the desire of the Soviet leadership not to have to resort to war. Indeed, Soviet negotiators stressed their desire to improve their security by controlling access to the Gulf of Finland in the case of any future aggression. In particular, Stalin sought a base at Hango. Stalin himself was personally involved in all the discussion, and provided assurances that at the end of any war between Germany, Britain and France, any Soviet bases in Finland would be evacuated. However, by the 3 November there was still no agreement over the use of Finnish territory, and Molotov announced that the matter would now be handed over to the Soviet military. Stalin himself still seemed keen to find a non-military solution and even proposed that various islands could be 'leased' to the USSR. The failure of these talks had interesting ramifications, apart from the purely military ones, and undermined any real hopes that the Kremlin had of 'doing business' with non-Communist governments. Therefore the failure of the Finns to accede to Soviet demands meant necessarily that, alongside military action, the Kremlin would also seek a change in regime in Helsinki to a more reliable 'Communist' colouring. This accounts for Stalin's attempt to install a puppet government under the Finnish Communist Otto Kuusinen, the Secretary of the Comintern, whose wife was languishing in a labour camp.

Stalin's plans went badly wrong when the Finns decided to contest them. The Winter War, which began on 30 November, defied general expectations: whereas the Soviet leadership had expected a quick and easy victory, in reality victory proved to be neither quick nor easy. However, it is worth noting that the Soviet military had been far from sanguine about their chances of a rapid victory, which might in part explain Stalin's desire to avoid a military option. Not least, when N. N. Voronov was sent as head of a military mission to the Karalian isthmus in mid-November, he warned that communications were abysmal and that the terrain would prove difficult especially for tank warfare,[19] and estimated that it would take at least two to three months to impose Moscow's will. As it turned out, he was right. Resistance in Finland led to a costly war that Stalin could ill afford: the reputation of the Red Army was hurt, while Moscow also suffered tens of thousands dead and wounded. The Peace Treaty was signed at the beginning of March 1940. Moscow actually imposed terms which were less than outright domination for the Soviet leader. Finland had to cede a tenth of its territory in the west and a base in the south of Finland at Hango, but it is clear that Stalin wanted to settle the war quickly, not least because the performance of the Red Army revealed military weakness. Stalin, aware of the state of the military, decided to replace Voroshilov with S. K. Timoshenko as Chief of Staff.

During 1939 and 1940 Stalin indicated the geographical requirements for Soviet security, namely buffer states on its periphery. He imposed conditions upon the Baltic states providing for bases in preparation for the war with Germany, and occupied Finland to give greater defensive depth. But Stalin had calculated upon the war between the Western imperialists lasting long enough for them to destroy each other before attention could be directed against the Soviet front, without expecting the West Europeans to succumb as quickly as they did. Nevertheless, he was one of the first to congratulate Hitler on his successes in Denmark and Norway. On 10 May the Germans notified Molotov of their invasion of Holland and Belgium. Stalin overestimated the military strength and resolve of other powers. Khrushchev later revealed that Stalin's nerve cracked when he learned about the fall of France and the withdrawal of the British from the continent. The Nazi–Soviet pact had been a gamble, and there had been intimations from the first that it could not be sustained for long. When Hitler took Paris in May 1940 Stalin knew that if Hitler did not then invade England he would turn eastwards. Indeed, Hitler signed the formal order for Operation Barbarossa on 8 December.

Stalin still did not expect the German invasion of the USSR which actually occurred in June 1941. Earlier in 1941 he had confidentially told his generals that war with Germany was possible; but in May and June, when information came in from all sides that the Germans planned to attack, he declared that this was meant as a provocation by the British Government. Yet he could not ignore either the evidence that German troops were massing on the border or the almost continuous reconnaissance by German aircraft of Soviet territory. The dictator's behaviour in the wake of the initial attack has been well documented. Gromyko recalls that Stalin was convinced that Hitler would honour the treaty.[20] This view is reinforced by others, who also tell of Stalin's shock and breakdown at the timing, if not the substance, of the German 'betrayal'.

On the day of the Nazi invasion the British offered unsolicited aid to Moscow. A few days later Washington proffered similar help. On 27 June Molotov proposed to the British a political agreement to define the basis of co-operation between the two countries. As Hitler threatened the very survival of the Soviet state, Stalin began negotiating with the British and the Americans to forge an anti-Fascist alliance, destroy Germany for ever and secure the future of the Soviet Union.

The United States

A second part of the story of the inter-war years concerns the attitude of the leadership in Moscow towards the United States. The Bolshevik leadership had sought to develop an economic relationship with the United States almost immediately after the Revolution: in May 1918 Lenin attempted to secure an agreement which would allow Bolshevik access to American credits, and during the Paris Peace Conference Bolshevik ministers tried to cultivate economic relations with the United States. While the Bolsheviks were at this time pursuing economic ties with any state that would actually trade with them, Lenin emphasised the importance of a strong trading relationship with the United States: 'America is strong, everybody is now in its debt, everything depends on it.'[21] In 1921 the Soviet newspaper *Izvestiya* recognised that 'the US is the principal force in the world ... all possible means will have to be employed somehow or other to come to an understanding with the US.'[22] However, despite this emphasis on American technological and economic strength, Lenin also argued that the United States over the longer term would face difficulties with the other capitalist states. Not least, he argued that, precisely because of its industrial strength, 'everybody hates America more and more ... everything indicates that America cannot come to terms with other countries because the most profound economic differences divide them, because America is richer than the others.'[23] Lenin believed that, in the longer term, the very strength of the United States would lead to schisms between the capitalist states, and that it would be possible for Moscow to 'exploit' these economic rivalries. In the 1920s and 1930s Lenin and Stalin both perceived the most profound cleavage in the capitalist world as that between the United States and Britain. Although there was little that Moscow could do at this juncture to profit from this capitalist split, this view would continue to inform their thinking about the West.

Throughout the 1920s and 1930s Moscow attempted to establish a closer relationship with the United States through offering economic inducements to American companies which, it was believed, needed both Soviet resources and its vast markets. The prevailing view held that Washington would be forced by economic necessity to recognise the Soviet regime. This view remained prevalent, particularly after the Wall Street Crash of 1929 and the ensuing economic depression. In 1930, Boris Skvivskii, the head of the Soviet Information Bureau in Washington, reported to Moscow that the importance of Soviet markets was felt in the United States and that the time was now opportune for Moscow to pressurise Washington. But Moscow was not interested just in a closer economic relationship with Washington; it hoped to use American power to influence the situation in the Far East as well.

Japan

The power and influence of the United States was perceived by those in the Kremlin as critical to the emerging struggle against Japan. Through a convention which was signed in Beijing in 1925 Japan had recognised the Soviet Union, and in return for coal and oil rights it also agreed to evacuate North Sakhalin, opening up what appeared to be a period of more constructive relations. But on 19 September 1931 Japanese forces moved into Manchuria and created a puppet state. By December 1931 Molotov had characterised the Japanese threat in the Far East and the emerging crisis in Manchuria as the most important problem of foreign policy. In an attempt to stave off conflict with Japan, the Soviet Union offered Tokyo the opportunity to conclude a non-aggression treaty. At the same time Stalin strengthened his Far Eastern Army, and attempted to find new allies to act with Moscow against Japan: in particular diplomatic relations with China were re-established after Litvinov's talks with the Chinese representative at the World Disarmament Conference in Geneva. The two countries concluded a non-aggression treaty in June 1932. Specifically, Moscow tried to use the Chinese Communists to pressurise Chiang Kai-Shek into opposing Japan. From 1932 onwards, Moscow felt its security threatened on two fronts, in both Europe and the Far East. While it sought alliances with the French and the British in the West, it saw the United States as a potential ally in the East. Moscow feared that it might face a Fascist Germany on one side and an aggressive Japan on the other; but its second greatest fear was the emergence of a German–Japanese axis.

In preparation for an alliance of sorts with Washington, Soviet spokesmen began to refer to a history of Soviet–American collaboration in the Far East. Indeed, official Soviet accounts of American military intervention in Siberia during the civil war period were now explained as intended not to hurt the new Soviet state but to halt Japanese expansionism.[24] This newly developed and rather benign view of past American actions was designed, at least in part, to signal Soviet willingness to co-operate with the United States; indeed, there were encouraging signs from Washington.

In January 1932 the American Secretary of State, Stimson, announced that the United States would not tolerate a situation resulting from any negation of the Pact of Paris in the Far East. He also reported that the American fleet would conduct extensive manoeuvres in the Pacific. Encouraged by this action, Litvinov proposed that the two states conclude a bilateral non-aggression pact and attempt to form a series of interlocking agreements to include Japan and China. Voroshilov, the Commissar of War, requested in a conversation with the American Ambassador to Moscow that Washington send military and naval attachés to Moscow to conduct talks over these issues, declaring the hope that this would lead to 'a relationship of the utmost intimacy with the military authorities of the Soviet Union'.[25]

In 1933 the new Roosevelt Administration established formal relations with Moscow which appeared to promise a greater degree of joint Soviet–American action. The American Secretary of State, Cordell Hull, explained that recognition by the United States would be a factor in preventing a Japanese attack on the maritime provinces. *Krasnaya Zvezda* commented that 'recognition would subdue the Japanese and that American power would tilt the correlation of forces if not in favour of the Soviet Union then at least in favour of the status quo'.[26]

Moscow's expectation that the establishment of diplomatic relations with the United States would deter the Japanese and lead to concerted action against Tokyo was soon disappointed. There were considerable reservations in

Washington about acting in the Far East, let alone in concert with Moscow. In particular, there was concern about the repayments of Tsarist debts and the activities of the Communist Party in the United States. In a meeting with Litvinov shortly before the USSR was formally recognised by the United States, President Roosevelt had made clear his anxieties over these issues. He required the Soviet Foreign Minister to sign a statement pledging that Moscow would not encourage or permit the formation of any organisation which aimed to disrupt the political and social system of the United States. In his memoirs Litvinov writes that this caused few problems and instead emphasised what he describes as Roosevelt's agreement to act against Japan. It is worth noting the willingness of Soviet spokesmen to downgrade the Comintern yet again to achieve important security objectives.

Washington expected that recognition would provide them with political leverage over Moscow. Specifically, some of Roosevelt's advisers believed that, in return for words of encouragement against Japan, Moscow should both resolve the issue of the debts and moderate the activities of the Comintern. When the negotiations began on debts and future credits in early 1934, Moscow linked payment of debt with open American support to prohibit Japanese expansionism.

This support was not forthcoming in the mid-1930s for two reasons. The first was that the United States still laboured under the influence of isolationism and was reluctant to become involved in international affairs. The second was the antipathy of some of Roosevelt's advisers to the Stalinist regime. Historians have pointed to the views held in the 1930s by George Kennan and Charles Bohlen, both of whom served on the embassy staff in Moscow and who warned in dispatches against the dangers of international Communism. Kennan pointed to Soviet pressure on the Chinese Communists to act with Chiang Kai-Shek as an attempt by Moscow to take over China, rather than as an attempt to bolster Chinese opposition to Japan. The scruples against acting with Moscow were strengthened by the bloody Stalinist purges, which confirmed for many in Washington the brutality of an undemocratic system.

Yet Roosevelt never ruled out the possibility of pragmatic co-operation with Stalin if it became necessary to subdue both Japan and Germany, and, following his re-election in 1936, he took steps to rebuild a more positive relationship. Accordingly, in November 1936, Joseph Davies was appointed as American Ambassador to Moscow. This was significant because Davies had continually espoused the value of working with the Soviet Union (despite his reservations about the nature of the regime). In January 1938 Roosevelt authorised Davies to find out from Moscow what the possibilities might be. In the subsequent discussions Litvinov sought the clear promise of a definite pact against aggression in the Far East, but the President, not least because of his worries over reaction from an isolationist Congress, refused to go this far.

Throughout this period clashes, some of them serious, were occurring between Russian and Japanese frontier troops. Stalin was not pleased with the performance of the Red Army during some of these encounters. In particular, during the Mongolian campaign of July and August 1938, the Japanese actually seized Soviet border territory above Lake Khasan. Voroshilov gave orders that the enemy was to be destroyed, but Vasily Blyukher, the Commander of the Far Eastern Army, argued that it made no strategic sense to bomb areas in which there might be civilian Korean casualties. Blyukher became another victim of the purges, and, dismissed from post on 22 October 1938, was subsequently arrested and died in prison. It appeared that, in the East as in the West, even though war was imminent Stalin was capable of destroying the command officer corps.

Despite overwhelming evidence as to the nature of the Stalinist regime, Roosevelt did none the less adopt a strategy of trying to mitigate against the possibility of alliance between Hitler and Stalin, choosing to maintain relations with the Kremlin while isolating Germany. To this end, he quite deliberately distinguished between the behaviour of the Soviet Union and Fascist Germany. (The Soviet assault on Finland had come close to undermining Roosevelt's strategy, but while Washington condemned Stalin's actions, it did nothing to aid the Finnish resistance.) After the fall of France in 1940, despite intense disapproval of Soviet actions, the American State Department began a lengthy series of negotiations to improve relations with Moscow and keep open the option of co-operation. For example, the option of providing lend-lease credits was not ruled out. Indeed, finally, when the worst Soviet nightmare materialised and the Tripartite Pact between Berlin, Rome and Tokyo signed late in September 1940 raised the prospect of a Berlin–Rome–Tokyo axis geared against the Soviet Union, Washington once again offered assistance. In addition, Washington actually alerted Stalin to evidence of the impending Nazi attack in the spring of 1941, but to no avail.

Conclusions

By 1933 the revolutionary Bolshevik experiment had been replaced – some would argue that it was usurped – by a security-minded Stalinist regime. The years between 1933 and 1941 left an enduring legacy. The first was the pre-occupation with borders against invasion, in particular a paranoia with German power and a desire on the Soviet side to push the borders West. Not least, on the Soviet side, whatever the reservations over the actual alliance with Hitler in some parts of the Soviet leadership, it presented opportunities, in particular for the incorporation of the Baltic states into a Soviet sphere of influence and the creation of the Ukrainian and Belorussian Socialist Republics. All of this was positive. Several lessons were learnt in these years: the first, as in the case of Finland, was that non-Communist governments were unreliable and unwilling partners, and that security required 'like-minded states' on the borders of the USSR.

A second lesson learnt by the Soviet leadership was that the Western states were inherently unreliable and reluctant to do business with the USSR. The very *raison d'être* of the Soviet state had threatened the West and made its states-men reluctant to even initially recognise the regime in Moscow. For both the Kremlin and the Western states, ideological differences did not preclude prag-matic dealings, but they did provide the basis for mistrust. This was a problem, as alliances of one sort or another seemed to be the only option available to the Soviet leadership at the end of the 1930s. Whom could Stalin trust? As we have seen, this was a key issue for him in both international and domestic affairs. Those who disagreed with him at home were destroyed. It is worth harking back to a point discussed in Chapter 1: that the Soviet Union was an inherently fragile regime. To the natural weaknesses of a post-revolutionary situation had been added very considerable internal political fragility. As a result of the dislo-cations caused by the industrialisation process of the 1920s and the collectivi-sation process of the early 1930s, an inevitable paranoia was created at all levels of society, expressed in the purges which took place in the middle of the decade.

It was, therefore, a fragile regime in more ways than one by the time the war came to the USSR in 1941. In the international sphere, this had impor-tant implications. Not least, it led to a lack of preparation by a military which had been savagely purged and, within the Kremlin, to an overwhelming mis-trust of any external non-Communist power. The failure of the British and French to act against Hitler, the reluctance of the Americans to aid the strug-gle against the Japanese in the East, as well as the policy of appeasement at Munich in 1938 left a legacy of enormous suspicion in Moscow which all shaped Soviet behaviour during the period of the Grand Alliance from 1941 to 1945. It was, of course, compounded by the series of miscalculations which the Stalinist regime made over the nature and timing of the Fascist attack. If the alliance with the British and the Americans was to have any purpose at all, it was to ensure that German power was destroyed for ever.

Notes

1   A. J. P. Taylor, *The Origins of the Second World War* (London: Harmondsworth, 1964). See also Geoffrey Roberts, *The Soviet Union and the Origins of the Second World War: Russo-German Relations and the Road to War, 1933–1941* (London: Macmillan, 1995).

2   Teddy J. Uldricks, 'Soviet Security Policy in the 1930s', in G. Gorodetsky (ed.), *Soviet Foreign Policy 1917–1991: A Retrospective* (London: Frank Cass, 1994).

3   *Izvestiya*, 16 October, 1933.

4   For Litvinov's views on collective security, see Litvinov speech to the central committee, 29 December, 1933: *Dokumenty vneshnei politiki SSSR* (Moscow, 1974).

5 See A. Bullock, *Hitler and Stalin: Parallel Lives* (London: HarperCollins, 1991), p. 577 and Z. Sheinis, *Maxim Litvinov* (Moscow: Progress Publishers, 1988), p. 259.

6 *Izvestiya,* 24 January, 1934.

7 'SSSR, Liga Natsii', *Kommunisticheski Internatsional,* 26–27 (20 September, 1934), pp. 3–11.

8 Anthony Eden The Earl of Avon, *The Eden Memoirs,* Vol 1 *Facing the Dictators* (London: Cassell, 1962), p. 148.

9 See A. Bullock, *Hitler and Stalin.*

10 Press statement by Litvinov 17 March 1938, in J. Degras, ed., *The Communist International 1919–1943,* Documents, vol. i. 1919–22 (London: Oxford University Press, 1956), p. 272.

11 Dimitri Volkogonov, *Stalin: Triumph and Tragedy* (London: Weidenfeld & Nicholson, 1991).

12 On the purges, see, John Gooding, *Rulers and Subjects: Government and People in Russia 1801–1991* (London: Edward Arnold, 1996), p. 218, and Amy Knight, *Beria: Stalin's First Lieutenant* (Princeton: Princeton University Press, 1993), ch. 4.

13 Volkogonov, *Stalin: Triumph and Tragedy,* p. 306.

14 A. Gromyko, *Memoirs* (London: Hutchinson, 1989), p. 37.

15 Jonathan Haslam, 'Litvinov, Stalin and the Road Not Taken', in Gorodetsky, *Soviet Foreign Policy 1917–1991.*

16 'Around the Non-Aggression Pact' (Documents of Soviet-German Relations in 1939); *International Affairs* (Moscow: October 1989).

17 See Charles Bohlen, *Witness to History 1929–1969* (New York, Norton: 1973).

18 S. Talbot, *Khrushchev Remembers* (Boston: Little Brown, 1970), pp. 127–8.

19 N. N. Voronov, *Na Sluzhbe Voennoi* (Moscow: 1963).

20 Gromyko, *Memoirs,* p. 38.

21 V. I. Lenin, *The Essentials of Lenin,* vol. 11 (London: 1947), pp. 690–700.

22 *Izvestiya,* 6 December, 1921.

23 V. I. Lenin, Polnoe Sobranie Sochinenii (Moscow: 1958–1965), XXXIX, 209; XL, 152.

24 *Pravda,* 24 December 1931.

25 Quoted in V. L. Mal'Kov, 'Soviet–American Relations 1917–1940. Paper prepared for seminar on the origins of the Cold War, sponsored by the United States Institute for Peace and the Research Coordination Centre', Ministry of Foreign Affairs (USSR, June 1990).

26 *Krasnaya Zvezda,* 20 November 1933.

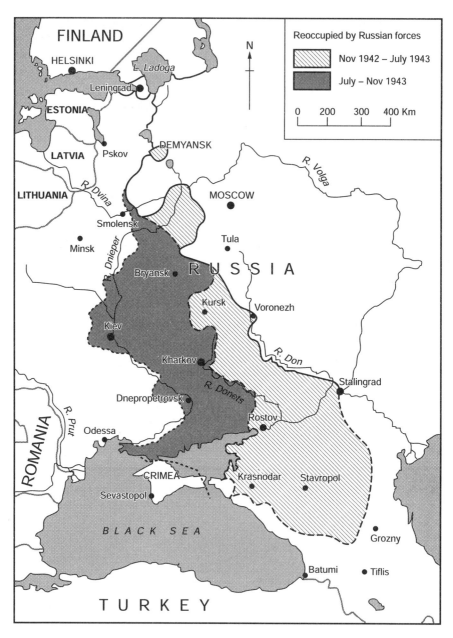

Map 1 Russian gains, 1942–1943

3

The War, the Grand Alliance and Victory over Germany 1939–1945

The German invasion of the USSR, under the code name Operation Barbarossa, appeared to have dealt the Soviet leadership a fatal blow. As discussed in Chapter 2, Stalin himself suffered a nervous breakdown when the news of the German betrayal was disclosed to him. Both the Soviet leadership and its military forces were in disarray. Within a few weeks, a million Soviet troops had been killed or wounded and a further million captured by the Germans. By the end of August 1941 Leningrad was besieged and Kiev in the Ukraine had collapsed. By October, German forces were quite literally at the gates of Moscow, and it seemed as if the Soviet capital itself would fall to Fascism. Lenin's body was removed from its mausoleum in Red Square to a place of safety. On 6 October Stalin cabled General Zhukov, one of the few survivors of the 1936 purge of the military elite, and ordered him to return to Moscow to help with its defence. Zhukov later revealed that on his arrival in the besieged capital he was summoned to an emergency meeting with Stalin. When he arrived in the Kremlin he found the dictator actually discussing with Beria the question of whether it might be possible to sue for a separate peace with Hitler.[1] Under Zhukov's command, however, Soviet forces began to halt the German offensive, and by early December a Soviet counter-offensive had begun. The Germans were repelled from Moscow, but redirected their efforts, this time moving troops into the Ukraine.

By 1942 the Fascists had increased their strength on the Russian front to 266 divisions, 193 of them German. The Germans forced the Red Army back until Soviet forces made a stand at the city of Stalingrad on the river Volga. A Soviet counter-offensive began on 19 November, inspired at least in part by Stalin's Order No. 227, issued on 28 July 1942. This demanded not a step backwards without an order from a superior commander, and officers who did not obey were placed in 'penal' battalions at the front.[2] The subsequent bloody battle of Stalingrad lasted over 4 months, during which a total of some 2 million soldiers perished; and it ended with a victory for the Red

Army and a turning-point of Soviet fortunes. The *Wehrmacht*'s strike force was destroyed at Stalingrad. Encouraged by the victory, the Soviet forces took back much of the Ukraine throughout 1943. On 18 January 1943 Zhukov was rewarded for his efforts when he was awarded the title 'Marshal of the Soviet Union'. By January 1944, after 900 days of misery and starvation, Leningrad was relieved. During nearly three years of siege 800,000 people in the city had starved or frozen to death, mortalities exceeding the combined British and American military losses suffered throughout the Second World War. Throughout all of the fighting in the East, the Kremlin urged its Western allies to aid the Soviet military effort through the opening of a second front in the West.

This chapter does not deal directly with the military history of the Second World War, but it is important to have an understanding of the military dimensions of the confrontation and the profound consequences of the military struggle with Fascism. The experiences of the Second World War left an indelible mark on the Soviet leadership and peoples. It was primarily on Soviet soil that the war was carried out, and it was the Red Army which bore the brunt of battle. While debate still rages over how many people died on the Soviet side, even conservative estimates place its losses at between 25 to 30 million dead. Given that the Soviet population in its entirety was estimated at this point as 200 million, this was a catastrophic experience for the USSR. Stalin's own son, Vasili, was killed by the Germans. It is also worth noting that in the course of the war much of the Soviet economic and industrial infrastructure itself was utterly decimated. It has been estimated that the Germans destroyed approximately 2,000 towns and cities and 70,000 villages, whilst over 25 million people in the USSR were rendered homeless by the destruction.[3] Despite these losses, the Soviet Union itself survived. Towards the end of the war Stalin took the title of Generalissimo in celebration of the victory of the Soviet Union.

Robert Tucker has described Stalin as a 'dark and deadly personality'. Despite his regime in the 1930s, however, he remained popular both within the Party and in the country as a whole. The Russian historian Dmitri Volkogonov has argued that part of Stalin's ability to rule, and his political skills, lay in the fact that he was a 'great actor' able to assume different guises.[4] Not only did he play the role of a great wartime commander with 'consummate skill', but he also successfully assumed other parts – that of fighter for the Party, theorist, father of the people or prophet. Although intellectually he had been no match for Lenin or Trotsky, he demonstrated in the struggle for leadership that he had purposefulness, political will, cunning and enormous ruthlessness: qualities which he deployed throughout the struggle with Germany and the negotiations with his allies over the peace.

The Generalissimo

By the time of the battle of Stalingrad the Soviet leadership had turned both a military and political corner. From this point on the Red Army proved capable of defeating the Germans. Given the circumstances of 1941, especially after the purges which had destroyed the Soviet officer corps, this was an incredible feat. The survival of the USSR was aided by the sheer size of the country and the harshness of the climate which, during the winters of both 1941 and 1942, provided difficult circumstances for the German troops to operate in. Yet, even if the USSR would survive, there was little to indicate that the Stalinist regime itself could do so. Stalin himself had been responsible for the lack of preparation of the Red Army and had left Moscow at the height of the crisis. None the less, once he recovered from the shock of the German invasion he proved masterly in 'pulling' the regime together. The process of centralisation which he had put in place in the late 1920s, together with the eradication of his political opponents in the 1930s, actually proved advantageous in wartime. During the war years Stalin headed a small but effective war government and chaired a state Defence Committee which had ultimate authority over every facet of Soviet life. It ordered a massive evacuation of peoples to the East and it oversaw the creation of huge military and industrial centres in areas beyond the reach of the Germans, in regions such as Central Asia. Most of all, though, Stalin successfully portrayed the war as a struggle not for Communism but one which was to safeguard the Soviet (especially the Russian) peoples. He was aided in this by Hitler's anti-Slavic manifesto and the behaviour of the German forces as they advanced into the country. It is a moot point as to whether Hitler might not have succeeded in his bid to seize power in the USSR if he had mobilised the anti-Soviet sentiments of the peoples of the Ukraine. As it was, the Soviet effort was justified as a defensive operation against Fascism. Stalin publicly justified the war effort as a great Russian effort and presented himself as the defender of the Russian peoples. In order to inspire national coherence he sought and achieved a *rapprochement* with the Russian orthodox church; and he ordered the opening of churches, many of which had been closed for 20 years.

This attempt to depict the struggle with Fascism as one of 'Russianness' twinned with the very essence of the Soviet state proved controversial. The emphasis upon Russianness involved a rewriting of relations between Moscow and the non-Russian peoples of the USSR. In 1941, for example, some of the non-Russian peoples, most notably those in the Ukraine, had been prepared at first to welcome German troops as 'liberators' from the Soviet yoke. The 1920s had seen a brutal repression of ethnic languages and rights in many areas, most notably in the Ukraine. These peoples did not subscribe to the Stalinist vision of a greater Soviet state. Stalin's role as heroic wartime leader defending the peoples also involved the rounding up of those minorities accused of co-operating or colluding with the Nazis. The Chechens, the Crimean Tartars and the Ingushes were just some of the minorities summarily deported during the war years away from their homelands and into new territories. Indeed, in some areas, again most notably in the Ukraine, a guerrilla war was waged against Soviet forces as they fought the Germans. Despite this local difficulty, Stalin succeeded in both convincing the Russian peoples and coercing other non-Russian groups to partake in his vision of the importance of the survival of the Soviet state.

Yet the sheer size and scale of losses and suffering during the war years and the fear that ethnic minorities within the USSR might betray the leadership irrevocably shaped the Soviet vision of the post-war world. In particular, it formed the manner in which decision-makers viewed the evolution of the Grand Alliance, the conduct of the war and the settlement which was to be imposed on Europe. Even in the depth of war, as it battled for its very survival, the Soviet leadership was planning its future foreign relations.

Wartime planning and spheres of influence

As early as December 1941, at the time of the Japanese assault on the US Seventh Fleet at Pearl Harbor in Hawaii, some figures in the Soviet leadership, most notably Litvinov, called upon Stalin to declare an open allegiance to the idea of a permanent Great-Power alliance with the British and Americans. Litvinov, who, despite his summary dismissal from the Soviet Foreign Ministry, had been appointed as Soviet Ambassador to Washington in 1941, was the most ardent adherent of this line. In a series of telegrams from Washington to the Kremlin he argued that invitations such as Roosevelt's offer to Moscow to join a Supreme War Council with the British and the Americans ought to be accepted. However, Litvinov was opposed by Molotov as he had been in his bid to promote a collective security agenda during the previous decade. The Soviet Foreign Minister objected to Litvinov's suggestion on the ground that a fully integrated alliance could prematurely propel the Soviet Union into a war in the Pacific. In 1941 Molotov believed that the USSR could not afford a dual confrontation. In these discussions, Molotov carried the day. The Kremlin did not support Roosevelt's scheme for a joint war council. However, Molotov did not always succeed in imposing his views on the formulation of Soviet policy *vis-à-vis* its new allies. For example, during May and June 1942 Molotov visited both Britain and the United States. He was interested in particular in the conclusion of a Soviet–British treaty. For some in the Soviet leadership the British were regarded at this point as the key ally in the formulation of any post-war settlement in Europe. Specifically, Molotov sought to gain from the British assurances that in the future they would recognise Russia's western frontiers as those of 1941. The British refused, and the idea was eventually relinquished. The Soviet leadership settled for a promise that a second front in Europe would be opened as soon as possible. Molotov himself did not favour this deal. Stalin, however, overruled his Foreign Minister and argued that the lack of a firm settlement on Soviet western borders did not really matter, as a degree of fluidity now might allow for greater opportunities later on.[5]

The Moscow Conference

As the war progressed after the Soviet victory at Stalingrad, the need for a greater degree of co-operation and coherence between the Allies became apparent, and a meeting was duly arranged between the three leaders. Stalin was reluctant to leave Moscow (as it turned out, he was afraid of flying) but he eventually agreed to hold a conference in Moscow in October 1943. The Western delegations approached the meeting with confidence that a military victory over Germany would be secured, and the British in particular wanted now to settle some aspects of the future settlement, being eager to secure some allocation of responsibility for liberated areas in post-war Europe. Churchill, the British Prime Minister, wanted agreement on how to treat the areas liberated by the advance of Allied forces. The American delegation agreed in principle with the aim of trying to construct a framework for post-war behaviour, but were not concerned at this juncture with the details of the arrangement. Indeed, Roosevelt made it plain that he was more preoccupied with finding acceptance of his scheme for a general security organisation which he envisaged could govern the behaviour of the great powers after the war. The Soviet delegation was concerned with the issue of the Second Front, as the Red Army was suffering massive casualties on the Eastern Front. Moscow put forward a very limited agenda, with the major proposal that the allies name the date of the setting of the second front in Europe. This demand caused some consternation among the British and Americans, who had not been expecting a discussion of military issues. The Soviet delegation, however, insisted that this issue be the first matter discussed. In particular, a guarantee of a Second Front in 1944 was demanded. Nevertheless, at the insistence of the British delegation, some issues of the post-war settlement were discussed. It suggested that none of the Great Powers should conclude separate bilateral treaties with other states. Anthony Eden, the British Foreign Secretary, wanted to ensure that no agreements were entered into by Moscow which might later prejudice the post-war settlement in Europe. The Soviet delegation rejected the proposal, and argued that Moscow had every right to enter into agreements on post-war questions with bordering states.

The Soviet delegation was interested in securing acceptance by the West that the Kremlin had a pre-eminent interest in Central and Eastern Europe. Moscow argued against any attempt by the British or the Americans to assert Western influence in these areas. Rather, Stalin argued that the Western powers should and could exert influence in areas such as Belgium, whilst the Soviet leadership took 'responsibility' for the Eastern parts of Europe. Moscow was not prepared to concede a veto over Soviet behaviour in Central and Eastern Europe; however, it was interested in 'horse trading' over territory, as was obvious in discussions over the future of Italy. The Italian surrender had been negotiated only a month before the beginning of the Moscow conference. The status of Italy as a co-belligerent had been accepted by the Allies on 13 October, but Stalin routinely expressed unease over what he perceived as his exclusion from the negotiations over the Italian surrender. To remedy this he proposed the creation of an Allied Military Political Commission, consisting of representatives of the three powers to supervise Italy. However, the nature of this commission caused disagreement. The Soviet delegation wanted the Military Political Commission to co-ordinate and direct all civilian matters in Italy as well as oversee the military organisation. Through this mechanism Moscow would have played a major role in the shaping of post-war Italy. Eden's counter-proposals were geared to limiting Soviet influence in Italy. He envisaged that the Military Political Commission should play merely an advisory role, and that real power should be entrusted to an Allied Control Commission. Molotov eventually accepted this proposal, and did not even insist on equal representation on the Control Commission, accepting a lesser role for Moscow in Italy. This Soviet concession can be explained, however. As Italy was the first country to surrender, Molotov recognised that a precedent would be set for the future treatment of other liberated territories, and the Soviet acceptance of a representative role in Italy established an important principle for the future: that the powers that occupied a territory at the surrender would have the predominant role in the settlement, with other Allies acquiring only a representative interest. Indeed, Molotov used the Italian example as one which had set a fair precedent. Despite relinquishing overt power, Moscow still maintained an interest in the political composition of Italy: there were several instruments that it envisaged using to exert influence in the post-war world, and one that any 'spheres of influence' argument has to take into account was that Moscow hoped to go on exerting influence through the international Communist movement. The Comintern had been officially dissolved in May 1943, but it did go on existing: its public dissolution had been a goodwill gesture towards the West, but there was little doubt that the Kremlin intended, if possible, to use foreign Communist parties as tools of Moscow in the spread of influence throughout Europe.

Most of the discussions at the Moscow Conference centred around the issue of Germany. Suggested guidelines for the future treatment of Germany from the American delegation envisaged radical revision of the German political system, the elimination of all Nazis, and *joint* occupation by the three Allied powers, to be effected and maintained by contingents of British, Soviet and American forces. This proposal was greeted enthusiastically by Molotov, who described it as depicting 'Russia's thoughts about Germany as if we had expressed them'.

At the Moscow Conference subjects of the post-war order likely to prove controversial were put firmly to one side, and there was an obvious desire to avoid tension. The most obvious bone of contention was that of the future treatment of Poland. The American Secretary of State, Cordell Hull, described the issue of Poland as a veritable 'Pandora's box'. Eden urged Molotov to re-establish relations with the Polish government in exile. Polish–Soviet relations had been severed over the 'involvement' of the Red Army in the Katyn Forest massacre of 1940. By 1943 the Polish Prime Minister, Mikołajczyk, put pressure on the Americans and the British to provide guarantees not only that Soviet demands for changes to the Polish–Soviet border be rejected, but that if it became necessary British and American troops would be involved in the occupation of Poland. Both Hull and Eden made it clear to Mikołajczyk that they were not prepared at this stage to sacrifice Allied unity to the demands of the Polish government in exile. When Eden did raise the issue, Molotov dismissed the demands of the Polish government in exile. Unwilling to antagonise Moscow, the issue was deferred by the Western Allies.

The Tehran Conference

The next major meeting between the three leaders was held in Tehran in Iran in December 1943. On the arrival of the American President in the city, Molotov insisted that the American delegation should occupy rooms within the Soviet Embassy for reasons of security. Roosevelt, unwilling to give offence, agreed. Churchill was further away in the British legation. As it turned out this was symbolic of his exclusion from some of the discussions. The most important issue discussed at the Tehran Conference was that of the Second Front. The American delegation advocated that the new offensive should take place in the spring of 1944, by a cross-Channel invasion of France. Churchill wanted Western forces to be used for operations in the Mediterranean theatre. Stalin had indicated at the Moscow conference that he had not ruled out the possibility of a landing in the Mediterranean or the Adriatic, but now he supported the American view. In the month before the Tehran conference, the Red Army had encountered fierce resistance in the Ukraine, and needed the Western powers to open a military operation to divert German attention away from its concentration upon the war with

Russia. Stalin seemed to realise that Churchill could hardly resist concerted Soviet–American pressure to open the offensive in France. Indeed, Churchill eventually conceded the point, and May 1944 was set as the date for the Anglo-American invasion.

All of these discussions were complicated because Moscow suspected that its Western Allies were trying to delay the launching of a second front. Kliment Voroshilov, the Soviet military representative at the conference, accused Western representatives of prevarication. When they tried to explain the operational difficulties of such a cross-Channel operation (Roosevelt argued that the English Channel was a disagreeable piece of water, not suitable for a crossing before May), Voroshilov argued that what was needed was more willpower not more planning.

Soviet leaders were acutely aware of Anglo-American differences over planning for the post-war world, and did try to take advantage of the degree of divergence between Churchill and Roosevelt on certain key issues. This impression of divergence was reinforced by Roosevelt's behaviour at the conference. The American President believed that it was important that Stalin did not receive the impression that the two Western states were ganging up on him. He refused to hold a meeting with Churchill before the conference itself. Churchill was also excluded from informal Soviet–American meetings at which the US President confided his thoughts to the dictator about the ordering of the post-war world. Roosevelt made clear his objections to either the British or the French maintaining their imperial possessions, and specifically informed the Soviet leaders that the United States supported the idea of self-government for the colonies in Asia. He also warned Stalin against bringing up the question of India with Churchill.[6] At the end of the conference Stalin showed his recognition of the power of the United States by toasting its great economic and industrial strength: its industrial and economic power, he said, was the most important factor on the Allied side.

Roosevelt also made clear his vision of a post-war settlement. He outlined a proposal for a three-tiered organisation consisting of, first, an association with a membership of 35 to 40 countries, and second, an executive committee of the four major powers, China, Britain, the Soviet Union and the United States, alongside six minor countries, with four 'policemen' who had the task of policing the peace. Stalin approved of the scheme in general, and also suggested that two security organisations should be created which would take responsibility for the post-war order in Europe and the Far East. The idea was rejected by Roosevelt on the grounds that, for historic reasons, Congress would not support any arrangement which involved America in a purely European organisation.

The issue of Germany was also discussed at the conference. The Americans suggested several ideas for its dismemberment. They proposed that it be split into five regions: Prussia, although much reduced in size; the north-western areas surrounding Hanover; Saxony and Leipzig; an area south of the Rhine; and a fifth region constituted from Bavaria, Baden and Württemburg. It was envisaged that Hamburg and the Ruhr would be controlled by the United Nations. The British proposal was not so radical, suggesting that Prussia and the southern states could be coalesced into a Danubian confederation; but, like the Americans, they perceived Prussia as the root of German militarism. Stalin, although favouring the American plan, declared that they were both inadequate, stating his belief that Germany would revive within 20 years unless it was restrained.

Stalin suggested that, as there was no hope of reforming the German character, the Allies should create a series of military strong points both within Germany and outside it. He proposed that the three Allies permanently occupy these points and be ready to act against any rebirth of German hostility. This was, he added, also a possible scheme for post-war Japan. His proposals are instructive, envisaging joint occupation, and demonstrating that the USSR envisaged all three Great Powers assuming responsibility for the occupation of post-war Germany. Despite the fact that Roosevelt had voiced doubts over a long-term political and military commitment to Europe, Stalin saw an American presence as an integral part of his scheme for Germany, and he foresaw the German question as requiring long-term political and military co-operation between East and West. No decision was taken on the proposals at the conference and the matter was referred to the European Advisory Commission.

The Americans did, however, ask Molotov to elaborate on the idea of creating 'strong points'. Indeed, the American delegation mentioned Belgium as a possible future site for air bases. Molotov did define the Soviet scheme more clearly, stating that the power responsible for securing these strong points during the war would provide the occupation forces. So, for example, in the countries liberated by the Red Army Moscow would be responsible for future security arrangements, while the Western states would be responsible for countries such as Italy. The American delegation reinforced this point by making clear that they had no intention of permitting any other power to hold bases in areas of American interest such as the Philippines. Logically this meant that in countries such as Germany, liberated by all the Allies, the 'strong points' would be jointly occupied. This principle was approved.

So far, it might be argued there was little for the Allies to disagree about; but at Tehran Stalin outlined his vision for Poland. His 'new' Poland would be between the Curzon line and the Oder river in the West, and would include East Prussia and Oppeln. The Soviet-Polish frontier would be on the Curzon line, but the USSR would also 'acquire' the cities of Tilizst and Königsberg, providing Moscow with the achievement of a long-held ambition to have an ice-free port on the Baltic.

Churchill eventually agreed to present these ideas to the Polish government in exile for two reasons: first, he felt that at this moment his hands were tied, and, second, the Red Army was approaching the Polish frontier and appeared intent on fostering a Communist-dominated government. Churchill considered it essential to obtain some agreement before that could occur. Roosevelt in private conversations with Stalin confided that he would prefer not to discuss the Polish issue as during the next year he had to face an election and there were six or seven million voters of Polish extraction. This, in effect, left the issue of Poland as a straight fight between Moscow and the British.

Stalin received confirmation on 7 April that a second front would take place in Europe. Once it began he moved quickly to assert Soviet influence and demarcate the areas of interest outlined at the Tehran Conference. The Red Army turned its attention to Poland, and despite the objections of the British, and, ignoring the Polish government in exile in London, recognised the so-called Lublin government.

The Red Army took Romania in late July and August 1944. The Romanians switched allegiance and joined the Allied side, fighting the Germans. Throughout the war the Soviet leadership had been planning to overthrow the Romanian leader, Ion Antonescu. In the spring of 1944 the Kremlin sent a former Romanian Army officer and trusted agent, Emil Bodnaras, to organise the underground Communist movement in Romania. After a purge within the Party, the Communists attempted to stage a *coup d'état*. Their plans were overtaken by the actions of the king who, along with some dissident generals, had also been planning a bid for power. Shortly after the Communist coup the king managed to overthrow Antonescu, and on his orders the Romanian forces relinquished their arms and the Red Army was able to sweep throughout the country. The king accepted armistice terms from Moscow, which included an acceptance of the Soviet–Romanian border as configured in 1940. It also provided for Soviet occupation. Although not the *coup d'état* envisaged by Moscow, it enabled the Red Army to assume control of the country.

On 5 September the USSR declared war on Bulgaria. This represented a change of policy by the Kremlin, and was inspired by a British demand that Moscow respond to the Bulgarian declaration of neutrality. Throughout the war the Soviet Union had sought to increase its influence in traditionally pro-Russian Bulgaria through negotiations with the Bulgarian leader, Ivan Bagrianov, and through the Communist Party. The Soviet Union had also sought to limit Anglo-American influence by blocking discussion of armistice terms for Bulgaria in EAC meetings. However, the British request provided the opportunity to invade and occupy Bulgaria.

In October the Red Army invaded Hungary, but met with fierce resistance from both the Germans and the Hungarians. The Soviet Union insisted that

Hungary turn its armies against the Germans and revert to its pre-war frontiers. The Red Army threatened to continue the war against Hungary if Miklos Horthy, the Hungarian leader, failed to comply with Soviet demands. Horthy eventually agreed to the Soviet demands, which included the establishment of a Hungarian Provisional National Assembly under the auspices of the Red Army. By the end of 1944 the Soviet leadership had control of Romania, Bulgaria and Hungary and was poised to assume control of Poland. It was at this point that Churchill sought to clarify exactly what degree of influence the West could expect to exert over the post-war settlement in Europe.

The Percentages Agreement

Specifically, Churchill sought to clarify Soviet intentions towards Western Europe. In October 1944 the British Prime Minster visited Moscow and presented Stalin with a proposal for the post-war settlement in Europe concerning the amount of 'influence' that the Soviet Union on the one hand, and the British and the Americans on the other, would exercise in certain countries. Churchill suggested the ratios as 90: 10 in the Soviet Union's favour in Romania; 90: 10 in the West's favour in Greece; 50: 50 in Yugoslavia; 50: 50 in Hungary; and 75: 25 in the Soviet Union's favour in Bulgaria.[7] According to Churchill's account, he wrote this on what he described as a 'naughty piece of paper' which Stalin studied and then ticked.

These ideas were taken up by Eden and Molotov the very next day. The Soviet Foreign Minister argued that some of the percentages should be changed. In particular he said that Moscow desired a greater degree of influence in Hungary. Molotov asked that the ratio to be changed to 75: 25 in the Soviet Union's favour in Bulgaria, Hungary and Romania. Eden actually refused, but then offered an alternative arrangement. This was 80: 20 in the Soviet Union's favour in Bulgaria; 50: 50 in the Soviet Union's favour in Yugoslavia; and 75: 25 in the Soviet Union's favour in Hungary. However, Eden and Molotov could not actually agree on the degrees of influence that each country should be 'allocated', and the matter of influence was left unresolved. A great deal of controversy surrounds these negotiations. First, although Churchill believed that he and Stalin understood each other, the American Ambassador in Moscow, Averell Harriman, disputed this and made it clear that Stalin understood perfectly well that the United States would never countenance any arrangement which divided Europe. Second, it was never an arrangement that could actually have been implemented, because it was not made explicit exactly what a percentage figure such as 75: 25 would entitle either side to. Stalin himself appears not to have taken the conversation with Churchill seriously, and there was little reference to it on the Soviet side.

However, Stalin clearly regarded Poland, Romania, Bulgaria and Hungary to be of primary importance to the Soviet Union and, in practice, in recognition of Soviet interests he was prepared to forego any potential influence in the West. Over Romania and Greece, for example, a trade-off does appear to have taken place; in return for the West accepting the pre-eminence of Soviet influence in Romania, Stalin was prepared to relinquish whatever interests he may have had, or claimed, in Greece. But by late 1944 this was really little more than a recognition of the existing realities of the military situation in Europe. The Red Army was already in control of Romania, Bulgaria and Hungary, and it was the disposition of military forces during 1944 into East and Central Europe which was actually the key to political influence.

Other areas were not so clear-cut. The strategy towards Germany and Austria was still unclear. At a meeting of the European Advisory Commission on Germany, Moscow had ignored British proposals for future conduct and seemed determined to obstruct progress on the German question. In February, though, Moscow submitted a proposal to the EAC accepting the British proposals both for a tripartite zonal occupation of Germany as a whole and for the city of Berlin. (The division of Berlin would later prove problematic.) Throughout the paper the principle of joint occupation was stressed. Yet, only a month before, the Soviet delegation had refused to discuss this issue. Reconciliation to Western views was founded in a Soviet fear that its Allies might negotiate a separate agreement with Hitler before the Red Army could reach German soil.

There were other considerations too. David Holloway has demonstrated that the advance of the Red Army into East and Central Europe brought the Kremlin important benefits, most obviously in the sphere of the Soviet atomic project. At the end of March 1945, the Czech government in exile, headed by Benes, was in Moscow for discussions. While there the Czechs signed an agreement with the Soviet leadership which provided Moscow with the right to mine uranium ore in Czechoslovakia. Earlier in the century the mines at Jachymov near the border with Saxony had been the world's main source of uranium, and the Soviet leadership knew that the British wanted access to them. The Kremlin was also concerned to get what it could from Germany. In May 1945 a special mission went from Moscow to Germany to study the state of the German atomic programme, but even before that the Kremlin had been concerned to take what they could. The competition in Europe at the end of the war was not just territorial, it was also about resources and, indeed, about humans. Many German scientists were interned by the Western Allies to prevent them 'falling' into Soviet hands, whilst on 15 March the US Army Air Force bombed the Auer plant north of Berlin, which had been used for the manufacture of uranium materials, not just to destroy German power, but also to prevent the Russians from gaining crucial technologies.[8] The Grand Alliance, as Germany was about to be defeated, had many different layers.

The Yalta Conference

In February 1945 the three Allied leaders met at Yalta in the Crimea. Churchill commented that if they had tried, the Allies could not have found a worse place in the world to meet, and that a decent supply of whisky would be necessary for him to bear the situation.[9] Of all the wartime conferences, it is the one at Yalta that has aroused most controversy. It has been alleged that it was here that the Great Powers divided the world into two camps and that the ailing Roosevelt was 'duped' by Stalin into making concessions concerning Poland. This is not accurate.

The idea that the division of Europe (or the world) took place at Yalta is wrong. The division of Europe had been defined in the 18 months before Yalta. Agreements on the composition of the control councils in East European countries had placed them within a Soviet 'area of interest', this was reinforced by the movement of Allied troops. The progress of the Red Army into Hungary, Romania, Poland and Bulgaria had established Soviet authority. If anything, what happened at Yalta was an attempt by the West to mitigate the reality of the Soviet control in the East.

The Americans attempted this through the Declaration on Liberated Europe. This, it was hoped, would place constraints on the behaviour of the Soviet Union. More critical for the United States, though, was its desire to obtain a guarantee that after the end of the war in Europe the USSR would aid the military effort against Japan. At Yalta, therefore, the two powers bargained over the price of Soviet aid.

Stalin's first concern was the future of Germany. Specifically, he sought guarantees on the destruction of Germany militarism, the dismembering of the German state and the question of reparations, hoping to fend off the more demanding of the attempts of the West to modify Soviet influence in Poland. Indeed, Soviet policy at Yalta may be characterised as a defensive exercise with Stalin protecting his 'interest' within Europe.

By February 1945 the Allied armies were converging on Germany from both East and West. The initial discussions at Yalta were military ones concerned with the timing and the character of the final blow against Hitler. The German counter-offensive in the Ardennes had been successful, but Roosevelt notified the Soviet leadership that, because of weather conditions, General Eisenhower, the Supreme Allied Commander in Europe, did not intend to cross the Rhine until March. The decisive assault on Germany from the West would be postponed until spring. There seemed, however, to be no impediment to the progress of the Red Army. It made spectacular gains throughout late 1944 and early 1945, covering 300 miles through central Poland, across the German frontier and to within 40 miles of Berlin.

Despite the apparent strength of Soviet troops, Stalin was concerned by the tenacity of German resistance. General Alexei Antonov, who had been made the Chief of the Soviet General Staff in February 1945 and who was in charge of the Soviet operation to take Berlin, predicted that the Germans would defend Berlin and that further fierce fighting was anticipated before the Red Army could move west. Stalin confirmed this forecast saying that, although the Red Army had established five or six bridgeheads on the west bank of the Oder, he anticipated stubborn resistance before Germany would fall. He was particularly concerned as the Germans were moving troops from the western battlefields to the Eastern Front. Stalin suspected that this was in fact preparation by the Germans to make a separate peace with the West, a deal that would deprive the Soviet Union of its share in the victory. Reassurances were sought that forces would maintain pressure upon the Germans so that the removal of troops from the west was impossible. Contrary to these Soviet anxieties, it was widely believed in the West that the Red Army would soon take Berlin.

The Declaration on Liberated Europe

The behaviour of the Soviet Union in the liberated countries of Eastern Europe caused anxiety. In particular, some within the American State Department were perturbed by the attitude of Soviet delegates towards Western representatives on the control councils in liberated territories. For example, the Soviet chairman of the control council in Romania had been issuing orders without consultation with the British or American representatives. To preclude this, the American State Department formed the idea of placing the behaviour of the Great Powers under a set of political principles, encompassed within a 'Declaration on Liberated Europe'. The Americans sought Soviet agreement to the declaration, which aimed 'to create democratic institutions' and had at its heart the idea that democratic elections were the key to the future in East and Central Europe.

The American intention was to regulate Soviet behaviour. Churchill was concerned that Stalin would regard it as an attempt to usurp the 'percentages' agreement. The fact that Stalin actually agreed to the proposal has been dismissed as a mere negotiating ruse to ensure continuing Allied unity. It is alleged that no attempt was made to abide by the principles of the declaration. Stalin, according to this line of reasoning, planned simply to install Communist governments throughout East Europe.

The second explanation for the supposed Soviet volte-face revolves around the question of expectations. It is here that John Lewis Gaddis's description of Stalin as a 'romantic revolutionary' comes into play.[10] It is possible that Stalin saw no reason at Yalta to oppose principles such as free elections in the liberated countries, because he expected the liberated peoples to vote Communist. It was widely believed within the Soviet leadership, despite the hostility that Soviet troops had met in Ukraine, that the Red Army would be welcomed and that this in turn would be expressed in support for indigenous Communist parties. In this spirit, 'free' elections did take place in Hungary in the autumn of 1945. The Communists, however, gained only 17 per cent of the vote. This result altered Soviet views and engendered a pragmatic response: political experiments were not to be attempted at the expense of Soviet security.

However, to the American delegation the proposal was a key factor in the post-war settlement. In some respects this was typical of American diplomacy. By securing Soviet agreement to a general principle to regulate the behaviour of the Great Powers the American delegation hoped to curtail Soviet activities. The declaration was closely linked to the Polish question: it was hoped that if Stalin actually abided by the principle of free elections, this could be resolved in a satisfactory manner. As it transpired over the next few months, however, Stalin preferred detailed and guaranteed arrangements to grand schemes.

The Polish question

The issue of Poland was discussed at seven of the eight plenary sessions at Yalta. The American delegation hoped that the Declaration on Liberated Europe would secure for the West a substantial voice in the settlement of the Polish question, but Western Allies had already conceded that the Soviet Union had a greater 'interest' in Poland. The crux of the problem was how far external influence should be permitted in an area regarded as a crucial security interest by the Soviet Union. Much of the discussion hinged on the future composition of a Polish Government. On 22 July 1944 the Lublin Committee had been installed by the Russians to form the core of any future government. At Yalta both the British and the Americans objected to the Lublin Government and sought the installation of a 'representative' government. Stalin and Molotov were insistent, however, that the Allies accept the Lublin Government. Churchill pointed out that the Polish question was one of honour, as the British had gone to war over the country; he conceded the Soviet demand over borders, but insisted that free elections take place. Stalin stated that Poland might be a matter of honour for Britain, but to the Soviet Union it was a matter of security, since Poland had twice been a corridor through which Russia's enemies had passed to attack. An uneasy compromise was eventually achieved. The Soviet Union agreed to a modification of the Lublin Government; additional representatives would be added in the form of émigrés, and elections were guaranteed.

Both the British and the Americans knew that they were in a weak position during the negotiations on the Polish issue. Charles Bohlen wrote afterwards that the Red Army gave Stalin the power he needed to carry out his wishes regardless of his promises at Yalta. Not only was it occupying Poland, but there was very little that the Western powers could do (short of military force – a strategy that was never contemplated by the Americans) if the Soviet Union violated the agreements. The position of the Western delegations was also complicated by the fact that, at Yalta, President Roosevelt wanted Stalin to commit himself to joining in the war in the Pacific as soon as Germany had been defeated. This Stalin did, agreeing that three months after the end of the war in Europe Soviet forces would be moved into action against the Japanese.

Germany

By the time of the Yalta conference in February 1945 the Red Army was actually within 40 miles of Berlin. The Americans and the British were concerned to secure 'legal' written assurances that the Red Army would respect 'Western' zones in Germany. On 1 February Edward Stettinius and Eden agreed that it was imperative they secure an agreement over the future of Germany before the Red Army entered Berlin. The concern was that the Red Army would move into Western zones and then refuse to leave.

Soviet plans did indeed exist to take Berlin in February. On 4 February general operational instructions were issued to Marshal Zhukov to consolidate, regroup and resupply up to 10 February before taking the German capital on 15 and 16 February. However, on 6 February those orders were cancelled because on the same day at Yalta agreement was reached on the division and the machinery to be implemented for the future control of Germany. The Red Army was redirected to a course of 'consolidation' in Eastern Europe. Stalin had been willing to take Berlin in order to assert Soviet rights in Germany, but once he obtained assurances that his allies had agreed to the Soviet zone in Germany this was no longer an immediate necessity. There were, however, disagreements at Yalta over Germany. Two areas in particular gave rise to dispute: the issue of French participation in occupation, and reparations.

Churchill urged that the French be used as a counterweight to German power. He pointed out that just as he had accepted that Poland's 'friendship' was necessary to the Soviet Union, so Moscow should concede a like role for France in relation to Britain. Roosevelt reinforced the need for a French military contribution to future European security by arguing that American troops could be withdrawn from Europe within two years. Stalin agreed to France aiding the military effort in the West and it was accepted that Paris would be given an occupation zone carved out of the proposed Anglo-American sector of Germany. Stalin, however, made clear his disdain for the

French and argued that, as they had fought so badly during the war, France might be better used as a large holiday camp!

On the issue of German reparations Soviet proposals had two aims. First, to ensure that Germany would never again be able to dominate Europe Moscow sought the destruction or reallocation of industrial capabilities. He proposed that 80 per cent of all German industries should be dismantled, and that Allied control should be established over remaining industry. Second, the Kremlin sought to rebuild their own devastated country with German industrial plant. Stalin proposed that a system be implemented whereby reparations would be allocated according to a country's contribution to the war effort and based upon direct material losses. It was suggested that German reparations should be based upon a figure of 20 billion dollars, with a Soviet share of 10 billion dollars.

Before the Yalta conference both Britain and the United States had considered at great length the question of a German settlement. On the one hand it was accepted that Germany should not be capable of posing a renewed threat to European security; on the other, it was understood that it should not be allowed to become an economic liability, literally dependent upon other powers. London and Washington wanted to find a formula whereby Germany would be economically self-sustaining but not capable of a standard of living higher than that of the Allies; but, while they were unwilling to implement Soviet suggestions, they lacked alternative proposals. The figure of 20 billion dollars was agreed upon as the basis for reparations, which later gave rise to much ill feeling between the Allies, although in the meantime the matter was referred to a reparations committee.

The Soviet aim at Yalta was patently to destroy German power and to affirm the agreement at Tehran for dismemberment. The British and the Americans had reconsidered the matter, however, and Churchill said that, although the British Government was still inclined to favour partition, in particular any scheme that would isolate Prussia, it still had doubts over any really drastic measures. Similarly, although Roosevelt still favoured the idea of Germany being divided into five or seven states, he preferred too to delay the decision.

Throughout the war the British had sought to bind the Austrian settlement with the post-war treatment of Germany. Initial British plans had favoured the idea that southern Germany be separated from the rest of Germany to form the basis of a Danubian confederation with Austria. At Yalta Churchill explained this scheme, proposing the establishment of a second German state, aligned with Austria, with a capital in Vienna. These schemes were opposed by Moscow as a return to the *Anschluss*: it was felt that Churchill was attempting to construct a *cordon sanitaire* which would involve a predominately German and Catholic state becoming the centre of an anti-Communist bloc. The Soviet Union demanded that Austria be dealt with in the same manner as it agreed to treat a defeated Germany, with tripartite or quadripartite occupation. However, Soviet proposals envisaged the restoration of Austria as an independent state, with allied occupation being seen as a short-term measure.

From a Soviet perspective the Yalta conference produced mixed results. The USSR failed to secure a definite Allied agreement on the question of reparations, but it was agreed that it was appropriate to divide future responsibility for Germany. This was the agreement Moscow had long pressed for. Western attempts to mitigate Soviet influence in Eastern Europe had failed. The Declaration on Liberated Europe had not registered as a threat: on the contrary, some Soviet commentators claimed that it legitimised their ambitions in Eastern Europe. However, the belief in the West that Moscow was failing to abide by the principles of the declaration led to an undoubted deterioration in Anglo-Soviet relations just as victory over Germany was about to be secured.

In particular, the Soviet action in Romania which resulted in the usurpation of the Radescu government and its replacement by the Communist Groza government was regarded with dismay in London. But it was actually Poland which once again caused friction. The commission which had been appointed at Yalta to 'compose' a new Polish government had failed to reach agreement. Stalin insisted that the Yalta agreements had intended the existing provisional (Lublin) government should be the basis of any new government and that new members had to be 'approved'. Grievance in London and Washington was fuelled when, in March, the Soviet leadership refused to accede to demands that captured American servicemen in Poland be returned home. On 13 March Churchill wrote to Roosevelt stating that the failure to resolve these problems meant that the Western Allies were confronted by a breakdown of the Yalta settlement.

Did Stalin betray the Western Allies? It is difficult to see that this was actually the case. The primary Soviet aim in terms of its western boundaries had remained unchanged from 1939 onwards: that was, the establishment and maintenance of 'friendly' governments on Soviet borders. Stalin recognised that his views of Poland were in total opposition to those of Churchill, remarking to Marshal Zhukov in reference to the Yalta agreements, 'Churchill wants the Soviet Union to share a border with a bourgeois Poland. That cannot happen.'

Up until the time of the Yalta conference, both sides had preferred to preserve Allied co-operation rather than risk a breakdown over the actual detail of agreement. For example, Averell Harriman wrote on 6 April, 'Up to recently the issues we have had with the Soviets have been relatively small compared to their contribution to the war, but now we should begin to establish a new relationship.' Churchill proposed that the West should use its military strength to compel Moscow to behave more reasonably. This could be done, he argued, by occupying as much territory in Eastern Europe as possible and by threatening not to relinquish it. However, Washington was reluctant to use its military power for such a purpose, especially as the Americans had yet to defeat the Japanese in the Far East.

From the standpoint of the Kremlin the immediate cause of the deterioration in Allied relations took place in March 1945, when Stalin was informed that negotiations had been under way at Berne (over the possibility of a German surrender) between General Wolffe, a commanding officer of the SS in Italy, and the American agent Alan Dulles. This constituted proof for the Kremlin that the Western powers intended to sign a separate peace, provoking a noticeable change in Soviet troop movements.

Immediately after the conference at Yalta, Soviet military strategy was designed to synchronise the moves of the Red Army with an anticipated Anglo-American advance into the heart of Central Europe. It was planned that the Red Army would begin moving towards Bratislava on the 10 March with an aim of reaching Prague within 40 to 45 days. Like Stalin's earlier decision to halt Soviet forces at the Oder river, the troops movement into Czechoslovakia appeared scheduled to wait for the Western advance.

The negotiations over the surrender of Germany conducted in March formed a watershed for Soviet views of the alliance. Suspicion of Western duplicity was fuelled by the fact that, since the discussion at Yalta, the military position had grown more complicated. The Red Army was bogged down in Hungary while Anglo-American forces had triumphantly crossed the Rhine at Remegan on 7 March. Western forces were rapidly advancing through Germany. The ease with which Anglo-American forces advanced engendered the belief in the Kremlin that the Germans were deliberately opening a route to Berlin and were transferring forces to the East. On 3 April Stalin voiced these suspicions in a letter to Roosevelt that 'the Germans have already taken advantage of the talks with the Allied Command to move three divisions from Northern Italy to the Soviet front'.[11] Marshal Zhukov believed that there must have been some collaboration by the Germans with the Western powers. He pointed out that only 8,351 men out of an army of 3 million died in combat during the Anglo-American crossing at Remegan, while the number of German prisoners of war ran quite literally into hundred of thousands of officers and men. Stalin again voiced suspicions in one of the letters he wrote to Roosevelt on 7 April:

> It is hard to agree that the absence of German resistance on the Western front is due solely to the fact that they have been beaten. The Germans have 147 divisions on the Eastern front. They could safely withdraw from 15 to 20 divisions from the Eastern front to aid their forces on the Western front yet they have not done so, nor are they doing so. They are fighting desperately against the Russians for Zemlenice, an obscure

station in Czechoslovakia, which they need just as much as a dead man needs a poultice, but they surrender without any resistance such important towns in the heart of Germany as Osnabruck, Mannheim and Kassel. You will admit that this behaviour ... is more than strange and unaccountable.[12]

These suspicions resulted in a shift in Soviet strategy towards Europe. Until March 1945 Western forces had been perceived as a necessary and integral part of the Soviet war effort against Nazi Germany.[13] However, even before Hitler surrendered, these same Anglo-American troops became a threat to Soviet ambitions. Stalin believed that they might yet be used to frustrate the agreements reached on Europe such as the zonal protocol which guaranteed Soviet occupation rights in Germany. The solution was to locate the Red Army where it could safeguard Soviet interests and, in addition, to take and hold 'Western' territory as a future bargaining chip. The Soviet Defence Committee decided to take Berlin before Anglo-American forces could get there. On 29 March Stalin showed Zhukov a letter from informants describing a clandestine meeting between Nazi agents and official representatives of the Western Allies at Berne. The letter alleged that the Nazi agents offered to cease resistance and conclude a separate peace. A free passage to Berlin was also offered to the Western Allies. According to Zhukov, Stalin replied, 'Roosevelt won't violate the Yalta accords, but as to Churchill, he wouldn't flinch at anything'.[14] Zhukov and Soviet Army General Sergi Shtemenko claim that Stalin took the letter seriously. As Shtemenko wrote, 'There remained no doubt that the Allies intended to capture Berlin before us.'[15] The Soviet High Command persisted in this belief even when Stalin received General Eisenhower's message on 31 March that instead of pressing for Berlin he intended to turn Anglo-American forces south. Stalin replied, agreeing that the plan was good and noting that Berlin had 'lost its former strategic importance'. However, this did not reflect his real belief. On 1 April 1945 the plan for the Berlin operation was reviewed at Soviet supreme headquarters. Stalin's conclusion that it was necessary to take Berlin before the Western Allies was illustrated by the encouragement he gave to two of his commanders, Zhukov and Ivan Konev, to compete for the prize of capturing it. On 1 April both commanders were summoned to the Kremlin and asked by Stalin, 'So, who is going to capture Berlin, we or the Allies?'[16] The Soviet leadership was also faced with a new American President, Harry S. Truman. The death of Roosevelt on the 12 April, who from all accounts was well regarded by Stalin, compounded Soviet fears that the Kremlin might yet lose out in a European settlement.

On 15 April Stalin informed Harriman that a major Soviet offensive was to begin and that Dresden would be the main objective. This was untrue – Berlin was the true objective. The Soviet leader grew ever more distrustful of his Western Allies. Zhukov reports that, by March, Stalin was anxious and fatigued and believed that his Western Allies might yet deceive him. Shtemenko recounted that on 16 April Stalin drew his attention to a claim by a captured German soldier that the remnants of the German forces had been instructed to 'open the gates in the West'. On 24 April, though, he agreed to General Eisenhower's suggestion that a common border be established along the Elbe–Mulde line. Stalin informed the American commander that after this border was formed the Red Army intended not only to occupy Berlin but, if possible, to clean out German forces east of the Elbe river. This meant that the Red Army would be moving into Schleswig-Holstein within the agreed British zone, signalling to the British and the Americans that a race was under way for the control of Denmark. Eisenhower informed Stalin that Anglo-American forces were launching an operation across the Lower Elbe to the Wismar–Donitz line. The military rationale behind the Western race for the Wismar–Donitz line remains unclear. If the priority was to exclude the Red Army from Denmark it was only necessary to hold the line south of Lübeck. However, holding the Wismar–Donitz line may be explained by the fact that it meant that the British occupied part of the Soviet zone in Germany and had acquired an area of Soviet territory with which to bargain. Following the collapse of Hitler's Germany, Western forces held nearly half the Soviet zone to the west of the Oder–Neisse line.

The battle for Berlin was a bloody one as the Germans continued to fight with ferocious determination. Both sides suffered huge losses: in some of Konev's units all the officers were killed. In the course of the battle Soviet soldiers liberated many British, American and other Allied prisoners of war. On 7 May Germany surrendered, and Prague was liberated by Soviet forces on 9 May. Once again Stalin had feared that the British and the Americans would try and take Prague for strategic and political reasons but, despite Churchill's protestations, when the Anglo-American forces liberated Western Czechoslovakia they were called to a halt well short of the capital, Prague.

When the war ended in Europe, therefore, Anglo-American forces were occupying parts of the Soviet zone in Germany. Churchill advised that the West hold on to the zone and refuse to withdraw. However, the new American President, Harry S. Truman, rejected Churchill's strategy and argued that the agreed zonal protocol for Germany had to be abided by. In an attempt to reassure Churchill that the British would not stand alone in Europe the President promised that, despite the Pacific campaign, American forces would not be removed arbitrarily from the European sphere. He guaranteed that only 30,000 of the 3 million men in Europe would be withdrawn within the coming three months.

Conclusions

By May 1945 the Grand Alliance had succeeded in its primary task – the destruction of Hitler and German power. While there was still a war against the Japanese to be fought in the East, the Soviet Union's primary enemy had been defeated. What did this mean for Soviet foreign policy? First, the Soviet leadership under Stalin had succeeded in extending its influence into the heart of Europe. In doing so, the borders of the Soviet Union were secure. The Kremlin had also secured an ice-free port and the Baltics, had taken Poland and subdued Germany. It is little wonder that Molotov commented, in the summer of 1945, that there was considerable satisfaction at Soviet gains. Stalin himself emerged from the war years with an enhanced reputation despite the catastrophe of 1941, and had secured an unassailable position within the Soviet political system (although this still did not prevent him removing Marshal Zhukov from power the following year because he feared that the successful military commander might emerge as a potential rival for power).

Yet the price of survival was high. As was noted at the beginning of the chapter, by May 1945 Soviet losses, both human and material, were phenomenal. These included the destruction of an eighth of the population and the wholesale destruction of Soviet industries and cities. Such losses mandated reparations from Germany and a period of prolonged co-operation with the West. The immediate task of the Soviet leadership in the spring and summer of 1945 was to repair the damage to the Soviet Union. The legacy of the war years was that the Soviet leadership believed that it deserved whatever gains, material or territorial, it had fought so hard and suffered so terribly to achieve.

Notes

1 Viktor Anifilov, 'Zhukov', in Harold Shukman (ed.), *Stalin's Generals* (London: Phoenix, 1997).

2 Paul Dukes, *A History of Russia, c. 882–1996* (3rd edn, London: Macmillan, 1998), p. 268.

3 For a description of the destruction of the Soviet Union during the war years, see John Gooding, *Rulers and Subjects: Government and People in Russia, 1801–1991* (London: Edward Arnold, 1996), ch. 7.

4 Dmitri Volkogonov, *Stalin: Triumph and Tragedy*, ed. and trans. by Harold Shukman (London: Weidenfeld & Nicolson, 1991).

5 Aleksei Filitov, 'The Soviet Union and the Grand Alliance: The Internal Dimension of Foreign Policy', in Gabriel Gorodetsky (ed.), *Soviet Foreign Policy 1917–1991: A Retrospective* (London: Frank Cass, 1994), pp. 97–105.

6 Robin Renwick, *Fighting with Allies: American and Britain in Peace and War* (London: Macmillan, 1996).

7 See W. S. Churchill, *The Second World War: Triumph and Tragedy* (London: Cassell, 1954), pp. 227–8.

8 David Holloway, *Stalin and the Bomb* (New Haven:Yale University Press, 1994).

9 Quoted in Renwick, *Fighting with Allies*, p. 82.

10 John Lewis Gaddis, *We Now Know* (Oxford: Clarendon Press, 1996).

11 *Stalin's Correspondence with Churchill, Attlee, Roosevelt and Truman 1941–1945* (London: Lawrence and Wishart, 1958), vol. II, pp. 205–6.

12 *Stalin's Correspondence*, p. 209.

13 See Caroline Kennedy-Pipe, *Stalin's Cold War: Soviet Strategies in Europe, 1943–1956* (Manchester: Manchester University Press, 1995), chs 2 and 3.

14 G. K. Zhukov, *Reminiscences and Reflections*, vol. II (Moscow: Progress, 1985), p. 347.

15 S. M. Shtemenko, 'The Battle for Berlin', in S. Bialer, *Stalin and his Generals* (New York: Peagasus, 1969), p. 499.

16 Viktor Anifilov, 'Zhukov', in Shukman, *Stalin's Generals*, pp. 343–60.

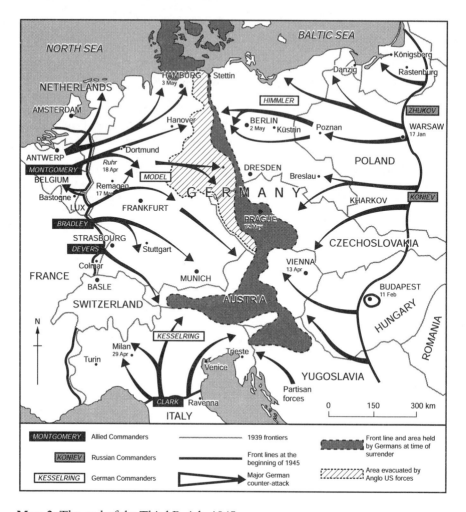

Map 2 The end of the Third Reich, 1945

4
The Cold War and Competition with the United States 1945–1953

It has been said that if we were to caricature the two main stories about the origins of the Cold War we would find two diametrically opposed interpretations of Stalin's behaviour. One has a power-crazed Stalin masterminding the subjugation of Europe and gloating at the inability of the Western Allies to deter him in his bid for expansion, whilst the other has a cowed dictator, the worse for drink, fearing imminent attack and driven into Eastern Europe in a desperate bid to protect Soviet wartime gains. Since the end of the Cold War, 'we know now', to paraphrase John Lewis Gaddis, that neither are accurate accounts of Stalin's foreign policy in the period after 1945. At the end of the Second World War the Soviet leadership under Stalin pursued a mix of ambitions. One agenda was obviously expansionist, necessitating the control of Eastern Europe and fulfilling long-held Imperial Russian and Soviet ambitions to secure western borders and effect a permanent resolution of the German issue through occupation. This control of East and Central Europe was for the Kremlin the *sine qua non* of the post-war settlement. A second agenda was to pursue co-operation with the Western Allies and to gain from the United States the economic and technological assistance needed for the reconstruction of USSR. Behind this seemingly pragmatic aim lay a complex set of calculations by the Soviet leadership which was dominated by the conviction that all the major powers had an interest in prolonged peace, mutual trading relations and the requirement for the emasculation of Germany. This chapter demonstrates that the Soviet leadership pursued both agendas until 1947. However, the announcement of the Marshall Aid programme in the summer of 1947 hardened attitudes in Moscow, and Soviet foreign policies underwent a fundamental reassessment as the Kremlin geared itself to the waging of a 'cold war' with the United States.

Consolidation

During the closing stages of the Second World War Soviet ambition in Europe had become one of the major issues on the East–West agenda. While, in general terms, the Soviet leadership was determined to fend off any demands by the Allies for a mitigation of its influence in East and Central Europe, the Kremlin did not engineer a breakdown in relations. This was clear during the Stalin–Hopkins talks in the spring of 1945. On 26 May Harry Hopkins, a close adviser to Roosevelt, was sent to Moscow to confer on the post-war settlement. From an American perspective, the primary purpose of the meeting was to secure a date for Soviet entry into the war in the Pacific, but inevitably the shape of the post-war settlement in Eastern Europe was discussed.

Indeed, Hopkins attempted to reassure Stalin that Washington did not object in principle to Soviet interests in Eastern Europe. However, he argued that while, for example, the United States understood the need for a Poland which was 'friendly' to Moscow, it would prefer it if the Polish government was more representative. In response, Stalin advocated a scheme whereby the present Warsaw Government could form the basis of any future administration but representatives from other Polish groups friendly both to the West and to the USSR would occupy a proportion of ministerial posts. Hopkins accepted this idea, although he must have known that, in reality, it did not fundamentally alter the political situation in Poland. Stalin alleged that the British were attempting to interfere in East and Central Europe and restore a *cordon sanitaire*. When Hopkins answered that neither the government nor the people of the United States had any such intention, Stalin repeated that he was speaking only of the British.[1]

This meeting with Hopkins is of some interest, revealing a mix of both insecurity and confidence on the Soviet side that Americans found rather baffling. On the one hand, Stalin said that he feared Western intervention in the politics of Eastern Europe, but on the other, he appeared confident that he could at least manipulate differences between the British and the Americans over the post-war order.

Soviet fears of some form of intervention in Eastern Europe were clearly demonstrated in the summer of 1945. Through a combination of political and military actions Stalin managed to exercise influence in both Austria and Germany. For example, under an agreement signed on 9 July Anglo-American forces should have been able to move into their zones of occupation in Austria, but it was only at the Potsdam Conference in July that Stalin actually agreed that Western forces could enter Vienna, and this was only after the British and the Americans had agreed that the remit of the pro-Soviet Renner Government could be extended to the whole of Austria. On 20 July it was anounced that Soviet forces would be withdrawn to a distance of 100 kilometres from the British zone in Austria. In this period Stalin also managed to secure the removal of Anglo-American forces from the Soviet zone in Germany. After the victory in Europe, British and American troops had held large tracts of territory within Germany which they had captured during the final days of the war. Some of this area had been originally designated to the control of Soviet forces. During the talks with Hopkins in May Stalin agreed to the inauguration on 5 June of an Allied Control Commission which would act as the supreme executive in Berlin. But before the commission could meet Marshal Zhukov required that Anglo-American forces be withdrawn from the Soviet zone.

Despite this insistence on 'spheres of responsibility', at the Potsdam Conference Molotov demanded that, for the purposes of economic planning, Germany should be treated as a whole, and he pressed for the creation of Central German 'agencies'. In particular, the Soviet Foreign Minister suggested that the Ruhr area (which had enormous economic potential) should be internationalised under the control of the Great Powers. The American Secretary of State, James F. Byrnes, who was present at the conference, wrote that Moscow's primary concern throughout the discussions was one of economic compensation and that the suggestion for the Ruhr was a ploy to exact as much reparation as possible. The Soviet delegation demanded that Germany should pay at least 10 billion dollars in reparations to Moscow. This idea encountered opposition, as the Americans had no intention of allowing the Western zones in Germany to be stripped of all economic potential, sinking them into poverty. They therefore countered the Soviet suggestion with the idea that reparations would be payable from within each individual zone of occupation. This was agreed, but only after Moscow was promised some additional deliveries of goods from Western zones. Soviet hopes of major gains from reparations were disappointed and the failure of the Western Allies to come to some form of satisfactory agreement with the Russians on this issue had immediate consequences in the East. In July 1946 a paper written by the Soviet Foreign Affairs Ministry stated that a 10-billion-dollar figure was the 'minimum' sum that should be accepted in compensation for the losses suffered by the USSR during the war with Germany. After the failure to get all they wanted at Potsdam, the Russians immediately intensified the procurement of reparations from their own zone, including the wholesale stripping of industrial plant, agricultural goods and precious minerals.[2]

The issue of how much was to be paid in reparations to Moscow was not the only bone of contention at the Conference. Indeed, there were a number of other thorny issues which had been deliberately postponed during the war years but which, after victory in Europe, could no longer be put to one side. Relations between the Western Allies and the USSR were not helped by the fact that Roosevelt had died suddenly and his successor, the former Vice-President Harry S. Truman, was regarded with great suspicion by those in the Kremlin. Potsdam was the first meeting between Truman and the Soviet leaders, and the new American President made a very poor impression. Molotov later provided a less-than-flattering assessment of Harry Truman which ran along the following lines: 'Malicious and unforgiving and not above offering you his hand to yank you off balance and work you over with a chair leg, a pool cue, or something out of his pocket.' Matters were not helped when Churchill lost the British General Election which had taken place during the conference and was replaced by the Labour leader Clement Attlee who, for the Soviet delegation, was an unknown quantity. Problems of adjustment to new personalities were further compounded by the fact that it was during the Potsdam Conference that Stalin was informed that the US possessed an atomic capability. Contemporary accounts record that Stalin displayed little emotion at this news and, to Western observers, did not seem to fully understand its implications. There is now evidence that Stalin already knew through Soviet espionage networks that the Americans had the bomb, so his lack of emotion was not surprising. What is interesting, however, is that the explosions over Hiroshima and Nagasaki in August 1945 made a particular impression on the Soviet leadership. In particular, they underlined US technological superiority. In the middle of August the People's Commissar of Munitions, Boris L'Vovich Vannikov, was summoned to the Kremlin with his deputies. Stalin ordered that the Soviet nuclear programme be accelerated to provide Moscow with atomic weapons in 'the shortest possible time'. The dictator noted that Hiroshima had shaken the whole world; the equilibrium had been destroyed (*ravnovesie navrushilos*).[3] In practical terms for the Soviet leadership the patent evidence of American power was significant for the post-war order, not least because the sudden end of the war in Japan had denied Moscow a major combat role in the Pacific region and had effectively ruled out any hope that the leadership had of a role in the post-war settlement in the Far East.

While the question of what role, if any, the USSR would be permitted to play in the Far East provided ground for disagreement between Moscow and Washington, it was not an impediment to the Soviet belief that co-operation with the West remained important to help the USSR develop its own technological base. Indeed, a complex picture emerges on the Soviet side. Whilst there was awe at the US atomic achievement and a patent desire to benefit from American technology, this aim coexisted with a second belief, which was that the American White House itself sought and indeed needed economic co-operation with Moscow. This notion was premised on certain assessments made in Moscow about the nature of the US economy. Soviet experts argued that, during the war, the economy in the United States had been producing at full capacity, which had had several beneficial effects – not least that of high employment. The end of the war, however, meant that demand would decrease and, as a consequence, Soviet economists argued that Washington would be compelled to find new overseas markets in order to continue to produce at full capacity. This search for markets, it was presumed, would lead the Truman Administration away from its traditional isolationism and would necessitate trade with the Soviet Union. Averell Harriman, the American Ambassador to the USSR, reported in amazement that some in Moscow believed that American business needed the development of an export market to the USSR as a matter of life and death

Issues of trade and aid, however, became more complicated as the negotiations over the European settlement continued. What is interesting is that Soviet tactics were not appreciably altered by American atomic power. This was evidenced at the London Meeting of the Council of Foreign Ministers which opened on 11 September 1945, arranged at Potsdam in order to prepare peace treaties with Germany and its allies. At the conference Molotov joked about the US nuclear capability, remarking that 'we must pay attention to the US, they are the only ones who have the atomic bomb'. On the Soviet side, however, at least in its public diplomacy, very little appeared changed by US nuclear power, and Molotov continued to pursue a linkage between Soviet and Western power in Europe. When the Americans refused to accept the peace treaties with Romania and Bulgaria, the Soviet delegation refused to sign the peace treaty with Italy. Molotov also linked any post-war settlement in Europe with that of the Japanese settlement, demanding an input into the Asian peace treaties.

In a meeting with Averell Harriman in October Stalin indicated that he had alternative courses to that of co-operation with the West, and argued that the option of isolationism and autarkism remained a viable one for his country. He added that, although he had personally opposed the adoption of this course, he might now consider it carefully, not least because of what he alleged was American intransigence over the Japanese settlement.

Throughout negotiations over the post-war settlement the Soviet leadership remained insistent that the USSR should maintain its predominant interest in East and Central Europe, but there were signs of flexibility over what it felt constituted influence and how to achieve it. In the autumn of 1945 Byrnes had proposed that American and Soviet troops should be withdrawn in tandem from Czechoslovakia. The Soviet leadership agreed. On 6 December, very much to the surprise of the Americans, the US Ambassador in Prague reported that the Soviet Government had kept to its agreement to evacuate its troops from the the country by 1 December. Whilst it might be argued that in the autumn of 1945 socialism had a firm grip in Prague, thus allowing Stalin to withdraw troops, it does indicate that there was leeway in Soviet thinking over the control of Eastern Europe. In part, in this initial post-war period, the old model of the Comintern with its adherence to a strict discipline between the Kremlin and other Communist parties, did not appear to be one that Stalin imposed with any degree of uniformity.

There was further evidence of flexibility on the Soviet side when, at the Foreign Ministers' Conference in Moscow in December 1945, Byrnes held a meeting with Stalin and agreement was actually reached on the Romanian and Bulgarian peace settlements. In return for Soviet assurances that free elections would be held and press freedoms respected (all of which would be monitored by a tripartite Allied Commission), it was agreed that Romania would be recognised by the West. Moscow also conceded that the Bulgarian Government would include two democratically elected ministers.[4] In return for what appeared to be at least a degree of compromise on the Soviet side, the Western Allies agreed that Moscow would have a consultative role in the Allied Control Commission for Japan.

It was striking how at this juncture Stalin pursued a mix of diplomatic and military manoeuvres to protect gains made in Eastern Europe. If concessions were necessary, as over the Bulgarian settlement, for example, they were made. Stalin proved masterful in repelling Western attempts for any real change in the status of Eastern Europe. Yet miscalculations were made over what the Western Allies would tolerate. In early 1946 Stalin provoked the first crisis of the Cold War when, in stark contrast to the Czech case, he refused to withdraw Soviet troops from Northern Iran. In 1941 British and Soviet troops had entered Iran under a joint agreement designed to prevent the oil fields from falling to the Germans and to ensure the security of the southern supply route to the Soviet Union. The Red Army had occupied the northern provinces whilst Britain controlled the southern parts of the country. In 1942 the Anglo–Iranian–Soviet Tripartite Agreement was signed, which provided for British and Soviet troops to remain in Iran until six months after the end of the war. During the period of occupation Moscow was concerned to exact long-term oil concessions from the Iranian Government, but it had also had an interest in exerting greater influence in Iran. Stalin told Byrnes at the Foreign Ministers' Conference in Moscow in December 1945 that if Soviet forces were pulled out, saboteurs might attempt to blow up the Baku oil fields. Nevertheless, he reassured Byrnes that he would accept the Western proposal that all troops would be withdrawn by March.

In January 1946 reports from Robert Rossow, the American Vice Consul at Tabriz, noted fresh Soviet troop movements into Northern Iran, and by March, when the deadline for the withdrawal of foreign troops was reached, Soviet forces still remained in place. American attitudes hardened. Reports of new and heavy Soviet troop movements in Azerbaijan confirmed the view of the need to act, and Byrnes took a forceful line. When informed of Soviet troops' movements towards Teheran he stated that this constituted 'military invasion' and meant that the United States could 'give it to them with both barrels'. A telegram was sent to Stalin asking for an explanation of the manoeuvres, but Moscow ignored the message.[5] Pressure continued on the Iranian Prime Minister Qavam to grant oil concessions, and Moscow remained adamant that its troops would remain in Iran. A combination of US diplomatic pressure and an Iranian appeal to the Security Council of the newly established United Nations organisation appears to have persuaded Moscow to change its mind, and in April Moscow reached an agreement with Teheran that Soviet forces would be withdrawn. President Truman recorded, 'The Soviet Union persisted in its occupation until I personally saw to it that Stalin was informed that I had given orders to our military chiefs to prepare for the movement of our ground, sea and air forces. Stalin then did what I knew he would do. He moved his troops out.' No documentary evidence has been found to substantiate this claim of such a drastic threat. Nevertheless, it was the combined Anglo-American pressure which compelled withdrawal. Moscow had not expected such a forceful American response, an understandable misperception given that, in December 1945, Byrnes had signalled a clear lack of interest over the future of any imperial possessions, and had reassured Soviet negotiators that Washington would not always side with the British. On the Soviet side, a probe into an area on the southern periphery which had promised influence had been repelled and had produced a reaction on the Western side which was unexpected.

The Soviet failure to withdraw from Iran indicated to some in the West that Moscow had territorial ambitions which overrode agreed limits. Analysts such as George Kennan, the American chargé in Moscow, made certain deductions from the Iranian crisis, most notably that Soviet conduct was untrustworthy in more general terms. George Kennan provided the rationale for a new approach to the USSR. For many months prior to the Iranian crisis, he had been sending dispatches from Moscow analysing Soviet behaviour in pessimistic terms and stressing the futility of policies which sought co-operation with Moscow.[6] He predicted that expansionist tendencies such as those displayed over Iran would dominate Moscow's foreign strategies. His analysis, which interpreted Soviet foreign policy as an outgrowth of an ideologically predetermined set of expectations and ambitions, provided the intellectual basis for a new Western strategy towards the Soviet Union. This was given its first public expression by the former British Prime Minister, Winston Churchill in March 1946.

The Iron Curtain

At a speech at Fulton, Missouri, in the United States, Churchill asserted that an 'iron curtain' had descended across Europe, and called for an Anglo-American alliance to counter it.[7] As he gave this speech, President Truman sat next to him, endorsing the view that Europe was divided. The Soviet response was predictable. *Pravda* published an indignant editorial, and on 13 March Stalin branded Churchill's speech a dangerous act and accused him of trying to incite war. From a Soviet perspective, in early 1946, the British and the Americans seemed determined to sour the prospects for co-operation as a series of disputes over economic reparations and the future status of Germany erupted.

In the spring of 1946 the US made a series of offers to test Soviet designs in Germany. In April Byrnes proposed to Molotov that the United States, the USSR, Britain and France agree to a treaty which would guarantee the disarmament and demilitarisation of Germany for the next 25 years. Four days later, on 4 May, US General Clay announced the suspension of further reparations from the American zone until all four powers had agreed to treat Germany as an economic entity.

During the spring and summer Washington and London moved towards the fusion of the Western zones which began in July 1946. This consolidated under one authority nearly 60 per cent of German and Austrian territory, and included the vast bulk of German industrial capacity. In this period the Americans also cut off reparations from their zone to the East and quashed any hopes that Moscow might have held of a future reconstruction loan. Washington also withdrew its support from the United Nations Relief and Rehabilitation Administration (UNRRA), with profound consequences for economic conditions in the Soviet zones of Germany. The issue of reparations also remained a bone of contention. At the Council of Foreign Ministers meeting in July, Molotov reiterated that what Moscow wanted was what he claimed had been agreed at the Yalta conference: 10 billion dollars in reparations, and the quadripartite control of the Ruhr region. The Americans refused to countenance such demands. The Soviet insistence upon huge payments and control of the Ruhr, it was believed in the West, would have led to a centralised German government, which could over time have been adapted for the seizure of absolute control of the country by Communists.

On 7 September 1946 Byrnes outlined Western policy in Germany. During a speech in Stuttgart, he stated that Washington was committed to the unification of the Western zones and to the economic, social and political recovery of Germany with or without Soviet co-operation.[8] For the Kremlin, this was alarming, signalling that the Western powers intended to rebuild and rehabilitate their zones of Germany. This had two implications for Soviet leaders. The first was that while the presence of US troops in Germany could act as a safeguard against a resurgance of German militarism, they also had the potential to form the basis of an anti-Soviet alliance in Europe. A second and more important implication of unification for the Eastern zones was that Soviet leaders feared that economic and political rehabilitation in Western zones might threaten Communist control in the economically precarious Eastern zones. This fear of a loss of control was also apparent in the negotiations over the timescale for the withdrawal of both Allied and Soviet troops from wartime positions.

In 1946 both the Americans and the British were keen to reduce the number of Soviet occupation forces throughout Eastern Europe. In May 1946 an

American estimate placed the number of Soviet troops at 700,000 in Romania, 65,000 in Hungary and 280,000 in Bulgaria.[9] The British War Office estimated that there was a rough total of 905,000 troops in south-east Europe.[10] Yet there was a problem as to how to persuade the Kremlin to withdraw its forces from Eastern Europe. Although the West was eager to persuade the USSR to remove its troops, they did not want to engage in the kind of 'troop trading' which had taken place over Czechoslovakia. Despite this reluctance, the Western Allies suggested that Soviet troops in Romania and Hungary should be measured against Western forces in Italy. This idea was vehemently rejected by Molotov, who argued that Soviet troops in Romania were necessary to protect Red Army lines of communication with occupation troops in Austria. Eventually Molotov appears to have carried this point. Byrnes and Bevin accepted the idea that troop levels in Bulgaria and Italy should be measured against each other, but also conceded that Soviet troops should remain in Hungary and Romania. This 'troop trading' has a degree of significance. Molotov did not concede that Soviet troops should be withdrawn, and the Soviet outlook remained subject to the need to avoid any substantial weakening of its grip on Eastern Europe. It is against this backdrop that the Soviet proposals for the demilitarisation and neutralisation of certain regions should be seen.

Throughout 1946 Soviet protests over the presence of American troops in Europe and the establishment of American bases throughout the continent had grown stronger. The objections in the first instance centred around the case of Italy. The USSR perceived the West as intent on turning Italy into a focus for air and naval bases which, it claimed, formed part of a wider plan to establish a military network throughout Europe stretching from Iceland to Italy. From May 1946 the Soviet military press began to comment unfavourably on the influence of Washington in both Reykjavik and Rome.[11] The post-war settlement for Italy had actually provided that all troops should be withdrawn within 90 days of a peace treaty coming into force, except those necessary to maintain lines of communication. Once it became apparent that the consolidation was the beginning of US air and military power in Europe, the Kremlin began to advocate schemes for demili-tarisation and neutrality on the European continent. These notions, it suggested, should be applied to Italy in the first instance, but later they could be a solution to the German 'problem'. Even if an 'iron curtain' had descended throughout Europe, it was a permeable or 'net' one. Both the Americans and the Russians were concerned to influence the nature of the political and military arrangements on the other side of the curtain.

The Kremlin's strategies of occupation in Eastern Europe, its intransigence over Iran, and its negotiating posture over Italy, confirmed for many in the West the view of the Soviet Union as an inherently aggressive and expan-sionist power. Although no extra pressure was exerted by Moscow upon Iran in 1946 and 1947, Washington remained concerned by what it perceived as aggressive and subversive Soviet actions throughout Europe. The United States was particularly anxious about what they perceived as a covert Soviet involvement in the civil war in Greece, which had broken out again in the winter of 1946. A report by the State Department concluded that the EAM (the Greek Communist Party) was being used by Moscow to undermine British influence in the region.[12] There was concern over the levels of Yugoslav aid to the Greek Communists. In Washington, it was assumed that Moscow was both co-ordinating and directing the Yugoslav leader Tito's activities. As it happened, Stalin actually found Tito's activities in Greece an impediment to his strategy of co-operation with the West: he had long conceded that Greece fell outside a Soviet sphere of influence. By February 1946 the State Department had been informed that the situation in Greece was so serious that the government might collapse at any moment.

While Greece was not a central strategic concern for Washington, the Truman administration perceived the civil war and the role of the Communists as part of a Soviet plan to dominate Europe. George Kennan noted that a Communist victory in Greece would be followed shortly afterwards by Communist control of Italy. It was believed that, once Italy had fallen, nothing would prevent the takeover of the Communists in France, Germany and Britain.

Communism was regarded as a particularly potent force during the winter of 1946–47 because of the growing economic crisis in Europe.[13] The winter was severe and by March 1947 the British Cabinet warned the American Ambassador in London that the country was heading for a financial crisis and that funds for British forces abroad would have to be reduced. During May 1947 the French Coalition Government did in fact fall, and Washington feared that the Communists would take power. During the spring of 1947 American officials considered that the situation in Europe was so serious that Moscow was being encouraged to take a harder line in negotiations. Not least, it was believed that Soviet intransigence over Germany was strengthened by the belief that Europe would succumb to Communism.

The American reaction to the threat to the stability of Western Europe took the form of the Truman Doctrine. This was announced on 20 June 1947 and made American financial aid available to both Greece and Turkey. It was followed by the announcement on 5 June 1947, by the Secretary of State, George Marshall, of Marshall Aid, a package of economic, industrial and technical aid which would be financed by the Americans and which was designed to help democratic governments rehabilitate their economies after the strains of the war. The purpose of both the Truman Doctrine and Marshall Aid was to strengthen the structures, economies and institutions of West European states to withstand the threat from Communism. The theoretical basis of these initiatives was wholly ideological – so that democratic structures based firmly on liberal ideals would not be subverted by Communism. Marshall's proposal was taken up by Britain and France, who on 19 June issued a statement welcoming the speech and inviting the USSR to a conference to discuss a common European recovery programme.

The Soviet decision to reject participation in the Marshall Plan is widely regarded by scholars as a turning-point in the development of the Cold War. Involvement in the Marshall Plan was, after all, in tune with Soviet objectives of co-operation with the United States in trade and the rehabilitation of the Soviet and East European economies: it appears odd, therefore, that Stalin eschewed this opportunity to gain aid. Why, then, did the Soviet leadership reject Marshall Aid? Initially, at least, the Kremlin was quite positive towards the plan. On 21 June the Politburo met and endorsed the idea of at least meeting with the British and the French to discuss the idea. Indeed, it was at Moscow's suggestion that the venue for the meeting should be in Paris. At the same time the Kremlin communicated instructions to the other East European states to ensure their participation in the plan.

At first, it appears that the Soviet leadership did not fully understand the implications of Marshall Aid – that is, that it was to be used to stave off the influence of Communism. The Soviet understanding of what Marshall Aid was intended for was rather different. Some in the Kremlin argued that it was a means of staving off a post-war depression in the United States through the creation of new markets for American exports. Others, however, argued that it was actually about the creation of a West European economic and political bloc which had an anti-Soviet agenda. It was only during the negotiations over aid with the French and the British during the summer of 1947 that the Soviet leadership finally decided that the Marshall Plan was indeed an anti-Soviet device and therefore unacceptable. Initially, though, the Kremlin had been willing to proceed on the basis that Marshall Aid could provide an opportunity for economic regeneration, although it was acknowledged that the programme did need careful handling. When Molotov arrived in Paris for the meeting he had 100 political and economic advisers with him: in itself an indication of the seriousness with which the Kremlin treated the negotiations. However, at the Paris Conference Molotov was confronted with Anglo-French plans which had at their heart the notion that all participating states would agree on economic modernisation programmes, to be supervised by a central European organisation responsible for the distribution of Marshall Aid. For the Kremlin this proved unacceptable, raising the real possibility that, in return for US aid, a central organisation would intervene in the economies of the Communist bloc. It also now transpires that the Soviet leadership had received information which told them of the central role that West Germany would take in any reconstruction plan for Europe. On 2 July,

after consultation with Stalin, who had remained in Moscow, Molotov publicly rejected the offer of Marshall Aid.

The Paris conference subsequently collapsed and the British and French
issued invitations to the 22 states in Europe to participate in a conference
that would form the European organisation to supervise Marshall Aid. After
the rejection of Marshall Aid by Moscow, however, it was always unlikely
that the East European states would participate. Standard histories of this
episode argue that pressure from the Kremlin, most notably on the Czech
leadership, prevented their acceptance of the terms. Geoffrey Roberts, however, has demonstrated that, at first, Moscow encouraged the Communist
parties of Eastern Europe to reply positively to the American offer, in the
hope that the East European states would receive Marshall Aid. Certain
political conditions had to be fulfilled though – specifically, that political
influence would not be undermined. Despite these instructions some East
European states, most obviously Tito's Yugoslavia, refused to countenance
participation in Marshall Aid. After the Yugoslavs had made their objections
clear, Moscow acceded to their objections. Moscow followed Belgrade. It
was at this point that Czechoslovakia, which had already accepted an invitation to discuss membership, was then informed that it had to boycott the
conference. There could be no question of a break in a unified Communist
front. So ended any hope on the Soviet side that it would be possible to
receive economic aid without political strings.

The final Soviet response to the Marshall Aid programme illustrated a
growing unease on the Communist side about the ramifications of both the
Truman Doctrine and Marshall Aid programme. The Soviet response was to
accept the division of Europe and, if possible, to tighten control over the East
European Communist parties. Here it should be noted that Tito was influen-
tial in advocating a unified Communist line. A decision was taken to found a
new co-ordinating mechanism for the international Communist movement,
to replace the Comintern, which had been abolished in 1943. Accordingly, in
September 1947 representatives of the Communist parties of the USSR,
Bulgaria, Romania, Czechoslovakia, Hungary, Poland, France, Italy and
Yugoslavia met in Poland to create an organisation to co-ordinate activities.
In the founding speech, Andrei Zhdanov declared that the 'two-camp thesis'
remained the predomiant theme in East–West relations. One interesting
aspect of this speech was that not only was it apparently a direct response to
the challenge of Marshall Aid, but it appears that the very establishment of
Cominform was a direct outgrowth of pressure from the Yugoslavs for
Moscow to develop a hardline militant popular front line, as practised by Tito
since the end of the war. Indeed, during the conference the delegates from
Yugoslavia launched attacks on the idea of alternative roads to socialism
which might involve alliances with non-Communist groups. The subsequent
disagreement between Tito and Stalin over the future of socialism provided

the grounds for an ongoing dispute between the two leaders, especially after Yugoslavia defected from the Soviet bloc in 1948.

It was at this point that those amongst the Soviet elite who had advocated a policy of post-war co-operation with the West came under attack. Eugene Varga, the eminent Soviet economist, for example, was roundly condemned for his thesis that, as a result of war, profound changes had taken place within the capitalist world. Specifically, Varga had argued that because of the degree of state planning which had been implemented in war economies, the nature of capitalism had changed. But during the summer of 1947 he was forced to recant, and throughout the autumn the Soviet leadership returned to a more militant and anti-capitalist line. Indeed, in 1949 the Council for Mutual Economic Assistance (Comecon) was formed by the Kremlin as an official and direct counterpart to the Marshall Plan. Comecon was designed to facilitate economic linkages between the USSR and the states of Eastern Europe and Mongolia.

During early 1948 the Soviet leadership used a range of instruments to try to maintain control in the East and to ensure the cohesion of a Communist bloc. While treaties of friendship and co-operation was one method, a less subtle means was tried in Prague when a Communist coup was engineered. Communist actions were triggered by the fear of losing power within the coalition: elections were actually set to take place in the spring of 1948, and there were indications that the Communists faced substantial losses. By mid-January the Czech Communist Party was entering a period of crisis. It was at this point, on 7 February, that the Soviet leadership intervened to prevent the Czech Government from accepting the offer of Marshall Aid. Moscow had been prepared to allow socialism to develop at its own pace in Czechoslovakia, but once this possibility began to disappear Stalin could not afford to allow Prague to turn westwards. Historians debate the extent to which Moscow was involved in staging the coup, but the very speed with which it acted afterwards seems to indicate foreknowledge of events. The right of passage through Czechoslovakia for the Red Army was requested, and Soviet officials such as the Deputy Foreign Minister, V. Zorin, were dispatched to Prague to supervise economic matters. Zorin, apparently, conveyed a message from Stalin to Gottwald, the leader of the Czech Communists, that, 'The USSR would not allow the West to interfere in Czechoslovakia's internal affairs.'

The process of consolidation of Soviet influence was also visible in Scandinavia. On 22 February 1948 Stalin sent the Finnish President, Paasikivi, a letter which contained a suggestion for a Soviet–Finnish treaty. In his proposal the Soviet leader directly alluded to the Soviet treaty with Hungary as a possible model. He suggested that the treaty provide for mutual assistance 'against a possible attack by Germany'. Molotov described the treaty as a joint defence pact.[14] This provoked widespread concern in both

Finland and in Western capitals that Moscow intended to 'swallow' Finland. Paasikivi believed, at least initially, that the Soviet intention was to bring Finland under military control and into the East and Central European bloc.

During February 1948, American diplomats in Helsinki reported fears of a coup similar to the one that had taken place in Prague. It was expected that the Communists in the Finnish Government would engineer a domestic crisis and that Soviet troops would then be 'requested' to help restore order.[15] Throughout January sources in Helsinki reported rumours of a build-up of Soviet forces on the Finnish border,[16] and Stalin himself pressed Paasikivi to agree to a treaty confirming a 'special' relationship. Moscow wanted to prevent Helsinki looking West, and in particular it sought to prevent the Finns from joining a prospective Nordic alliance. Moscow wanted to keep Sweden, and possibly Norway, neutral. By not obviously 'browbeating' the Finns into the treaty, Moscow achieved its security aims without frightening the other Nordic countries. In a conversation in mid-February, the new Soviet Ambassador to Finland, General Savonenkov, revealed these intentions. He suggested that the Finns should take the initiative over the treaty in public, because such action would make it less likely to create tensions in Scandinavia and affect the security choices of other Nordic powers.[17] This type of persuasion worked, Soviet influence in the north was secured and Moscow's tactics were successful. However, in the case of Berlin they were almost entirely counter-productive.

Berlin

The Soviet leadership hoped to achieve a range of objectives through the imposition of the Berlin blockade in 1948. First an attempt was made to coerce the West into abandoning its strategy of building up a coalition encompassing a new West German state. Second, an attempt was made to persuade the West to reopen negotiations with Moscow on the question of Germany as a whole. A third and not entirely compatible aim was also pursued. This was to build a separate state structure in the Eastern half of Germany, to consolidate control within Eastern Europe.

By the spring of 1948 the Western powers had succeeded not only in merging their zones of occupation in Germany, but also in laying the foundations for military-political integration into a Western coalition. The Soviet government was implacably hostile towards this idea, claiming it to be an attempt to create an anti-Soviet Western bloc utilising German military-industrial strength. A variety of tactics was used by Moscow to persuade the Western Allies to negotiate on the issue of Germany as a whole. The Soviet leadership sought discussion of the demilitarisation and denazification of Germany. It continued to demand participation in the control of the Ruhr area, and a uniform German currency to avert the introduction of a separate currency for the Western zones. Currency reform was regarded as detrimental to Soviet economic rehabilitation in the East. It was perceived as part of a strategy, inherent in the Marshall Plan, to build up the West against the Soviet Union, and was a powerful symbol of the intention to unify the Western zones and reinvigorate the West German economy. Soviet actions over Berlin in 1948 were closely linked to Western measures aimed at German military and political integration.

In March Marshal Sokolovsky, the commander of the Soviet sector in Berlin, walked out of the Allied Control Council. Berlin, because of wartime arrangements, lay deep within the Soviet occupation zone. The Russians controlled all ground access to the city. On the 31st of that month the United States Military Government in Berlin was informed that, as from 1 April, new restrictions were to be imposed on Allied personnel travelling into Berlin by rail and road. On 18 June the Western Allies informed Marshal Sokolovsky of their intention to implement a new currency reform in the Western zones of Germany two days later, and on the same day the Soviet military authorities ordered 'obstructions' in Berlin and the Western zones. Sokolovsky followed this with a decree announcing a currency reform for the Soviet zones of Germany and the whole of Berlin. Sokolovsky was officially informed of the Western intention to introduce currency reforms into the Western sectors of Berlin on 24 June. On the same day the remaining waterways, road and rail links were closed by the Soviet military authorities. Throughout the spring of 1948 Moscow attempted to persuade the French to oppose Anglo-American plans for Germany. Moscow at this stage counted upon traditional French fears of German militarism.[18] Here, the Kremlin did seem to have hit upon a weakness in the Western camp. In April and May there was intense discussion in Paris over the future of Germany. Anxiety over the military potential of a new German state competed with a desire to benefit from US economic aid. The French considered a range of options through which they hoped to gain both military security and economic assistance. Some French ministers argued for a policy of Franco-German reconciliation through a Western federation. The paramount concern was that, if Paris did not agree to the merging of all the Western zones in Germany, the British and Americans would simply proceed without France.

On 3 August the American Ambassador in Moscow, Walter Bedell Smith, held a meeting with Stalin and Molotov. The Soviet leader agreed to lift the blockade, but called for a conference of the Council of Foreign Ministers on the future of Germany. On 24 August the USSR dispatched a note proposing a meeting of the Council of Foreign Ministers to discuss any unresolved matters regarding either Germany as a whole or Berlin in particular. Moscow proposed numerous alternatives to the creation of a West German state throughout the period of the blockade. The Warsaw statement of June 1948, made after a conference of Soviet and East European representatives in Poland, concluded by proposing that the four major powers should adopt a five-point programme for all of Germany. This would include the implementation of measures ensuring the final demilitarisation of Germany by agreement between Great Britain, the USSR, France and the United States. Another requirement would be the institution of a quadripartite control regime for a definite period over the heavy industries of the Ruhr to preclude the re-establishment of a German capacity to wage war. Moscow also asked for the conclusion of a peace treaty with Germany to enable the withdrawal of occupation forces within a year of the treaty. The latter proposal was reiterated on 21 September 1948, and throughout 1949 the Kremlin reaffirmed its support for the withdrawal of all foreign troops from German soil.[19]

As William Taubman has commented though, 'Stalin always made the worst of a bad job.'[20] The Soviet provocations over Berlin merely hardened Western actions. The Soviet leadership was surprised by the determination with which the Americans operated the airlifting of supplies into the city, and were careful not to interfere with US actions. An estimate has been made that of the 162,275 flights from the West that took place into Berlin between June 1948 and June 1949, less than 1 per cent were interfered with.[21] There is little doubt that Stalin underestimated the lengths to which the Western powers would go to ensure the success of the airlift, especially through the winter of 1948–9. This was understandable, since many in the West doubted its ability to sustain the airlift.[22] Second, though, Stalin recognised that any interference with Western air access could push the conflict into an area where the margins for error and accident might be reduced and might result in war. Following the single incident in which Western and Soviet aircraft collided over Berlin, Western officials received the impression that the USSR was deeply concerned over possible repercussions from the incident.

As the success of the airlift became ever more apparent Stalin moderated his political demands in an attempt to salvage something from the standoff. By January 1949 he no longer made the withdrawal of Western currency reforms a *sine qua non* for lifting the blockade. A non-nuclear Soviet Union obviously had an interest in avoiding military conflict with the US. In the 1940s the USSR was striving to create its own nuclear force. Soviet concentration upon the production of nuclear weapons in the 1940s signalled clearly the recognition of the strategic power of such weapons: a recognition which must have been reinforced by the examples of Nagasaki and Hiroshima. The Soviet fear of a strategic air attack in the late 1940s is indicated by the emphasis upon the forward integration of East European countries into Soviet air defences; the fact was that Soviet conventional military power in Europe was not what it was assumed by the West to be at the time. Soviet appreciation of the US nuclear potential was acute. The Berlin crisis, therefore, was a localised confrontation (albeit one with much wider possibilities and dangers) in which Moscow eventually had to accept defeat. Stalin had hoped to force the West to negotiate on larger issues through the application of pressure on a small isolated enclave in Germany, but succeeded only in providing the rationale for Western rearmament.

On 8 April 1949 it was announced that the United States, Britain and France had agreed 'on all questions relating to the establishment and control of a West German Federal Republic'. As soon as the Republic was established it was agreed that, for security reasons, occupation troops would remain under a new occupation statute. In April 1949 the defence ministers of the five Brussels Treaty powers, with American and Canadian participation, announced their agreement on a sweeping plan for the defence of Western Europe, and on 12 April the United States and Britain reached agreement on establishing facilities in Britain to provide for the stationing of atomic bombers.

Soviet ideology still maintained that intra-state conflict existed within the Western bloc. Such apparent theoretical confidence in intra-Western-bloc conflict appears at variance with the reality of progressively closer military-economic co-operation in the West. Yet during 1949 the Soviet Union made immense efforts to exploit what they percieved to be structural weaknesses in the capitalist system and manipulate both elite and public opinion to the advantage of Communism. These attempts to utilise the public in the Western states were apparent in January 1949, when P. N. Pospelov, the editor of *Pravda*, announced that 'peaceful coexistence' was the order of the day. The Kremlin began to advocate a strategy designed to appeal to those elements in the West opposed to nuclear weapons and remilitarisation in Europe. For example, the Peace Movement was designed to gather popular support for such an issue. The instrument for this campaign was primarily the Cominform, but also Communist parties throughout Europe. Yet it should not be thought that Moscow managed at all times to control or direct foreign Communist parties. (The rift with Tito had demonstrated that this was palpably not the case.) On 11 January the leading French Communist, Marcel Cachin, talked of the possibilities of peaceful coexistence. Three days later he visited Italy and, with Togliatti, the leader of the Italian Communists, began to talk of socialism 'winning' by peaceful means. Although it had sparked the initial campaign in the West, Moscow was quite often surprised over the activities of the French Communists and on more than one occasion worried as to how far their 'comrades' might go.

The first so-called 'peace offensive' was a brief affair, launched by Cachin in January, 1950 and followed by a declaration by the leading French Communist, Thorez, of full support for the Red Army in the event of any future war. This radical pronouncement apparently alienated many supporters and was judged too extreme. The second wave of the peace offensive did, however, have more success. On 24 February, the International Liaison

Committee of Intellectuals for Peace, appointed at the Wrocław Congress, met in Paris and announced a series of meetings to be held in several major cities. Even though Moscow was not directing every move of the international peace movement, in the West it served only to increase fears of a Soviet desire to usurp democratic governments.

There is little doubt over the relief that the Kremlin felt in August 1949 when Soviet scientists succeeded in exploding an atom bomb. One commentator openly stated that the United States could no longer blackmail the USSR. Indeed, in a speech in November 1949 Malenkov included the possession of the atomic secret as a contributory factor to the strength of the Soviet position, proclaiming that the global balance was now tilted in favour of socialism and the Soviet state and listing factors which had contributed to this favourable trend. The Communist victory in the civil war in China was regarded as a particular triumph. However, the emergence of Mao as victor in the Chinese civil war had ramifications for Soviet foreign-policy conduct, not least because Stalin came to fear that the Chinese leader would challenge him for leadership of the Communist movement. It is against this backdrop of triumph and anxiety that the Soviet actions on the Korean peninsula have to be judged.

Korea

At the Cairo meeting in 1943 Korea had been promised independence, but had been divided into occupation zones along the 38th parallel. Moscow controlled the north and Washington the south. Soviet troops were withdrawn in January 1949, with US troops leaving a few months later: both, however, left separate regimes in place. The character of the north Korean regime was of dependency on Moscow, certainly for military supplies, and of ambition to unite the two zones. In the summer of 1950 the North invaded the South. Up until the 1990s the Soviet version of events in Korea was very simple: this was, that North Korea intervened in South Korea on 25 June 1950 in response to a provocation by the south. This version of events, however, was simply false. The North Koreans had planned a full-scale assault on the south to begin on 25 June, the goal being unification of the two Koreas. Stalin, 'we now know', approved the plan, provided the arms and equipment to make the attack possible and sent military advisers to assist. Moscow had been excluded from influence in the settlement of the Japanese question despite its protests, and if the North Korean invasion of the south could have been accomplished quickly, without American opposition, Stalin would have recouped control of the whole of Korea under the influence of Communist powers at little cost to Moscow and gained a foothold in the region.

According to Khrushchev's memoirs, which record the discussions between Stalin and the North Korean leader Kim Il Sung, the latter appears to have reassured Stalin during preliminary talks that the invasion could be achieved quickly and without opposition from the United States.[23] Volkogonov's biography of Stalin, which also analyses the discussions between Stalin and Kim Il Sung, confirms that the Soviet dictator knew of the North Korean plan but made many attempts to distance himself from the attack in public, and that from the outset he tried to avoid direct confrontation with the USA.[24] The Soviet dictator was also in part motivated by the victory of Mao in China: Stalin was afraid that Mao would emerge as a rival for the leadership of the Communist bloc in Asia. This also in part seems to have propelled the Soviet dictator to accept Kim Il Sung's assurances that an easy victory was possible on the Korean peninsula. The idea itself came from Pyongyang. Kim Il Sung pressurised Stalin with no less than 48 telegrams in a bid to gain the approval and support of the Kremlin over the intervention in Korea. Stalin supported the idea, at least initially, because he believed there was little chance of an American challenge.

Washington had signalled its lack of interest in Korea very clearly. By mid-1949 Washington had withdrawn the bulk of its forces from the Korean peninsula, while American spokesmen had defined US strategic interests in the region in such a manner as to exclude Korea. Senator Tom Connally, the Chairman of the Senate Foreign Relations Committee, for example, during an interview on 5 May 1950 had stated that Korea was not an essential part of the defence strategy of the United States. Despite this, the American military reaction to the North Korean aggression was rapid. On 27 June the Security Council of the United Nations (UN), from which the Soviet delegation had absented itself, condemned the invasion of South Korea and called upon the North Koreans to withdraw. On 30 June US ground units under the auspices of the UN were ordered into action. The Americans developed a double-pronged response to the Korean conflict, a military response in the East and a building up of defences in Europe. There was recognition within the US Administration that the European allies believed that this was an attempt by the Kremlin to probe American resolve globally. This was an assessment that President Harry Truman shared and decided to act on.

The importance of China

The American intervention prevented the attack by the North Koreans from being successful. Within weeks the military situation had changed. The Kremlin then appeared to be witnessing a collapse of a fellow Communist regime in North Korea. The Soviet leadership appeared undecided between encouraging the initially reluctant Chinese to intervene or withdrawing Soviet support of Kim Il Sung. According to Khrushchev, there was a move within the Kremlin to write off North Korea, but by late August the Chinese and the Soviet leadership had agreed to use Chinese troops in Korea. It is interesting that, from the time of the Chinese intervention in late 1950, Stalin remained constant in his determination to aid the Chinese troops enagaged in the conflict both with Soviet air power and personnel. The first clear-cut encounter between Soviet personnel and American forces occured the day after US troops had crossed the 38th parallel on 8 October. Two US F-80s strafed a Soviet airfield 60 miles north of the Soviet-Korean border. Despite this back-up for Chinese forces, Stalin remained anxious over a possible confrontation with Washington. After American troops had crossed the 38th parallel he actually ordered Kim Il Sung to abandon the defence of North Korea and pull out the remnants of military forces into northeast China. Almost immediately the dictator changed his mind over withdrawal, not least because Mao was determined to fight on. This reveals both the limits of Stalin's commitment to Third World allies and the influence that Mao exercised over the conduct of the war. It was Mao and the Chinese who led the war against the Americans at this point.

The situation in Korea though worsened considerably by the spring of 1951. The Chinese forces had been halted and Seoul had been retaken by UN forces. A second Chinese offensive failed to make any real impact on UN troops, and a line was established near the 38th parallel. It was at this point that Moscow suggested a ceasefire. On 23 June 1951 Yakov Malik, the Soviet Ambassador to the United Nations, called for a mutual withdrawal from the 38th parallel. Ceasefire negotiations took place, but the fighting continued. What this signalled on the Soviet side was an acceptance that an armistice could be arranged in Korea without a formal settlement of the issues which had up until this point formed an integral part of their conditions for peace – that is, the withdrawal of US troops from the Korean Peninsula. Although the war in Korea dragged on until 1953, by the summer of 1951 Moscow had to face the fact that the Western alliance had not only remained united over resisting the Communist threat in Korea, but, worse, in the light of the Korean War had moved irrevocably towards a coherent military-political unit in Western Europe which would include West Germany.

On 30 November Otto Grotewohl, the head of the government in East Germany, wrote to Adenauer, the West German leader, taking up the Eastern-bloc suggestion for the creation of an 'all-German Consultative council' which he suggested might eventually form the basis for a provisional government for the whole of Germany. At this stage the East Germans were mobilised to form a bridge between East and West Germany to try and impede the inclusion of the Western part of Germany into an anti-Soviet alliance. At an extraordinary meeting of the GDR *Volkskammer*, on 2 March 1951, a resolution was passed to ask the Federal Bundestag to press the four Great Powers to conclude a peace treaty with Germany and create a German state, a Germany which would be unified, democratised and *demilitarised* and, after the signing of the treaty, free of all occupation forces.

The Soviet Union also protested in this period against the establishment of the North Atlantic Treaty Organisation (NATO), a permanent military alliance led by the Americans and set up in 1949. In fact, the Soviet leadership argued that it would not participate in any further diplomatic meetings unless there was a discussion of the issue of US military bases in both Europe and Asia. Once again the issue of US bases was linked to the issue of a German settlement. While historians have on the whole ignored the details of the negotiations that took place between 1951 and 1952, it is here that we see Soviet suggestions for neutralisation and demilitarisation in Central Europe. For example, on 4 February 1951 Moscow had suggested in a telegram to Washington that it might be possible to limit the size and position of NATO forces on the European continent. This implied a pragmatic acceptance of the existence of NATO but an attempt again to exclude German might. But the Soviet initiatives to block the full integration of West Germany into a Western alliance failed. On 9 July 1951 the Western allies announced their intention of ending the state of war with Germany. From the summer onward, Soviet diplomacy consisted of a constant reiteration of the arguments against the incorporation of Germany into NATO. This was the theme of a Soviet initiative in early 1952. On 10 March the Soviet Government proposed a peace treaty with Germany and once more outlined conditions for peace that would mean the withdrawal of US troops and a demilitarisation of Germany. The draft contained the provisions, first, that Germany be re-established as a unified state and second, that all occupying forces be withdrawn from Germany within a year. Another clause explicitly banned the new Germany from entering into 'any coalition or military alliance directed against any power which took part with its armed forces in the war against Germany', and a further one insisted also that all military bases on German soil be liquidated. The Soviet initiative was dismissed as yet another attempt by Moscow to divert Western military attention. In their response, the West made it a condition of the unification of Germany that the UN should supervise general elections throughout the whole of Germany. This, however, was unacceptable to Moscow. There was a readiness to sacrifice East Germany in exchange for a 'neutral' Germany but not a democratic Germany.

By the time Stalin died in March 1953, the Cold War had taken on several characteristics. The first and most obvious one was the division of Europe between a Soviet-controlled East and an American-dominated West. It has to be said that, for the Soviet leadership, this was in many ways a satisfactory outcome to historic security concerns, not least control of the heart of Europe. Yet it had been achieved at high cost. The control of Eastern Europe and the Soviet refusal to mitigate political conditions within the bloc after 1947 ended any realistic hope of positive trade and aid packages from Western states. This effectively consigned the Soviet leadership to a long-term management problem in the East – how to reinvigorate poor economies, control restive peoples and establish the legitimacy of the Communist model. The task was made more difficult by the visible economic 'success' of the capitalist model in the other half of the continent.

It is in this period that we can observe the beginning of a clear development of two competing systems. On the one side there was a Communist bloc characterised by economic autarky and authoritarian political structures while, on the other, the Western alliance remained dedicated to the spread of liberal political and economic institutions.

The second characteristic of the Cold War was the emphasis placed by both sides on the importance of nuclear technology. After the American explosions over Japan in August 1945, the Soviet leadership strove to achieve a nuclear capability. But what is odd about the period is that, despite the symbolic importance of nuclear power, it appeared to make little difference to the conduct of the Cold War in Europe. Indeed, it is striking how little either Soviet or American diplomacy was affected by the nuclear age. Nevertheless the Soviet side placed the highest premium on equalling US technological strength. Indeed, one of the most interesting and striking consequences of the nuclear age was that this determination had important ramifications for what might be termed the 'human' story of the Cold War. The demands of the Soviet nuclear programme required an intensification of the stripping of parts of the Eastern bloc to supply Soviet scientists with the material necessary for the arms race. Not least in East Germany, the consequence of this 'stripping' was a drop in living conditions; while at home in the USSR the demands of the nuclear and military programme retarded the development of a competitive consumer industry.

A third and final characteristic of the Cold War established in this period was that, until the Korean War, the confrontation between East and West remained focused on Europe. Only after that war can we really talk of a general Cold War that had gone global. The fact that it spread can be attributed to Mao's relationship with Stalin as much as to anxiety over American power. The Soviet leadership feared that, after the triumph of Mao in China, Beijing could become a potential rival for leadership of the Communist cause in both Asia and in the Third World. Communist allies were not, as Stalin had found out with Tito, always easy to control. Indeed, it is interesting just how problematic Moscow found the international Communist movement. Although in public the growth of centres of Communism was lauded, in private the Kremlin worried over its control. Stalin's international legacy to his successors was twofold: the problem of how to contain the threat from the West, as well as how to manage allies.

Notes

1 US Department of State, Foreign Relations United States, FRUS Potsdam, vol. 1, pp. 26–32.
2 Norman Naimark, *The Russians in Germany: A History of the Soviet Zone of Occupation, 1945–1949* (Cambridge, Mass.: Harvard University Press, 1995).
3 David Holloway, *Stalin and the Bomb* (New Haven: Yale University Press, 1994).
4 Enclosure 2. Memorandum of the US Delegation at the Moscow Conference of Ministers (Moscow, December 18, 1945). FRUS 1945, vol. II, pp. 567–76.
5 Department of State Memorandum, FRUS 1946, vol. VII, p. 347.
6 The Charge in the Soviet Union (Kennan) to the Secretary of State (Moscow, 22 February, 1946), FRUS 1946, vol. VI, pp. 696–709.
7 *New York Times*, 6 March 1946.
8 *Department of State Bulletin*, XV (September 15, 1946).
9 FO 371/58633, Hayter letter to Holman, Bucharest. Quoted in E. Barker, *The British Between the Superpowers 1945–1950* (Oxford: Macmillan), p. 61.
10 US Delegation Record. Second Session Sixteenth Meeting, Paris, 14 May 1946. Quoted in Barker, *The British Between the Superpowers*.
11 See 12 May 1946 *Krasnaya Zvezda*; 11 June, 1946, *Krasnaya Zvezda*.
12 State Department, Lot 55 D 638, January 1947.
13 PPS/1/Policy with Respect to American Aid to Western Europe, 23 May, 1947.
14 US Department of State: 30 March 1948. 760D. 6111./3–3048.
15 US Department of State: 28 February 1948. 760D. 6111/2–2848.
16 US Department of State: 22 January 1948. 760D. 6111/2–2248.
17 US Department of State: 27 February 1948. 7460D. 6111/2–2748.
18 Bidault Papers, Box 21 (6 April). Quoted in J. Young, *France, the Cold War and the Western Alliance 1944–1949* (Leicester: Leicester University Press, 1990), p. 188.
19 *Pravda*, 3 January 1949.
20 Francesca Gori and Silvio Pons (eds), *The Soviet Union and Europe in the Cold War 1945–53* (London: Macmillian, 1996).
21 Robert Rodrigo, *Berlin Airlift* (London: Cassell, 1960), p. 214.
22 Record of meeting on 'Berlin Situation', Forrestal Papers (27 June 1948: Princeton Library).
23 Nikita Khrushchev, *Khrushchev Remembers*, ed. Edward Crankshaw (Boston: Little Brown, 1971), pp. 33–4.
24 Dmitri Volkoganov, *Stalin: Triumph and Tragedy* (London: Weidenfeld and Nicolson, 1990), pp. 540–1.

5
The Stalinist Legacy and Khrushchev's Foreign Policy 1953–1964

Certainly, by the time of his death in 1953 Stalin had left his successors a complex legacy. On the one hand there were considerable achievements, the extension of Soviet frontiers into East and Central Europe, the defeat and subjection of Germany and the not inconsiderable feats of the Soviet atomic programme. In addition to this, the victory of Mao in China gave at least a veneer of strength to global Communism. Yet the Stalinist legacy was not quite this clear-cut. Soviet achievements had been achieved at great cost. The occupation of the states of East and Central Europe had resulted in a forcible and coherent Western response, signalled by the Marshall Plan and the creation of NATO. Worse still, from a Soviet perspective, was that the division of Germany had resulted in a reinvigoration of the Western bloc, evidenced through the obvious superiority of living standards and conditions in the West. Perhaps most worrying of all, however, the green light given to Kim Il Sung to invade South Korea had caused the West to redouble its rearmament efforts and had led to NSC 68. In April 1950 the Truman Administration announced National Security Council Directive 68 (NSC 68). This called for a tripling of the US defence budget to defend against the threat of Soviet expansionism. Indeed, the actual conduct of the Korean war had meant that Mao and Chinese forces had had to dig Stalin out of the Korean quagmire. It was also the case that, with the forcible Western response to the Soviet 'probe' in Asia, the superpower competition for influence had spread out of the European arena. After the death of Stalin his successors had to decide what form the Soviet response would take throughout new areas, most notably in the Middle East and Africa.

At the same time as the Soviet Union confronted the new pattern of global politics, it was faced with a series of internal problems; most notable of these was the effect that the emphasis on a large-scale Soviet nuclear programme had produced. There was a shortage of consumer goods and consequent disquiet with the economic situation. A general attempt to release the political and economic system from misery was attempted through the process of destalinisation. This in itself was problematic; the release of political controls might engender forces that would not be easily contained. These worries were compounded for the Soviet leadership by the need to control the East and Central European states. Intriguingly, recent research from the Soviet archives demonstrates that Soviet leaders continued to worry that the unrest throughout the Eastern bloc might result in a 'spill-over' effect which could affect the USSR itself. Stalin's Communist allies, whether in the Eastern bloc, China or Western Europe, gave cause for concern. All of this mandated the need for a 'breathing space' with the West.

After the death of the dictator, however, a power struggle ensued within the walls of the Kremlin. Individuals jostled for position, and the consequent leadership competition was not really resolved until 1957, when Nikita Khrushchev, the mine worker from Donbass, emerged clearly as leader. The extent to which an individual can impact upon the making of foreign policy is often debated. Certainly, the story of Soviet foreign policy after 1957 is to a great extent that of Khrushchev's attempts to bring the USSR into co-equal status with the United States, while at the same time struggling to modernise both the economy and the political system.

The institutionalisation of the Cold War 1953–1955

Immediately after the death of Stalin, however, the Soviet story is one of uncertainty and insecurity. Stalin's death removed the hope that the cult of personality could be used to overcome the difficulties of the USSR. This left the problem of who was to rule: a difficult situation because there existed no clear mechanisms by which to choose a new leader. All of this was compounded by the tensions which had arisen within the Kremlin as Stalin began to ail. In particular, the 'doctor's plot' had revealed the extent of elite feuding. During this episode, nine doctors were 'purged', accused of trying to remove elements of the higher levels of the Party and the military. Subsequently a campaign was launched to eradicate anti-Marxist feelings. In this power struggle, three contenders for the position of leader emerged: Malenkov, the Prime Minister; Beria, the Chief of Police and Minister of the Interior; and Khrushchev, the Party chief.[1] Initially they ruled as a triumvirate, and it appeared that they were determined to follow a coherent line in foreign policy and seek a *rapprochement* of sorts with the Western bloc. At Stalin's funeral on 9 March, Malenkov called for the possibility of a lasting coexistence and for a peaceful competition between the two different systems. Almost at once the Soviet press became less anti-Western, and the leadership demonstrated a greater willingness to negotiate the end to the Korean War and raise the issue of a Great-Power conference to discuss once again the future of Germany.

Even before his death in March 1953, those around Stalin had moved to address what they saw as some of the most counterproductive aspects of his regime. In domestic politics this took the form of trying to remedy the shortage of consumer goods and mitigate the excesses and arbitrary nature of the political system. In foreign-policy terms it meant a reinvigoration of policies which might prohibit Western defence integration, and specifically the continued development of a coherent Western bloc, with the West German state at its core. It was noted in Chapter 4 that in early 1952 the Soviet leadership had presented the Western Allies with a note which envisaged a comprehensive peace treaty with Germany. Under this agreement Moscow had proposed that Germany be reunited, although it was required that it would have to cede all territories east of the Oder and the Neisse line. It had also contained the clause that all occupation forces be withdrawn a year after the conclusion of the treaty.[2] Government structures based on elections would also be instituted. Soviet notes were sent to the Western Allies in May and August which continued to urge the Western Allies to take this notion seriously.

The Soviet notes, however, met with almost uniform cynicism in the West. The leadership of the German Federal Republic under Adenauer was not prepared during this period to risk what had been accomplished in West Germany for the price of an all-German solution. Indeed, the West Germans were not prepared to countenance any form of arrangement in which a Soviet leadership would have had an input into the future composition of an all-German government. The American leadership, which in the wake of the outbreak of war in Korea had already moved towards a policy of military containment, took barely any notice of the Soviet initiative. In particular, the Americans rejected any possibility of a Four-Power Conference on the German question.[3]

The initiatives appear to have been taken at the instigation of Beria. This is interesting, because, at least initially, it was Beria who appeared to be dominant in the policy-making process and specifically in Soviet–German policy. After the death of Stalin, it has been argued, it was he who was instrumental in ordering a relaxation of the regime in East Germany. Supported by Malenkov, he attempted to prevent the GDR from blocking itself off from unification, and he ordered the SED (Socialist Unity Party) leadership to reduce the pace of the building of socialism. In part at least this was an attempt to mitigate the considerable dissatisfaction of the East German population which had resulted in an endless flow of refugees to the West. In particular it was this haemorrhaging of people that appeared to have unnerved the Soviet leadership. The East German reform programme was the subject of intense debate within the Kremlin, but was not endorsed by Khrushchev. He later accused Beria of having been willing to give up East Germany in return for preventing Western defence integration.[4]

The relaxation of the regime in East Germany had profound consequences. Workers in East Germany staged large-scale disturbances and attacked Communist officials. In Berlin, Halle and Leipzig strikes affected industry and communications; prisoners were released, and the resignation of Ulbricht and Grotwohl was demanded. Communism in the East appeared under threat. The Soviet regime had to respond to the collapse of the SED regime, and it appeared that Soviet control in East and Central Europe might collapse. It also demonstrated how risky a neutral Germany could prove to be. On 17 June the Soviet leadership decided to re-establish Ulbricht and not to consign the SED to retirement. Soviet tanks were used to quell the uprising. Beria was removed from his posts at the Party plenum, and was eventually shot on 24 December.[5] On 22 August, meanwhile, Moscow had agreed a deal with the SED leadership which included the cancellation of all reparation payments and post-war debts, as well as a clause agreeing that Moscow would supply goods and credits to the value of 465 million roubles. At this point it appeared that the GDR was fully integrated into the Eastern bloc, and the preoccupation of Soviet foreign policy, particularly after the uprisings, was consolidation in the East.

Throughout all of this, however, the Soviet leadership did not forego the notion that it would be able to manipulate the differences it perceived as existing among West European states on defence integration. The Kremlin hoped in particular to retard the growth of the European Defence Community, or EDC. The Soviet leadership tried to renew notions of neutralisation and reunification. The idea of a reunified Germany was revived as a negotiating ploy, to prohibit what the Soviet leadership believed would turn out to be a new, coherent Western alliance centred around West Germany – in the shape of the EDC. Soviet commentators claimed that Germany would dominate any such defence alliance. In early 1954, at the Berlin conference, the Soviet delegation proposed that Germany should be both united and neutralised. The idea was mooted that troops would be withdrawn and Germany would then be prohibited from joining any defence alliance. In addition, Molotov called for the abandonment of NATO and the creation of a pan-European organisation without American participation. Eisenhower's Secretary of State, John Foster Dulles, who attended the meeting, recounted that when this proposal was tabled it was regarded as so preposterous that laughter rippled around the Western sides of the table, much to the dismay of the Communist delegation.[6] The Western delegation countered with a suggestion that the future of Germany should be decided through free German elections. The Soviet regime obviously could not, after the 1953 rebellions, accept any plans for reunification which were based on the free choice of the German people. In March a Soviet note finally conceded the point that Western defence structures would include the West Germans and a permanent American contingent. However, the note also requested that the USSR be allowed to join NATO.

The Soviet leadership did, however, draw some comfort from the collapse of the EDC. The French resisted pressure to be drawn into the European military alliance, and refused to ratify the EDC treaty. Soviet attempts to undermine the proposed alliance centred around exerting pressure on the French. Here two tactics were apparent. One was to raise the spectre of German revanchism: in particular, the USSR tried to depict the EDC as an instrument through which the Germans would once again dominate the continent. Second, the Kremlin sought to play upon tensions between Paris and Washington over the French involvement in Indo-China. At this stage the Americans had refused to support the French effort in Asia, and Moscow offered to use its influence in Indo-China if Paris rejected the EDC. Soviet triumph at the failure of the EDC did not last long, however; Moscow was almost immediately confronted with the British idea of a West European Union. The British revived the idea of a Brussels Pact, first raised in 1948, which would include both Italy and the Federal Republic of Germany. French fears over possible German revanchism was met through the suggestion that all key decisions would be taken by NATO and that the US would make a permanent military commitment to Europe. These ideas were formalised in the Paris Treaties of October 1954, and what they meant in practice was that Germany was formally divided.

This proposal provoked from Moscow another determined attempt to mitigate any prospect of a formal military alliance with the Federal Republic at its heart. The Social Democratic Party (SPD) organised a series of strikes, and Moscow mobilised a campaign which once again aimed at promoting the idea of a neutral and unified Germany. In the early part of 1954 Moscow had actually offered to join NATO, and proposed a new collective security arrangement for the continent. By early 1955, however, it had to settle for the division of Germany, the consolidation of the Eastern bloc and renewed attempts to harness the technological power of the Western bloc. On 25 January Moscow ended its state of war with Germany and announced an intensification of its links with the GDR. In November 1954, immediately after the signing of the Paris Treaties, Moscow had threatened that if the West went ahead it would create a defensive organisation in the East. The Paris Treaties were ratified on 26 March 1955, and the Warsaw Treaty Organisation (WTO) was formally established on 14 May 1955. The new organisation included the USSR, Poland, Czechoslovakia, Hungary, Romania, Bulgaria, Albania and the GDR. Article 5 of the organisation's founding documents was the establishment of a political consultative committee to co-ordinate foreign polices. Not unintentionally, the Warsaw Pact mirrored the structures of the NATO Alliance. Soviet sources claimed at the time that the creation of the Pact arose out of the refusal of the Western powers to include the USSR in the Western security alliance, although the official *raison d'être* of the Pact was the threat from German revanchism.

However, even if Moscow presented the creation of the WTO as a second-best substitute to the pan-European security arrangement it desired, in reality the Pact bestowed several not inconsiderable benefits. First, it formalised military relations between Moscow and the East European states. Up until 1955 the relationships had been of a bilateral nature, and there had been no systematic attempt to integrate East European forces with each other or with the Red Army. The Pact allowed for the setting up of a joint command of the Soviet and East European Armed Forces to oversee defence arrangements. This was, of course, in no way an alliance of equals: Moscow, and its Soviet commanders remained firmly in command.

Second, the new arrangements provided Moscow with a justification for the stationing of troops throughout East and Central Europe. This was useful, because when a peace treaty was signed with Austria on 15 May 1955 Moscow would have lost its wartime pretext for maintaining troops on Hungarian soil, which had been justified as a necessary conduit for the Soviet occupation troops in Austria. Indeed, with the Paris Treaties and the creation of the Warsaw Pact, both the USSR and the Western powers had secured spheres of influence and had at least tacitly signalled that there would be no large-scale intervention in the affairs of the other half of the bloc. Although Khrushchev continued to attempt to manipulate what he perceived as tensions within the Western alliance following the Geneva conference, improved relations with the West permitted a period of détente. The agreement over Austria in May had been one important example of a Soviet willingness to negotiate on some of the outstanding issues of the Second World War. It should be noted that the Soviet withdrawal of its troops from Austria made little difference, as there was little chance of Communism developing there. Indeed, the population within Austria had been noticeably anti-Communist, and it was unlikely that Soviet-style ideals would have gained ground. The example of Austria, however, was held up by the Soviet leadership to other states – particularly the West Germans, but also some Third-World states – as demonstrating the advantages of what could be achieved by a state which was officially neutral.

Despite difficulties over the issue of Germany, the Soviet desire for a *rapprochement* with the West was clearly demonstrated at the Great Power meeting which was held in Geneva in July 1955. Khrushchev went to Switzerland to meet the American President Eisenhower, the British Prime Minister Eden and Faure, the French Prime Minister. In terms of concrete achievement, the Geneva meeting was noticeable for the Great-Power colloboration over ending the war in Indo-China and the establishment of an International Control Commission for the country, chaired by the British and the Soviet Union. Whilst little else of substance was actually achieved, the delegates discussed a number of questions: most notably, West Germany and the issues of reunification and disarmament. Nuclear power and disarmament was also an issue high on the agenda, and the Soviet delegation made an attempt to transfer control of nuclear production to a UN organisation. The American counterproposal to have a so-called 'open-skies' verification regime for nuclear arms not surprisingly met with little enthusiasm on the Soviet side.[7] The Soviet account of the meeting at Geneva is interesting for the light it sheds upon the newly emergent superpower. There appears on the part of the Soviet leadership to have been a genuine desire to lower Cold War tensions, and there was also a genuine feeling of inferiority *vis-à-vis* the American delegation. In his memoirs, Khrushchev revealed the awe with which the Soviet delegation greeted the Americans and in particular their chagrin over the inferior Soviet aircraft! Soviet officials had arrived in a two-engine plane, in contrast to the four-engine aeroplanes that transported its Western counterparts.

Whilst this vignette from Khrushchev's memoirs is amusing (and is actually evocative of the accounts of the feelings of inferiority which the Soviet delegates who attended the Genoa conference had felt in 1922) it revealed a serious side of Soviet thinking. This was the clear understanding of the rather precarious nature of their superpower status. Soviet insecurity in this period was manifested in two ways: one was the management problem of the Eastern European states, and the other was the question of how to rival US nuclear power. By 1955–6 the issue of Soviet control over Eastern Europe had become an urgent one.

As noted above, the creation of the Warsaw Treaty Organisation was not an expression of genuine solidarity on the part of the Eastern bloc. This worried the post-Stalinist leadership. During 1955 Khrushchev had moved rapidly to invoke a programme of destalinisation through which some of the worst excesses of the Soviet regime had been eradicated, and he also sought to reform the command economy to produce greater benefits for citizens. The uprisings in East Germany during 1953 had provided a dire example of what could happen in a regime that failed even at a basic level to meet the expectations of the people. At the 20th Congress of the Communist Party of the Soviet Union (CPSU) in February 1956 Khrushchev took the opportunity to make some major pronouncements. The first related to foreign policy. The Soviet leader asserted that the main feature of international relations in the contemporary era was the evolution and strength of the socialist camp and the pursuit of peaceful coexistence with the West. Khrushchev reinforced the notion that a temporary alliance against the imperialist enemy was possible, although he noted that, in the longer term, socialism would triumph through peaceful competition. However, he asserted that war was not an inevitable part of this process. Thus far, Khrushchev was paving the way for a period of peace with the West. (He also noted, despite the recent show of Western unity over Germany, that the fierce struggle within the capitalist camp would continue and intensify.) Khrushchev argued that Soviet foreign policy should follow and pursue peaceful coexistence as its primary goal with the West, and should strengthen its relationship both with Yugoslavia and so-called fraternal allies in the Third World. There was little hint that the West might find this unacceptable.

In foreign-policy terms, the Soviet leader criticised Stalin for his lack of military preparation in 1941 and for his unrealistic assessment of the risks involved in the Korean War.[8] The second crucial aspect of this speech was Khrushchev's assessment of Stalin's behaviour during the 1930s. In one speech, which lasted for four hours, he denounced Stalin's autocratic and cruel rule, laying the blame personally on the dictator for the mass repressions, the torture and the execution of thousands of Soviet citizens which had characterised the period after 1934. During this criticism of what he called the crimes of the Stalin era, he read out extracts of letters from those who had suffered during the purges. All this constituted a major questioning of the Stalinist regime and the nature of government in the USSR. With his criticism of the Stalinist system, Khrushchev was attempting to make a new compact with the Soviet people in which, in return for the eradication of the most fearful aspects of Stalinism such as the arbitrary nature of the judicial system, people could be brought more into a willing acceptance of the regime. There were limits to this reform process, however. As one commentator argued, 'We were afraid that the thaw might unleash a flood, which we wouldn't be able to control and which could drown us.' Limits were also imposed as to the nature of reform, because Khrushchev himself feared that he could be implicated in the crimes of the Stalinist era.

This initiative proved the old adage that reform can lead to revolution. Beria had leant this to his great cost in East Germany, but during 1956 Khrushchev confronted a similar situation in Poland. The crisis in Poland was provoked by the death of the Communist Party leader, Bolesław Bierut, which had led to the release of some political prisoners and the removal of some of the old hard-liners. Part of this thaw in Poland was attributed to the publication of some of Khrushchev's pronouncements. Worker strikes and riots ensued in Poznań. By October the situation had deteriorated, and the Polish Communist Party wished to install Gomułka as leader. This was a worry for Moscow, as Gomułka had actually been purged by Stalin. Khrushchev believed that Gomułka might move Poland into an anti-Russian position and leave the USSR facing a hostile power. On 19 October Khrushchev flew to Poland to persuade the Polish Communists not to elect Gomułka. Khrushchev was actually refused permission to enter the plenum at which the matter was to be discussed and which elected Gomułka. Despite Khrushchev's fear, he promised to keep Poland within the Warsaw Pact but also warned that if the Russians attempted military intervention the Poles would resist.[9] Even though the Polish crisis of 1956 was defused, albeit in a rather eccentric manner, by Khrushchev, a crisis arose in Hungary.

Pressure had been building within Hungary since the spring of 1955. (The reformist Prime Minister, Imre Nagy, had been dislodged by an old Stalinist Party leader, Mathias Rakosi, who had earlier been forced by Moscow to cede the post to Nagy.) When Khrushchev managed to oust Malenkov in early 1955 he decided to reinforce the leading role of the Communist parties throughout Eastern Europe. In the case of Hungary, the new Soviet leader was worried that Nagy's attempts at reform might go too far. Rakosi's rule, however, sparked popular protests, and the Russians authorised his removal in July. However, this proved to be a temporary expedient, and popular unrest continued to mount throughout the summer. The surge of discontent culminated in October, when a huge demonstration was organised in Budapest by students who had been inspired by the recent changes in Poland. The security forces were unable to contain the crisis, and senior Hungarian figures appeared overwhelmed by the situation. Until very recently little was known about what actually occurred in the Kremlin when news of the crisis broke. The Soviet leader ordered that the Presidium discuss the crisis, but failed to reach an immediate decision on whether troops should be sent into Hungary. Despite this lack of unanimity, Khrushchev sent an order through the Soviet Defence Minister, Zhukov, to 'redeploy' Soviet units already in Hungary into Budapest so that they could assist Hungarian security forces. They were joined by two divisions stationed in Romania and two divisions from the Ukraine. Yet the arrival of Soviet troops proved to be largely counter-productive.

Khrushchev ordered the Red Army into Budapest to restore order, but it failed to do so. The Hungarians resisted the commands of the Red Army and, in fact, engaged in resistance activities. It appeared that even some of the Communist internal security forces might join the anti-Soviet forces. This provoked a crisis in the Kremlin, and the leadership had great difficulty in deciding on a response. On 30 October the new Hungarian Party leader, Imre Nagy, announced that he was accepting the demands of the rebels and returning to a government more in line with the Hungarian political tradition of a democratic coalition of parties. On 31 October, the workers' councils which had been created in most regions established a parliament for all the country. The leaders of the insurgents also demanded the complete withdrawal of Soviet troops from Hungary, a rejection of the WTO and an acceptance of the neutral status of Hungary. On 1 November, in line with these demands, Nagy withdrew from the Warsaw Pact. In short, the Hungarians rejected both Communism and Soviet control.

Khrushchev believed that this declaration could precipitate a wholesale crisis through the East European states, as well as igniting groups within the USSR, and decided to act decisively. On 31 October he secured the approval of the Supreme Presidium for an all-out intervention in Hungary, and he also managed to rally the Polish and other East European leaders behind this move. On 4 November the Hungarian–Austrian border was sealed and the Red Army moved in. Three days of fierce fighting ensued, in which there were some 25,000 casualties, including 5,000 dead. The anti-Communist movement was brutally suppressed and Hungary was secured for the Kremlin, but at a high price.

Throughout this crisis, Khrushchev also had to take into account the possible response to it in the West. Ironically, the Soviet leader had had a degree of luck in that the Americans, the British and the French had actually been focused on the crisis in the Middle East over Suez. Bordered by Egypt on one side and the Sinai peninsula on the other, the Suez canal was a vital waterway for European shipping to the Gulf states and beyond. For the British in particular it was of key strategic importance because it led to the oilfields of the Arabian peninsula. On 26 July 1956 the new Egyptian leader, President Gamal Abdel Nasser, had announced that he was nationalising the Suez Canal Company, so that money levied upon ships travelling through the canal, which had been going to the Suez Canal Company (in which the British and French Governments were major shareholders), would now go to the Egyptian Government and could be used to finance the Aswan Dam project. In response, the British and the French engineered a crisis in collaboration with the Israelis, who perceived it as an opportunity to deal a blow against Nasser and Egyptian power in the Sinai. The British, the French and the Americans had made a determined effort throughout the summer to persuade Nasser to revoke his plans, but failed. In late October Israeli forces, backed by the British and the French, moved into Egypt and launched air attacks. The British and French issued an ultimatum calling for the removal of both Egyptian and Israeli troops to a distance of 10 miles either side of the canal. The Egyptians refused, at which point the British and French sent troops to ensure the free navigation of shipping though the canal. Unexpectedly Washington sternly condemned the Anglo–French–Israeli alliance, and exerted pressure for military withdrawal. Despite the crisis in Hungary, Khrushchev attempted to make political capital out of the situation in Suez, backing Egypt and proclaiming Suez a disaster for the imperialists. He made a series of crude threats, such as, 'We are fully resolved to use force to crush the aggressors and to restore peace in the East.' On 5 November the Soviet foreign minister sent notes to the three 'aggressors' and to Washington. The note to the US proposed the joint use of Soviet–American naval forces to bring a halt to the aggression to Egypt.[10] Not surprisingly, this was rejected by the United States.

Khrushchev, though, drew two lessons from the Suez débâcle. He held it up as an example of protracted and counterproductive action by great powers, something he did not want to emulate in Hungary. He also deduced from the crisis in the Middle East a belief that Suez would in fact prevent the Western powers putting together a coherent response to any Soviet intervention in Hungary. This was not the critical decision in the debate which took place amongst Soviet leaders over whether to intervene, but it certainly helped strengthen the position of those who advocated a military solution. What is fascinating is that Khrushchev believed in late October that unless he acted decisively in Hungary, Soviet foreign policy would be damaged, since indecision might, he argued, provide the imperialists with evidence of Soviet weakness.[11]

Yet the decisive factor for Khrushchev in ordering the intervention in Hungary was the belief that, unless the revolution was quelled, there would be a spill-over into the USSR itself. This anxiety was heightened by a series of intelligence reports from both Romania and Czechoslovakia. KGB sources transmitted evidence that in border areas there had been contacts between Hungarian rebels and Czechs and Romanians. Both countries had suffered from student demonstrations. Quite apart from the worries over the satellite countries, there was evidence that destalinisation had resulted in a series of protests against authoritarianism within the USSR, most notably in Tbilisi and other Georgian cities.

The Warsaw Pact survived the challenges of 1956, but what was evident was that the façade of unity was one based on Soviet military power rather than any form of political or social unity. It also demonstrated for Khrushchev the difficulty of pursuing a domestic reform process when the Communist bloc itself was so insecure. Indeed, as a result of the events of 1956, Khrushchev's position as leader came under serious threat. At the December CPSU Central Committee meeting, it was noticeable that he did not make a speech. On 5 May 1957 there was an attempted political coup against him within the Presidium which demanded his resignation. Khrushchev refused to resign, and instead rallied the support of key figures such as Marshal Zhukov.[12] He then summoned the Central Committee and managed to gain a reversal of the Presidium's decision. (Rather ironically, in October 1957 he accused Zhukov of 'Bonapartism' and removed him from high office.) In the course of the debates of June and July 1957, Khrushchev accused his rivals of not supporting his foreign policy initiatives and, during the course of the debates, managed finally to oust his most serious rival, Malenkov. Yet even as he secured his domestic position (after the 1957 showdown, Khrushchev has been described as a dictator, enjoying total power), the foreign-policy agenda became yet more complicated. The difficulties, as in 1956, centred around the issue of alliance solidarity within the Communist world, but this time the issue was relations with Mao's China.

China: the problematic partner

If Khrushchev's pronouncements had unleashed a wave of unrest throughout the Soviet bloc, it had also fundamentally altered the Soviet relationship with

China. Khrushchev had not informed Mao of what would occur at the Twentieth Party Congress, although this may have been because he himself had not really decided on whether he would actually go ahead with his denouncement of Stalin or not. The Chinese, unlike other delegations, decided to protest over the contents of the speeches. In particular they objected to the criticisms of Stalin. As Mao pointed out in the aftermath of the Party Congress, Stalin had been leader of the Communist Party, and to criticise him and to criticise his achievements, yet still wish Moscow to continue to head a global Communist movement, was somewhat contradictory.[13]

At first Khrushchev's relations with Mao had appeared good. In 1954, during a visit to Beijing, he had offered to return the Port Arthur naval base to Chinese control, and substantial trading credits were agreed. Although there was a degree of personal antipathy between Khrushchev and Mao, it did not really surface until 1956. Mao decided that Khrushchev was 'unreliable' and, according to one source, barely concealed his irritation and dislike for Khrushchev during a visit to Moscow in November 1957.[14]

Mao had serious concerns over the unmasking of Stalin within the Communist movement. Stalin remained within China an important symbol of the stages through which China had to progress to achieve Communism. There was no example of a successful socialist revolution other than that in Russia. Although Chinese experience did differ significantly from that of the USSR, Mao believed that the Soviet example was critical to the development of China. Mao initially supported the Soviet handling of the uprisings in Eastern Europe in 1956, but was quite clear that Khrushchev was wrong in his political reforms. Not least, he worried that the Soviet example would encourage those around him to warn against autocratic tendencies within the Chinese Communist Party. Mao's attitude towards Moscow hardened during 1958 as he launched the attempt to reform the Chinese economic system, known as the 'great leap forward'. Part of the reform was intended to reduce Chinese economic dependence upon Moscow. At the same time, Khrushchev asked for a Soviet radio station on Chinese territory to communicate with its new nuclear-powered submarines. Mao demanded that Khrushchev visit Beijing to discuss the matter properly, and when Khrushchev arrived he found his welcome less than warm. The Soviet suggestion for reciprocal rights in using naval bases to develop a 'common fleet' to counter the American Seventh Fleet met with open derision on the Chinese side.[15] Mao's attempts to prove that China remained independent of the USSR continued shortly after the visit, when the Chinese shelled the two offshore islands of Quemoy and Matsu which were part of Taiwan without prior consultation with Moscow. Part of this appeared to be a consequence of Mao's desire to show that Khrushchev could not control Chinese actions, but it was also to demonstrate his displeasure at what he perceived to be attempts by the Soviet leader to 'please' the Americans through his strategy of peaceful coexistence. The growing rift in Sino–Soviet relations was confirmed in 1959, when Khrushchev made a third trip to China and was rebuffed on a number of issues, not least the Soviet request that Mao release two American prisoners who had parachuted into China during the Korean War. By 1960, Khrushchev was attacking Mao by name, while, in the mid-1960s, the Chinese leaders were openly ridiculing 'Khrushchevism' and his failure to draw the proper lessons from the Stalinist model. In July 1960 the Soviet leader decided to withdraw all advisers from China immediately and tore up over 300 contracts which had been signed with Beijing.

At least part of the problem in Sino–Soviet relations was the issue of nuclear weapons. Mao could not understand Khrushchev's attitude towards capitalism, given what the Chinese leader believed to be the advanced state of the Soviet missile programme. The Chinese could not understand why Khrushchev failed to press military advantages home in the international environment. The problem for Khrushchev was that despite his public pronouncements he knew that Soviet nuclear forces were vastly inferior to those of the US.

A strategy of bluff: the impact of nuclear power

One of the major areas of disagreement between Khrushchev and Malenkov had been the impact of atomic power on foreign and military affairs. After the Soviet Union had achieved an explosion of the hydrogen bomb in August 1953, Malenkov had developed new ideas about international relations. Specifically he argued that, given recent Soviet achievements in fusion, a state of deterrence existed between the two blocs; war would now be disastrous for either side, and therefore peace was necessary and possible. This represented a radical break with the standard Stalinist line in thinking about nuclear weapons. Stalin had held that war was inevitable between the two camps and that nuclear weapons made no difference to this state of affairs. Under Stalin, military affairs had been paralysed by the notion of the 'permanently operating factors'. Even the Soviet achievement of a fission bomb in 1949 had made little impact upon this idea.[16] Stalinist 'military science' held that factors such as surprise attack could make little decisive difference to the outcome of war. There were obvious reasons why Stalin had held to this type of thinking. Not only did it excuse the blunders of 1941, when surprise had almost proved decisive, but it justified the Soviet position in the period from 1945 to 1949, when the US had held a monopoly on atomic power. Immediately after the death of Stalin, however, military theorists changed the mission of the armed forces to take account of nuclear weapons. It was now admitted that a surprise attack could prove paralysing, and surprise might prove decisive.

Throughout 1954 Malenkov continued to claim that a form of deterrence existed between East and West. Malenkov also argued that, because of this, the USSR could now afford to divert some of its military spending away from the defence sector into the production of consumer goods. After the successful test of the hydrogen bomb, Malenkov had argued to the Supreme Soviet, 'Now we can and consequently we must accelerate the development of light industry in every way in the interests of securing a faster rise in the living standards ... of the people.'[17]

This position was not endorsed by Khrushchev or the Soviet military, and shortly after he had first aired his views Malenkov was forced to retract. By April 1954 he said that a nuclear war could actually only bring about the downfall of the capitalists. The Soviet service chiefs were adamant that Malenkov was wrong in seeing nuclear weapons simply as a deterrent; rather, they argued, nuclear weapons should be incorporated into conventional force structures. But what this debate did point to was a recognition that, certainly, nuclear weapons had changed international relations and that some accommodation with the US had to be sought.

This view was reinforced by Khrushchev's attempts during the mid-1950s to find a peaceful coexistence with the West, and to have a 'breathing space'. The strategic balance was actually weighted in favour of the US at this point. The USSR could not and had not matched the extensive strategic modernisation programme that the US had carried out in the 1950s. The US Strategic Air Command by this stage had 1,300 aircraft capable of nuclear strike missions against the USSR. It had B–46s and B–52s capable of carrying bombs from the United States to the USSR and then returning to the US.[18] The Soviet strategic bomber force at this stage only had medium range aircraft. Despite this weakness, or more probably because of it, Khrushchev felt compelled to conceal its weakness and bluff about its strength. On Aviation Day in July 1955 the Soviet Union made an ostentatious display of Bear and Bison bombers, although in fact the same squadron of bombers flew over Red Square time and time again. This actually set off a fairly intense debate within the United States as to whether in fact a 'bomber gap' existed or not.[19] The launching of Sputnik, the Soviet satellite, in 1957 provided Khrushchev with the impression of strength, as did the development of the Soviet Intercontinental Ballistic Missile (ICBM) force. From this point Khrushchev continually gave the impression of the development of an immense and increasingly accurate strategic rocket force. These exaggerations masked the fact that, in reality, the USSR had only four ICBMs. The Americans did not know this at the time and, as John Lewis Gaddis has put it, Khrushchev's 'rhetorical rockets' made an enormous impression upon both the US public and government.

It is difficult to know what Khrushchev hoped to achieve through bluffing over Soviet nuclear achievements, apart from perhaps an enhancement of

Soviet status, particularly valuable in the Third World, and a clumsy attempt at nuclear deterrence. He was to be disappointed, however. The Eisenhower administration accelerated its military programmes and, to reassure West European allies in particular, he created a NATO nuclear stockpile and offered to station Thor and Jupiter intermediate range missiles at bases in Europe. These were actually of little military or strategic significance in the longer term, for while they might counteract Soviet intermediate-range missiles until the American strategic rocket force was fully in place, in the medium term they could only provide 'cover' for NATO allies facing Soviet intermediate range ballistic missiles (IRBMs). They had a disastrous portent for the Soviet leadership, though – NATO missiles could reach Soviet soil from their European bases. This initiative, to Soviet minds, confirmed the fears long prevalent that the West Germans were to be given nuclear weapons.

On 1 May 1960 the Soviet leader was informed that an American U–2 plane had penetrated Soviet air space. Khrushchev believed that this constituted a violation, and he ordered that it be shot down. The plane was brought down and the pilot, Gary Powers, was captured. Khrushchev attempted to embarrass President Eisenhower, though only gradually revealing that they knew the full story of the spy plane, first allowing the Americans to release a cover story and then going public to demonstrate its falseness. Eisenhower decided to take full and public responsibility for using spy planes. The problem for Khrushchev was that U–2 flights had revealed that his 'rhetorical rockets' were just that – rhetoric. His strategy of bluff was exposed; it was a shambles, and at the Party Central Committee plenum on 4 May there was a realignment within the Party leadership.

At the mid-May summit in Paris in 1960, the Soviet leader demanded an apology for the incident from Eisenhower. This was not forthcoming, and the summit broke down. By 1960 Soviet foreign policy appeared to be in complete disarray. Khrushchev would not negotiate whilst Eisenhower was still in the White House, the Chinese continued a barrage of criticism against Khrushchev and finally, at the United Nations in September, the Soviet leader quarrelled with the Secretary-General Hammarskjöld over his handling of the UN operation in the Congo, and banged his shoe on the top of the table in anger.

During 1960–1, despite the bleak general outlook, Khrushchev still found Soviet nuclear weaponry useful, not least in helping him push forward conventional arms cuts as part of a cost-cutting exercise in the Soviet armed forces. On 12 January 1960, for instance, he suggested a radical reduction in Soviet troops levels, proposing that the army be reduced by one-third. This, he argued, would be possible because the Soviet strategic rocket force was the backbone of the armed forces (despite the fact that the USSR still had only four R-7s on a launching pad near Plesetsk in Northern Russia!).

Khrushchev claimed that he had thought through all the implications of such a proposal, and had recognised the fact that such a massive demobilisation could have ramifications for those involved. Indeed, throughout January 1960 continual assurances were given by both the political and military leaderships that those demobbed would be looked after. The Soviet newspaper *Izvestiya* even carried the headline for those awaiting demobilisation, that 'You are being awaited everywhere Dear Friends'.[20] The government promised a package of economic benefits which included the promise of jobs primarily at industrial enterprises, and construction projects in transport and in agriculture. Loans were also promised worth 700 roubles to soldiers to engage in home construction. The evidence, though, shows that 250,000 Soviet officers were forced into premature retirement without actually receiving adequate compensation or housing. The Soviet military were caught by surprise; indeed, Marshal Malinovsky warned on 20 January against being caught once again in the position of 1941.[21] As part of the reform process, Khrushchev had hoped that the living standards of ordinary people could be raised; yet, in June 1962 in the USSR, the Red Army had had to fire upon strikers in Novochevkassk who were protesting about food prices. This sat uncomfortably with the tone of the Twenty-Second Party Congress in October 1961, in which Khrushchev once again launched a public assault on the 'monstrous crimes' of the past.

Strategy of deception: the Cuban missile crisis

In 1961, Khrushchev was aware of the sustained efforts of the Kennedy administration to eliminate Castro in Cuba. Whilst the Bay of Pigs episode in which a group of Cuban émigrés were equipped and supported by the US to overthrow Castro was the most infamous incident, it was followed by others. This included Operation Mongoose, the code name for the massive covert operation by the CIA undertaken to topple Castro after the failure of the Bay of Pigs invasion in April. Various parts of the US government were determined to overthrow the Marxist-inspired dictator who occupied islands embarrassingly close to the US mainland. During the spring and summer of 1962 there was a series of US military manoeuvres in the Caribbean area, and it was not clear whether or not the Americans were planning an invasion. From the Soviet point of view the portents did not look good. Indeed, JFK himself had said, following the Bay of Pigs débâcle, that the Americans could not stomach having Castro's Cuba right next to them. There is little doubt that there was genuine concern within the Kremlin over what the Americans might have in store for Cuba, and that the Russians felt committed to its defence; but it is still unclear as to whether Khrushchev expected to supply direct Soviet military intervention. The interesting question in 1962 was why and how Khrushchev came to the conclusion that the deployment of nuclear missiles onto Cuba might be the best way to defend the Revolution.

According to his memoirs, Khrushchev argued that he had had the idea during his visit to Bulgaria in May.

> I had the idea of installing missiles with nuclear warheads in Cuba without letting the US find out that they were there until it was too late to do anything about them … I thought … my thinking went like this; if we installed the missiles secretly and then if the US discovered the missiles were there after they were already poised and ready to strike, the Americans would think twice…. In addition to protecting Cuba, our missiles would have equalised what the West likes to call the balance of power. The Americans had surrounded our country with military bases and threatened us.[22]

If this account is to be believed, there are several factors that Khrushchev identifies which were central to his decision to place missiles on Cuba. The first was obviously the desire to protect Cuba from the Americans, and this was a genuine concern. The 'loss' of Cuba, had the Americans succeeded in overthrowing Castro, would have resulted in a loss of prestige for the USSR both in Latin America but also in the Third World in general. A successful placement of missiles would have served as a symbolic but also very real display of Soviet power *vis-à-vis* the Americans. The second factor identified by Khrushchev, however, was equally important. This was that the Americans had placed missiles in a state bordering the USSR. Jupiter missiles had been placed in Turkey and were operational under American command in 1962. Khrushchev had continually displayed his hostility to the deployment of the Jupiter missiles in Turkey and American influence in the region[23] and, after the Bay of Pigs fiasco, he had linked the situation in Cuba to that of Turkey. Missiles on Cuba would have been the quid pro quo. Khrushchev also had in mind the overall strategic position. On 21 October 1961 the US Deputy Secretary of Defence, Roswell Gilpatric, in a speech to businessmen in Hot Springs, Virginia, had alerted the world to the fact that the USSR was vastly inferior to the US in nuclear arms, arguing that because this weakness the USSR would not provoke a nuclear conflict. The public exposure of his strategy of bluff in the Gilpatric speech had damaged the Soviet leader internationally as well as domestically. Whilst Khrushchev later claimed that the so-called balance of power had always been a secondary consideration, it was still important.

How exactly did the Cuban missile crisis unfold? In September the Soviet leadership assured the American president that there would not be trouble in either Berlin or Cuba before he had to face congressional elections in November. This was less than honest, as the Russians were planning the deployment onto Cuba. However, on 14 October an American U-2 overflight of Cuba showed that missile installations were under construction. On 18 October Kennedy held what had been a pre-planned meeting with Gromyko, who lied to the President about the nature of shipments to Cuba, claiming that they consisted of 'defensive armaments'.[24] The American President was equally duplicitous. He commented that he took Soviet statements on trust, although he knew it to be otherwise. Gromyko's pleasure with this meeting was revealed by a cable that he sent back to Moscow, declaring after the meeting, that the 'overall situation' was 'completely satisfactory'. On 22 October 1962, in a TV address Kennedy informed the US people that the Soviet leadership were engaging in missile construction on Cuba. Kennedy warned that he would consider any attack from Cuba as the equivalent of an attack from the USSR. Kennedy also announced a naval blockade (or 'quarantine', as it became known) to prohibit further shipments to Cuba. This was a high-risk and possibly confrontational strategy, as there were several Soviet vessels already on their way to Cuba.[25]

Indeed, some Soviet officials did suggest that Khrushchev staged a 'diversion' in Berlin as a response to Kennedy's speech. The Soviet Ambassador in Washington, Dobrynin, cabled an analysis to the Kremlin which recommended a rebuff to Kennedy that might include a hint that Western powers in Berlin might suffer. There were also suggestions that Khrushchev could respond with a troop build-up around Berlin. This 'linkage' between Soviet actions in Berlin and on Cuba had been suggested at an earlier point in the crisis, when parts of the Soviet leadership had thought that 'pressure' on Berlin could distract attention away from the deployment on Cuba. However, Berlin at this point was not the primary focus of the attention of either superpower. That remained firmly on the drama in the Caribbean.

With the imposition of the quarantine, Kennedy had placed the initiative for any resolution of the crisis firmly upon Khrushchev. US military strength, in a conventional and nuclear sense, was far superior to that of the Russians, and Khrushchev was aware of this. He was therefore placed in the position of having to rapidly scramble and save whatever Soviet prestige he could from the situation. On 26 October he sent Kennedy a long letter that appeared to contain a 'solution' to the crisis. In part the letter still justified the presence of the missiles as 'defensive', but Khrushchev proposed that if the US declared that it had no intention of invading Cuba, future shipments would not carry any kind of armaments. In earlier versions of the story of the Soviet missile crisis, it had been thought that a Soviet counsellor in the Soviet embassy in Washington, Alexander S. Fromin, had played a key role in the crisis. At a lunch with an American TV reporter Fromin had more or less reiterated the Khrushchev proposal which was then relayed to the White House. It now appears that this particular piece of history from the Cuban missile crisis was actually irrelevant! However, the very next day a second letter arrived from the Soviet leader demanding the quid pro quo of the removal of US missiles in Turkey. On 28 October, however, the Kennedy administration chose to ignore the second letter and accept the terms of the first, believing that the second letter had arisen out of factionalism within the Kremlin.

While a superpower military clash was averted and Khrushchev could claim to have saved the peace, the crisis had irrevocably damaged the Soviet leader in several respects. The first was in the relationship with Castro. Soviet–Cuban relations had become strained during the crisis anyway because of a series of disagreements. The first of these was that Cuban zeal might actually provoke a US response. In particular, the Kremlin had been concerned by the Cuban shooting down of a U-2 plane on 27 October. Indeed, Castro had advocated recourse to the use of nuclear weapons if it became necessary. Here it is worth noting that, like Mao, Castro found Khrushchev's caution entirely mystifying. In particular, however, Castro had been infuriated by the resolution of the crisis, which had taken place without any prior consultation over Kennedy's terms. The lesson taken by the Cuban leadership from the crisis was that they had been entirely mistaken if they had ever really believed that Khrushchev would have protected Havana at the expense of Moscow.[26] Castro later declared that had he been aware of the 'real' state of the Soviet strategic arsenal, he would have 'counselled prudence'. (It is also worth noting that none of the Warsaw Pact allies were informed of the installation of the missiles in Cuba before the US government revealed the fact.)[27]

The second immediate ramification of the crisis was that Khrushchev's actions and the American response weakened his domestic position. It is difficult to judge how far the débâcle in the Caribbean was directly responsible for his downfall as, by this stage, his domestic reforms were failing. He was subsequently removed as leader, rather ironically, given his success in 1957 and at the Party plenum in 1964. Officially, at least, he was released from his duties because of his advanced age and deterioration in the state of his health.[28]

The Khruhschev legacy

By the time that Khrushchev was removed from office, the international system had changed dramatically since the Stalinist era. Two blocs had developed which confronted each other directly in Europe and Asia and maintained a form of stability through nuclear deterrence. Indeed, the Khrushchev era had seen a high degree of mirror-imaging between the blocs, particularly with the creation of two military alliances in Europe. Apart from the vexed question of Germany and particularly the status of Berlin, a form of *modus vivendi* had been reached in Europe with a grudging recognition that 'spheres of influence' existed, although this should not ignore the constant Soviet belief, witnessed through the sponsorship of the Peace Movement, that the political consensus in Western Europe could be undermined.

Yet, this apparent stability both between and within the blocs was a chimera, certainly on the Communist side. The rifts which had developed between Khrushchev and Mao had proved fatal to Communist solidarity and, by the 1960s, global politics had developed into a triangular contest, with Moscow facing competition with both Beijing and Washington. The schism with China was particularly dangerous to the Soviet regime, as it questioned the Soviet leadership of the Communist world at a time when the allies in Eastern Europe, most noticeably Hungary, had proved unreliable.

The crisis in Cuba had also damaged the USSR. Khrushchev's strategy of deception had led to the unmasking of alleged superpower nuclear strength and had finally stirred his enemies in the Kremlin to move against him. But, worse, it meant that the Soviet Union had to 'catch up' with American strength to avoid any such humiliation in the future. This mandated a massive effort in the research and development of nuclear technologies, and a consequent emphasis upon the USSR's military-industrial complex.

Despite his success against the anti-Party group in 1957, Khrushchev not only faced opponents of his foreign policies in 1964, but also faced those who felt that his programme of destalinisation and domestic adjustment was erroneous and somewhat harebrained. Perhaps, though, the final testament to Khrushchev and his part-battle against Stalinism was that he was able to live to write his memoirs. His successor faced a rather different set of challenges.

Notes

1 Joint Meeting of the Plenary Session of the Central Committee of the Communist Party of the Soviet Union, USSR Council of Ministers and Presidium of the USSR Supreme Soviet, *Pravda*, 7 March 1953.

2 See 'Draft of Soviet Government of Peace Treaty with Germany', *Diplomatic Correspondence Relating to Germany. Soviet Note to the United States, the United Kingdom and France*, 10 March 1952. C.W. Baier and R. P. Stebbins (eds), *Council on Foreign Relations: Documents on American Foreign Relations* (New York: Harper and Brothers, 1953).

3 Wilfried Loth, *The Division of the World 1941–1955* (London: Routledge, 1988), pp. 267–73.

4 See 'O prestupniix antipatiniix antigosudarstveniix diestviax Beria, Plenum of the Central Committee of the Communist Party of the Soviet Union', 2–7 July, 1953, reported in *Cold War International History Project Bulletin*, 1 (Washington, DC: Woodrow Wilson International Center for Scholars, Spring 1992).

5 Amy Knight, *Beria, Stalin's First Lieutenant* (Princeton, NJ: Princeton, 1993).

6 Quoted in John Lewis Gaddis, *We Now Know: Rethinking Cold War History* (Oxford: Clarendon Press, 1997).

7 Nikita Khrushchev, *Khrushchev Remembers*, ed. Edward Crankshaw (Boston: Little, Brown, 1970).

8 Stephen F. Cohen, *Rethinking the Soviet Experience: Politics and History Since 1917* (Oxford: Oxford University Press, 1985).

9 Mark Kramer, 'New Evidence on the 1956 Polish and Hungarian Crisis', in *Cold War International History Project Bulletin*, 8–9 (Washington, DC: Woodrow Wilson International Center for Scholars, Winter 1996/7).

10 Mark Kramer, 'New Evidence'.

11 Mark Kramer, 'New Evidence'.

12 R. F. Miller and F. Feher, *Khrushchev and the Communist World* (London: Croom Helm, 1984).

13 William Taubman, 'Khruschev vs. Mao: A Preliminary Sketch of the Role of Personality in the Sino–Soviet Split', in 'More New Evidence on the Cold War in Asia', *Cold War International History Project Bulletin*, 8–9 (Washington, DC: Woodrow Wilson International Center for Scholars, Winter 1996/7).

14 Mark Kramer, 'More New Evidence on the Cold War in Asia'.

15 'More New Evidence on the Cold War in Asia'.

16 David Holloway, *The Soviet Union and the Arms Race* (London and New Haven: Yale University Press, 1983).

17 *Pravda*, 13 March 1954.

18 *Pravda*, 9 August 1953.

19 John Lewis Gaddis, *We Now Know*.

20 *Izvestiya*, 26 January 1960.

21 *Krasnaya Zvezda*, 20 January 1960.

22 *Khrushchev Remembers*.

23 *Pravda*, 31 October 1959.

24 James G. Hershberg, 'More New Evidence on the Cuban Missile Crisis', in *Cold War International History Project Bulletin*, 8–9 (Washington, DC: Woodrow Wilson International Center for Scholars, Winter 1996–7).

25 'More New Evidence on The Cuban Missile Crisis'.

26 *Cold War International History Project Bulletin*, 8–9 (Washington, DC: Woodrow Wilson International Center for Scholars, Winter 1996/7).

27 *Cold War International History Project Bulletin*, 1 (Washington, DC: Woodrow Wilson International Center for Scholars, Spring 1992).

28 *Pravda*, 16 October 1964.

6

Towards a Global Role? Foreign Policy in the First Brezhnev Era 1964–1970

Allies, ambitions and opportunities

Khrushchev's 'resignation' was without precedent. The 'palace coup' organised against him altered several facets of Soviet politics. The first was that the post of First Secretary and Prime Minister were separated to prevent any individual from securing the level of personal power which Khrushchev had acquired. Leonid Brezhnev, therefore, became Party First Secretary and Aleksei Kosygin was appointed as Prime Minister. (At the Party Congress in 1966 Brezhnev took the title 'General Secretary'.)[1] A second consequence was that Brezhnev moved swiftly to end the programme of destalinisation in domestic politics which had been initiated by his predecessor, and a greater element of caution entered the conduct of Soviet foreign policy. After the Cuban débâcle the leadership was not prepared to directly confront the United States whilst labouring in a position of strategic inferiority. There was a wholesale rejection of the 'harebrained schemes' of the Khrushchev days. Whilst he might have been willing to 'bluster' his way through the nuclear age, his successors were not, and they embarked on a determined effort to 'catch up' with the United States in the quantity and quality of strategic arms. Unlike Khrushchev, they were unwilling to rely solely on nuclear forces, and determined efforts were made to diversify Soviet strategic and military forces. The aim of the Brezhnev leadership was not only to catch up with the American lead in strategic arms, but also to be able to compete more effectively in the growing competition between the superpowers in the Third World. As well as displaying caution, therefore, Brezhnev's Kremlin in certain areas of the Third World also displayed ambition. Soviet objectives, however, were tempered not just by US nuclear superiority, but also by the unpredictability of some of Moscow's allies. Khrushchev's successors sought to mend the holes which had been knocked into the Communist world. This was not easy. The Chinese, in particular, had proved difficult for Khrushchev to contain, and the schism between the two great Communist powers worsened in the 1960s, exacerbated by tensions over struggles within the Third World. The Kremlin experienced problems with other allies too. This was most notable in Eastern Europe, where the Romanians and the Albanians demonstrated a greater degree of independence from Moscow.

Brezhnev takes over

Brezhnev demonstrated a clear break both in style and substance from his predecessor. While Khrushchev had spent his youth under the regime of a Tsarist Russia, Brezhnev represented a different generation, having lived his entire life under a Soviet Communist regime. He had been born in the Ukrainian town of Kamenskaye and later claimed that this gave him a rather different perspective to those in the leadership who had had a wholly Russian experience. The great gain of the Brezhnev years in political terms, however, was that the notion of a collective leadership was maintained. The men around Brezhnev were, on the whole, those who had survived the purges of the 1930s, and they were allowed to grow old in post. Brezhnev had been appointed by Khrushchev in 1954 to supervise the 'Virgin lands' scheme in Kazakhstan, and had reputedly brought 87 million acres of land under control and made it cultivable. From this experience he had gained the reputation of being a good manager who could deliver economic reform. Indeed, part of the reason for the appointment of Kosygin was that he was associated with the consumer industries and considered expert in consumer production. In foreign policy Brezhnev had several goals. One was to increase the import of technology from the United States, which necessitated some form of *rapprochement* with Washington. Brezhnev, however, argued that this could not be fully attempted until the USSR could negotiate from a position of military and strategic parity. The middle years of the 1960s were therefore an interregnum spent in pursuit of this objective.

Strategic arms, Third World competition and the China card

One of the main stories of the 1960s in terms of Moscow's relations with the outside world was that of renewed competition with the United States in both the military and political spheres. In 1960 Khrushchev had declared that the USSR would try to catch up with the USA in the production of missiles by 1965. Yet when he was ousted from office the USSR lagged behind in terms of its strategic forces. The Soviet military took the opportunity to reassert their position and encourage the new leadership to initiate a major military build-up. In the early 1960s Soviet policy had given priority to the deployment of intermediate-range missiles such as the SS-4 Medium Range

Ballistic Missiles (MRBMs) and the SS-5 Intermediate Range Ballistic Missiles (IRBMs) which had ranges capable of striking targets in Western Europe. The next generation of intercontinental ballistic missiles (ICBMs) production, the SS-7 and the SS-8, was initiated in 1962. While the main production decisions did take place before the winter of 1964, some of them presumably following the Cuban missile crisis, it was under the Brezhnev regime that the USSR moved rapidly to acquire a stockpile which could match that of the United States. In 1965 there were signs of substantial construction at missile sites throughout the USSR as the Soviet Union began a massive deployment of SS-9 and SS-11 ICBMs.[2]

One of the debates of the 1960s concerned the type of strategic arsenal the USSR should build, and specifically whether it should continue with its plans to build and deploy anti-ballistic missile systems (ABMs). Such a defensive system actually fitted rather well into Soviet thinking about nuclear deterrence, because defensive systems might lessen the destruction inflicted on the homeland; but it also meant that the leadership were not simply dependent upon the strategic whims of enemies. Throughout the 1960s there was discussion in Soviet military periodicals of the importance of surprise in any future war, and a stress on the need to frustrate or forestall such an enemy attack on the Soviet homeland. In the mid-1960s the USSR actually began to deploy a defensive system around Moscow. Soviet leaders justified this investment as protection for the people. For the Americans, though, the Soviet deployment of the system had more sinister connotations. In particular, assertions by the Soviet military and political leaderships of the need to take the strategic offensive and win any nuclear encounter led many American analysts to believe that Moscow was indeed preparing to 'fight and win' a nuclear war. Scholars in the West claimed that the Soviet Union had a predilection for fighting wars, as opposed to what was claimed was the American reliance upon mutual deterrence.

This was a classic case of misunderstanding (perhaps deliberately) the Soviet approach to warfare. For the military in Moscow, preparation for fighting a war was not necessarily incompatible with deterrence. Indeed, some Soviet theorists claimed that the most credible form of deterrence was to have the capability to fight and win a nuclear war. However, the Soviet buildup resulted in a compensatory improvement of US offensive capabilities, of which the development of MIRVs (Multiple Independently Targetable Re-entry Vehicles) was the most important step. This decision, and the subsequent one in 1967 to invest in and deploy a 'thin' ballistic missile defence system, caused the Soviet leadership to reappraise the value of defensive systems. Whilst the Brezhnev leadership had initially refused to engage in a programme of comprehensive arms control, because of the fear of being frozen into an inferior strategic position, by 1967–8, with the prospect that the Americans might actually deploy effective defensive systems, the Kremlin let it be known that they were ready for talks on both offensive and defensive arms.

However, it was not just the rivalry with Washington that influenced the Soviet strategic view. Once again tension with China meant that the USSR had to make a complex series of calculations. In October 1964 China had detonated an atomic bomb, and two and a half years later it managed to develop a hydrogen bomb. Whilst attention in Washington focused primarily on the superpower arms race, some of the sharpest debates of the decade over nuclear strategy took place between the Russians and the Chinese. Triangular diplomacy was evident also in the competition in the Third World, and particularly in South-East Asia, where all three powers to varying degrees became embroiled in the politics of Vietnam.

The Vietnam quagmire

The status of Indo-China had been contested throughout the Second World War. For five years during the wars Indo-China was a French-administered possession of Japan. In September 1940 after the fall of France the French Governor-General concluded an agreement with Japan that permitted the stationing of Japanese troops in Indo-China. After the Japanese surrender of August 1945 the Communist-led Vietminh launched a general uprising and took control of Hanoi in the north. The independence of Vietnam was proclaimed by Communist leader Ho Chi Minh in September but contested by the French. In 1954, after a prolonged struggle between the Vietminh and the French, an agreement was concluded at Geneva on 21 July which provided for a ceasefire and a division of the country into two zones. All Vietminh went to the north and all French and state troops to the south. This agreement left the Hanoi regime – recognised by the USSR and China since 1950 – in control of the north.

American support for the regime in South Vietnam can be viewed as a logical step in the process of containment that had begun earlier in Europe. The containment of Communism was the rationale, at least in public, for the deployment of US troops and equipment in the early and mid 1960s. In May 1965 President Johnson told Congress, 'Wherever the Americans had stood firm, aggression had been halted.... This was true in Iran, in Greece and Turkey and in Korea.... It was true at the Cuban Missile crisis. It will be true again in South-East Asia.' For Johnson a US failure in Vietnam would lead inevitably to a demonstration that the American commitment against Communism was worthless. Yet in pursuit of this aim, and somewhat ironically, given that the original target of containment was Moscow, during the middle years of the 1960s Washington came to believe that it was the Kremlin which could help resolve the war in Vietnam. Johnson argued that Moscow had a very large stake in resolving the crisis. This expectation placed the Kremlin in a delicate position, not least because the Soviet leadership itself was caught between several competing tensions in South-East Asia. On the one hand, Moscow believed that it had a duty to support Communist North Vietnam in its struggle against the Americans. (If the Kremlin chose not to, then the Chinese might prove willing and able to assume the mantle of Communist leadership in South-East Asia.) There were benefits in providing material assistance and aid to the North Vietnemese, not least that the Kremlin could help prolong and escalate the costs of involvement for Washington, thus rendering it less potent elsewhere. On the other hand, however, there were significant risks in this strategy: Moscow also wanted to stabilise and reduce the risks associated with Third World conflicts, particularly if they might involve a direct conflict with the United States. The position of the USSR was therefore a complex one.

There had been signs shortly before Khrushchev was removed in October 1964 that he had attempted to effect some form of resolution in South-East Asia. After the Cuban missile crisis the Soviet leader had little incentive to encourage 'adventurism' in his allies. In the summer of 1964 there were indications that Khrushchev was prepared to forego a central role in the Asian conflict. Yet shortly after this, Moscow became significantly more militant over the crisis. Brezhnev moved quickly to enhance levels of co-operation with North Vietnam. In December 1964 a permanent mission for North Vietnam, or the Democratic Republic of Vietnam (DRV) was established in Moscow and the material assistance given to the DRV and the National Liberation Front which operated in the south increased substantially. In February Kosygin headed a delegation to North Vietnam and, according to reports on the front pages of *Pravda*, he issued a number of public warnings to the United States over their actions in the south.[3] This appeared to have some effect, and Washington delayed any military actions against North Vietnam in the hope that, during his visit, Kosygin could exert a sobering effect on Hanoi. Kosygin had actually informed the Chinese, on his way through to North Vietnam, that he hoped to find a way of helping the US disentangle itself from Vietnam. Hanoi, however, had its own agenda. On 7 February, the Vietcong attacked the American barracks at the Pleiku air base and Camp Holloway. More than 100 men were killed and wounded. After the attack Moscow, through a series of announcements carried in the pages of *Pravda*, signalled to the Americans that it would render the DRV further assistance to aid its struggle. In response and to coincide with the end of the Kosygin visit, the US bombed the southern regions of the DRV. By February 1965, in response to the escalation in the American military campaign, the Soviet Union increased its support for Hanoi. It is worth noting, however, that the war in Vietnam provoked a lively debate within the Brezhnev leadership. Opinions varied over American motivations. Aleksandr Shelepin and

Marshal Malinvosky believed that the war in Vietnam was not an isolated case, but represented an attempt by the United States to wage a global battle against Communism. Brezhnev himself perceived Vietnam as an isolated arena into which the Americans had been dragged, and argued that it was not necessarily representative of US actions globally. Whatever the divisions within the Politburo, the Soviet leadership gradually increased its support for the north. In March 1965 Moscow recognised the National Front for the Liberation of South Vietnam as the sole representative of the people in the south, and provided increasing levels of material aid intended to 'match' an American contribution. From 1963 to 1967 Soviet supplies to North Vietnam exceeded one billion roubles. As early as 1965, American intelligence reports discovered the first SA–2 SAM site under construction, whilst in June 1965 Mig–17s were supplied to the regime in the south. In April 1966 this was followed by a supply of Mig–21s. During the spring of 1965 Brezhnev even floated the possibility of Soviet volunteers going to fight and work in Vietnam. By the summer of 1966, the Kremlin openly publicised its role in training Vietnamese pilots to fly the Mig–21s. In October *Krasnaya Zvezda* described the key advisory role of Soviet missile specialists in the conflict. From February 1965 until 1968, when the bombing was halted, Soviet personnel were engaged in ground-to-air combat against the American forces.

Throughout this period the Soviet Union hoped, through its actions, to deter American forces from attacking Hanoi as well as escalating the costs of the conflict in South-East Asia for the United States. Moscow also wanted to prevent the Chinese from claiming the primary role opposing US imperialism in Vietnam. Yet there were a series of problems for the Soviet leadership in all of this, not least of which was how far Moscow might be dragged into an open conflict with Washington because of the unpredictable behaviour of either Hanoi or China. From this perspective, Moscow had every reason to hope for an early settlement to the conflict, especially if it could derive benefits from brokering a peace. However, the details of any such settlement remained problematic. Moscow sought a solution which was in the main advantageous to Hanoi, whilst the Americans sought a negotiation to satisfy Saigon. The Americans believed that Moscow, too, would seek a mutually beneficial peace in the area. President Johnson argued that he 'sought in Southeast Asia an order and security that we think would contribute to the peace of the world and in that we think the Soviet Union has a very large stake.'[4] In this vein the Americans made a number of approaches to the Soviet Union to facilitate a settlement. In August 1966, for instance, a meeting took place between the military attaché of the US embassy in Moscow, a Colonel Fitzgerald, and officers of the Department of External Relations of the Soviet Defence Ministry. The Americans attempted to stress the importance they attached to a Soviet role in Vietnam. Details of the contacts, all high-level, although unofficial, between Americans and Soviet officials, remain sparse; but there appear to have been intense efforts on behalf of the Americans to use the Russians as a back channel. For example, the Austrian Ambassador to Moscow, Vodak, was used throughout the summer and autumn of 1965 to provide such a channel of communication.[5]

There has to be a question mark over whether the Brezhnev leadership was actually capable of influencing Hanoi. The leadership in Moscow relied upon assessments made by its embassy staff in Hanoi as to whether the North Vietnemese would countenance some form of settlement at this stage. The Embassy staff were universally pessimistic over the willingness of the North Vietnamese to accept a settlement. In particular, during 1965–6 reports sent back from officials in the field, based on conversations with North Vietnamese politicians, ascertained that Hanoi had great hopes of 'beating' the United States and that discussions at this stage would not have been in Hanoi's interests. Perhaps because of these assessments, the Kremlin was reluctant to be used by Washington as an official channel or formal mediator in the dispute.[6] The Kremlin left this job to other countries such as Canada and India. The Soviet Union did, however, convey on a regular basis the various American proposals for settlement to Hanoi, but in 1967 the North Vietnamese refused to accept a negotiated settlement.

Progress did not seem any more likely at the beginning of 1968. Hanoi had rejected a solution put forward by Johnson. This was the so-called 'San Antonio formula', an initiative outlined by the President in a speech he made in Texas on 29 September 1967. During this, Johnson declared that Washington would stop bombing North Vietnam if it was assured that this might lead to a 'productive discussion'. This was rejected by Hanoi. In turn, Moscow denounced the decision and informed the North Vietnamese that the Kremlin could neither afford a policy of brinkmanship with the US or any prospect of a greater involvement in Vietnam. Whilst it is difficult to judge whether Moscow's intervention on this issue was decisive for Hanoi, peace talks finally started on 13 May 1968. The opening of the talks were aided by the decision of Johnson not to run again for the Presidency. The official quadripartite negotiations over Vietnam opened in Paris on 18 January 1969. In this period Moscow, through the Soviet Ambassador in Hanoi, maintained channels of communication which simultaneously attempted to push the North Vietnamese to negotiation and away from a reliance on military methods to defeat the Americans. As the talks in Paris began, but then dragged on, the Americans openly asked the Soviet leadership for additional assistance in pressuring Hanoi to take a more flexible position. The new American President, Richard Nixon, believed that the Russians could, if they so chose, exert a decisive influence on Hanoi. By the end of the decade, however, little had been achieved in terms of a settlement, but in the meantime the Soviet leadership was caught between supporting a fraternal ally and nudging them to a compromise with the Americans. The Soviet position was complicated by the continued criticism from Beijing that it lacked commitment to its revolutionary Communist allies.

The China card

The Chinese remained highly critical of Soviet foreign policy in the Third World, particularly after the crisis over Cuba in 1962; throughout the 1960s Beijing was particularly vociferous in its criticisms of Soviet behaviour towards Hanoi. These differences over the Third World, however, were part and parcel of a general deterioration in the Sino–Soviet relationship. Several issues were causing tension between Beijing and Moscow. The most obvious bone of contention was the issue of the border between the two vast nations. Differences over the actual location of the Sino–Soviet border had a long history stretching back as far as the seventeenth century, but from 1962 onwards serious military clashes began to occur. In March 1963 Beijing indicated its intention to lay claim to south-eastern Siberia and half a million square miles of Soviet Central Asia. This territory had been obtained by Tsarist Russia during the nineteenth century under what the Chinese termed the 'unequal treaties'. In 1964 some negotiations did take place between the two governments over border issues, but talks were marred by mutual allegations over the mistreatments of populations in border areas. Tension arose in particular over the Central Asian border which divided the Chinese province of Sinkiang from the Soviet republics of Tadjikistan, Kirghizia and Kazakhstan. During 1965, as the border talks proved inconclusive, Moscow began to build up its military strength in the East, and intermediate-range nuclear missiles were deployed throughout the Eastern provinces of the USSR. In January 1966 Moscow reaffirmed a defence pact with Mongolia and negotiated a new 20-year mutual assistance treaty. Soviet troops were deployed into Mongolia for the first time in a decade.[7] Relations were such that the USSR was identified as China's number one enemy, and in March 1966 the Chinese refused to attend the Twenty-Third Party Congress in Moscow. The impact of the Chinese cultural revolution, which began in August 1966, also had a detrimental effect on Sino–Soviet relations, and diplomatic relations were eventually severed between the two states. From 1967 Soviet forces were increased along the Sino–Soviet border, increasing from 15 divisions in 1968 to 30 divisions in 1970.

The attitude of China forced the Soviet leadership to pursue two different but not necessarily incompatible aims in Indo-China. The first was to prevent the United States from destroying the regime in Hanoi and inflicting a defeat on Communism in the Third World. This was important after the Cuban missile crisis and the allegations by Beijing of Soviet weakness in the face of Communism. The second ambition was to prevent the Chinese from usurping the Soviet role as the guardian of Communism. Mao remained publicly critical of Soviet actions in Indo-China, and accused Moscow both of collusion with the Americans and the assumption of a neo-imperalist mantle. The Soviet leadership countered such criticism by pointing to several gains for the Communist world from the prolonged US engagement in Vietnam. Soviet leaders were delighted to witness what they perceived as a disintegration of NATO, caused by the French withdrawal from the alliance's integrated command structure in 1966. In addition to discord over Vietnam within NATO, the Kremlin watched keenly the growth of the anti-war movement within the United States over the military involvement in South-East Asia. Despite this rebuttal of Beijing's criticism, however, the Soviet leadership remained sensitive to Chinese criticisms that Moscow was less than forceful in its Third-World strategies.

Chinese criticism on this issue was not just confined to Asia but extended also to Africa. China had long been critical of the Soviet attitude during the Algerian war of liberation. This had started in November 1954 as a rebelllion (although not a Communist-led one) against French rule. During most of his time in power, Khrushchev had ritually castigated the French and colonial rule in Algeria. When it came to actually providing assistance to the rebels, Khrushchev proved cautious, and the first shipment of Soviet aid was not made until February 1958. Soviet policy remained cautious, especially after 1959, when de Gaulle returned to power in France. The Soviet leadership banned a shipment of Chinese arms from crossing the USSR to the rebels, fearing that it might alienate de Gaulle: the Kremlin hoped that he might prove capable of splintering the Western alliance. Of that more will be said later, but in the late 1950s Moscow kept a watchful eye on how the Chinese might provoke the West over the colonial struggle in North Africa. Throughout the 1960s the Chinese ridiculed Moscow's lack of militancy over Algeria. Whereas Moscow *talked* about extending recognition for the provisional government in Algeria, Beijing actually did so in 1960. When Algeria did finally achieve independence it did so without substantial Soviet help. This, though, was simply one case in which the Russians proved themselves selective in which colonial struggles they aided.[8] There was little to be gained from outright involvement in Algeria and North Africa, but in other areas of the globe, especially those contiguous to the border of the USSR, Brezhnev proved capable of using any opportunity to further Soviet political and military influence. This was true in particular of the Middle East in the late 1960s. It was under Brezhnev that the preparation of a wholesale military commitment to that region was made.

Towards an imperial strategy?

From 1964 onwards the Soviet leadership implemented a strategy which was designed to enable it to penetrate more fully into the Arab world. The USSR had obvious connections with the external Islamic world, and there was a concern over the control of the Islamic population within Central Asia and how it related to the external world. Not the least of these concerns was a worry that the Muslim populations within the USSR could be used as a channel of influence by foreign powers. After Khrushchev's removal from office there was a dramatic reversal in the official treatment of Islam. Whilst Khrushchev had overseen a strong anti-Islamic campaign, during which mosques within the USSR had been closed down, his successors embarked on a different strategy. This involved a new initative to aid investment in the analysis of Islam, and the creation of policy-related institutions to examine questions of Islam. A generation of young Soviet scholars were trained in Islamic studies and began to play an active role in the area of policy relating to the Islamic world. This reappraisal led to the conclusion that Soviet Muslims were far more militant than had been thought, and that Islam could not be contained within the structures that Stalin had created.

The Soviet regime abandoned the anti-Islamist propaganda of the Khrushchev years and adopted instead a more sophisticated policy of differentiating between fanaticism within Islam and moderate Islam. This did not mean that an anti-Islamic line was wholly abandoned; it was not. Rather, the Soviet leadership decided to be more flexible in its approach to Islam for both domestic and foreign-policy reasons. At home, the dangers of Islamic radicalism were stressed, but abroad Brezhnev argued that Islam could act as a progressive and radical tool. Where Khrushchev had stressed the retrograde nature of Islam, Brezhnev saw it as possessing positive revolutionary features which could be utilised against capitalism. The development of an 'Islamic' channel was used in this period to enhance Soviet influence in those countries with which it had no official diplomatic relations. In particular, emphasis was placed on the development of relations with Morocco, Jordan, Tunisia and North Yemen. An array of channels were put in place to appeal to the Islamic world. In November 1968 Ziauddin Babakhanov, a Soviet mufti, led a delegation to the Islamic conference in Rawalpindi, where he assailed American, Israeli and British imperialism. In 1969 Babakhanov visited Morocco for the first time[9] in a propaganda attempt to reach Muslim communities abroad. This marked a serious departure by the Brezhnev leadership, and was to have significant influence. In the meantime the Kremlin also pursued more 'traditional' routes in attempting to exercise influence in countries on the Soviet periphery.

The Soviet 'courtship' of Egypt which had been started under Khrushchev was pursued with some energy by Brezhnev, and encouraged by the Soviet military, who sought access to ports and permanent naval facilities. This was held to be necessary to compensate for the loss of Albanian naval facilities when Tirana evicted the Soviet presence in May 1961. In the period between 1964 and 1966 Soviet economic and military assistance to Cairo was increased, but it reached a peak in the crisis of 1967. During May 1967 Nasser called for the expulsion of the UN observer force in the Sinai desert which had been put in place after the Suez crisis of 1956. He also closed the Straits of Tiran to Israeli shipping. Israel treated Nasser's actions as an act of war. On 5 June 1967, Israel launched a devastating attack on Egyptian forces in the Sinai peninsula. The subsequent Israeli response, and in particular the rapidity of Israeli advances into the Sinai, caused the collapse of the Egyptian Army and ended in a ceasefire on 10 June. This in itself was an embarrassment to Moscow, who had supplied most of the equipment to the Egyptian forces. On 12 June, two days after the ceasefire took effect, Moscow began a massive operation to resupply military equipment to Egypt, sending units of its Mediterranean fleet to Port Said and Alexandria to prevent any more Israeli air incursions. In addition, it severed diplomatic ties with the Jewish state. The first Soviet combat forces were openly committed in the Middle East in defence of Egypt. In the autumn of 1968, in a bid to attract international attention to the occupation, Nasser began a series of low-level military actions along the Suez canal against Israel. The response from the Israelis was to mount a number of air attacks deep into the Egyptian hinterland, including military and industrial installations around Cairo. After a plea from Nasser in January 1970, Moscow decided to provide an effective air-defence system, including the provision of some 8,000 technicians and Soviet pilots for the aerial defence of Egypt. This number had doubled by December. The Soviet military position appeared at a peak, and was explained at least in part by the fact that the Kremlin was concerned that they could lose influence in the Middle East, especially as the Americans were supplying the Israelis.[10]

Yet the 'alliance' with Egypt proved problematic in many ways, not least over the issue of the Yemen. In 1962 Egypt intervened in the conflict in Yemen. Cairo decided to shore up the Republican cause against the Royalist forces who were backed by the Saudis. Nasser did not consult with Moscow prior to this. Once the Egyptians were engaged, they realised that Soviet military and logistic support was essential to the enterprise. Moscow then backed Nasser in the hope that it would gain military privileges in Egypt and perhaps a strategic foothold in Yemen. Yet, as a result of Egypt's crushing defeat at the hands of Israel in the June war (otherwise known as the Six Day War) of 1967, Nasser was forced to withdraw his troops in the Yemen. The last Egyptian soldier left in early October, and the Royalist forces, backed by the Saudis, closed in on San'a and appeared on the verge of recapturing the capital. To prevent this, Moscow intervened directly, providing the Republican forces with large-scale logistical support and military advisers. By the end of the year the Republicans, well armed by the Soviet Union, were in control. Soviet intervention had proved decisive. It was control of the air by Soviet pilots in particular that had proved a key instrument in defeating the Royalists. This was one of the first instances of the engagement of Soviet fighter pilots in the Third World, and it led to increased tension with the United States, which had been supportive of the Saudi backing of the Yemen Arab Republic.[11]

The years at the end of the 1960s, therefore, saw a mixed set of results for the Kremlin in its foreign policy. There had been some success in certain areas, such as the Yemen, and it appeared as if the crisis in Vietnam could be resolved without souring superpower relations. Most importantly of all, however, in terms of the relationship with Washington, Moscow had finally approached its goal of achieving a strategic nuclear equivalence with the United States. On 19 August 1968 Moscow proposed that President Johnson visit the Soviet capital to start negotiations on the limitation of strategic nuclear arms as a precursor to discussions on other issues. All of this good news though was interrupted by what was the perennial problem for the Kremlin – how to deal with rebellion within the Communist world. For Moscow, the question of the management of allies was once again paramount.

The intervention in Czechoslovakia

Soviet hegemony over the states of East and Central Europe was changed by the events of 1956 and the Sino-Soviet split. After the intervention in Hungary, Soviet control rested in part upon military forces, but it was also dependent upon economic linkages and the loyalty of East European Communist Party leaders. Moscow's ability to ensure the loyalty of high-ranking individuals was critical to its control of Eastern Europe. There were a number of circumstances which could threaten this and substantially undermine Moscow's control.[12] The first of these was the coming to power of an indigenous elite which was independent of Moscow, and who relied for power on a domestic base of support. A second threat was that a Party leader installed by Moscow might gradually move away from Soviet influence, using nationalistic tendencies to accrue power at the lower and middle ranks. A third threat was that, as a result of an intra-party split, a pro-reform faction might gain indigenous support. The Yugoslav case had illustrated the first type of threat. Tito's refusal to join either the Warsaw Pact or Comecon meant that Khrushchev had been forced to recognise Tito as a rather independent member of the socialist commonwealth.

The Romanian example was illustrative of the second type of independence which could be achieved with East and Central Europe. Although initially solidly within the Soviet camp, Romania possessed a strong anti-Soviet tradition, and the Soviet annexation of Bessarabia during the Second World War had intensified anti-Soviet tendencies. The Romanian leader, Gheorghi-Dej, had managed to steer a middle course through the Sino-Soviet dispute, but, more importantly in terms of independence, despite intense Soviet pressure he had maintained Romania's economic independence. In 1964 the Romanian leader rejected any attempt by Moscow through the auspices of Comecon to turn Romania into a primary supplier of raw materials for the USSR. In 1965 Nicolae Ceauşescu succeeded to power in Romania and continued the tradition of balancing good relations with Moscow with economic independence and the maintenance of relations with the West. In April 1967 Romania established diplomatic relations with West Germany. The West did try and profit from these trends; as early as 1964 President Johnson had initiated a campaign to build bridges to Eastern Europe. This project was enthusiastically endorsed by the Brandt-Kiesinger coalition which had came to power in West Germany in 1966. (Somewhat ironically, later on, as part of the détente process, Moscow would follow Romania in developing technical and economic co-operation with West Germany.)

These were two examples of how it was possible to operate within the Soviet orbit but remain semi-independent and even, on occasion, defy Moscow. The Czech crisis of 1968 presented the Soviet leadership with an unprecedented challenge. By 1968 Czechoslovakia was ripe for reform. The country had been badly ruled by Antonin Novotny, and in particular the economy presented serious problems. Indeed, the Soviet leadership was not sorry to see Novotny go, and there is no evidence that Moscow made any attempt to save him when on 5 January he was pressurised to resign as First Secretary. He was succeeded by Alexander Dubček, the first Secretary of the Slovak Communist Party. When he came to power the Party was divided between progressive and conservative factions, neither of which had full control of the Party organs. Novotny had used the conservatives to run the party. In the ensuing power struggle, the progressives, led by Dubček, relied increasingly on the rank-and-file Party members for support. The reformers tried to take control of the Party, and at the Czech Party Congress in late June they won an overwhelming victory. Socialism with a human face became the story of the next few months, posing in the process a number of problems for Moscow. The first was that the reform faction was independent of Moscow, and the second was that the reform movement initiated democratic changes which threatened to erode Party control.

Between January and August six summits were held between Brezhnev and Dubček. Two of these meetings were held in the context of Warsaw Pact meetings in a bid to persuade Dubček to mend his ways. On 14 July a conference was held in Warsaw between the USSR, the GDR, Poland,

Hungary and Bulgaria. Dubček, however, refused to attend. The other Warsaw Pact members made public the so-called Warsaw letter, which made a number of accusations against the Czech Communist party.[13] In July Brezhnev called for a meeting with Dubček which was duly arranged at Cierna on the Czech border. Nothing came of it and another meeting at Bratislava was convened. The subsequent Bratislava statement talked of all-round co-operation among the countries of Eastern Europe. Despite this pressure from Moscow, the reform process continued apace in Czechoslovakia. Popular pressure had been building for censorship to be more or less abandoned, and on 16 April an action programme was adopted which sought in effect to introduce a division of political powers. All of this activity was worry enough for Brezhnev, but it was compounded by an approach by the Czech leadership to Bonn for trading links in imitation of the deal made by Romania. There was even talk that the Czechs might get a loan from the Germans to reform the economy. This was too much for the Kremlin: the Soviet leadership could not afford to see the Czechs pulled westwards.

Yet, in dealing with the Czechoslovak situation, the Kremlin confronted a number of serious problems. Within Czechoslovakia itself there was no evidence either of internal disorder or resistance to the government. There was, therefore, no obvious reason for intervention. There was also a second problem. The USSR did not actually have troops stationed in Czechoslovakia as it had in Hungary and Poland; Soviet troops had been withdrawn in 1945. Whilst it is true that some troops had been moved into Czechoslovakia in May under the guise of Warsaw Pact manoeuvres, these had proved to have had no influence on the Czech government – so far.

Brezhnev made massive efforts to resolve the crisis without military intervention. From the beginning of the year political leverage was constantly tried by both the Kremlin and the other Warsaw Pact states. Some analysts claim that stress over the Czech situation led to Brezhnev's first heart attack shortly after its resolution. Military intervention was not an easy option. Gomułka, the Polish leader, explained in his memoirs,

> To intervene … was not a simple or easy matter … it was necessary to weigh very carefully on the scales the pros and cons of the situation. Even in the Soviet leadership itself there was no unanimity as to the final balance of that account. I will tell you very frankly that the scale was tipping both ways until the last minute.[14]

When Brezhnev did finally decide to carry out the invasion, it appeared as if he had actually had his hand forced by Marshal Grechko, the Defence Minister, and Walter Ulbricht, the East German leader.[15]

Despite political hesitancy, the technical preparations for invasion appear to have started as early as April. Estimates vary as to the actual number of troops involved, but it appears that around 400,000 troops were used from the USSR, Poland, Hungary, East Germany and Bulgaria:[16] twice as many as those used in Hungary, and almost as many as the United States had in Vietnam. These troops were used to take control of key targets, such as the Ruzyne airport near Prague, which was seized on 11 August, allowing a large airlift of troops and equipment to begin, including 250 landings on the morning of the 21 August, bringing in trucks. Despite this there was no resistance, although Soviet troops had been told to prepare for this eventuality. Adams Roberts noted shortly after the invasion that white stripes had been painted on many of the military vehicles, and argued that this would have been useful for identification if the USSR had to use air power to quell opposition. There was, however, no outright opposition, although Soviet propaganda announced the loss of two or three men and the Czech side announced casualties. Soviet troops found themselves the target of abuse but little outright violence. Few arrests were made, apart from the holding of the Party leadership, including Dubček. He was taken to Moscow to 'negotiate' some form of settlement between 23 and 26 August. Brezhnev in the presence of the Soviet Politburo explained why the Soviet leadership had resorted to force. Zedenek Mlynar, who was present, reported in his account of the meeting that Brezhnev had spoken at length about the sacrifices made by the USSR in the Second World War to defeat Fascism and preserve socialism. The Soviet leadership, it was argued, could not afford to have the gains of 1945 negated.[17] The public version of these events was anodyne, stating that troops which had temporarily entered Czechoslovakia would not interfere in internal matters and would be withdrawn as soon as the situation normalised. The secret protocol, however was, rather different. The Czech leadership had to promise to expel those associated with reform, and maintain those conservative elements which had supported the Soviet intervention. New laws and regulations were also promised for press, radio and television. On the issue of troop withdrawals, the only explicit agreement was the withdrawal of non-Soviet forces. However, this was not the end of the affair. Although he was allowed to continue in power, Dubček was regarded as unreliable. Pressure was brought to bear on him, including monthly meetings between the Soviet and Czech leaderships and the maintenance of the Soviet troops' presence in the country, as agreed in a document on 16 October.

Rather ironically, however, the final denouncement came in early 1969. In January a young man, Jan Palach, set fire to himself in protest at the Soviet occupation. This brought about a renewed upsurge in nationalist fervour within Czechoslovakia, compounded in March when the Czech ice hockey team beat the Russian ice hockey team at the world championships in Stockholm. Among other incidents, the Aeroflot offices were attacked in Prague. Marshal Grechko arrived in the Czech capital on 31 March and demanded that the government contain the situation (this included the reim-position of censorship) before the WTO were compelled to intervene.[18] Grechko feared a general military crisis within the Warsaw Pact, and was fear-ful that other states might imitate Romania's action of 1961 and withdraw from the alliance. This ultimatum succeeded practically because the conserv-ative forces within the Party had gained ground after the Soviet intervention and because Dubček himself seemed exhausted from the prolonged battles with both conservative colleagues and Moscow. Dubček resigned and was replaced by a more pliable figure, Husak.

In the aftermath of the intervention, the Brezhnev leadership put together a new announcement of what rules governed the relationship between Moscow and the East and Central European states. Western observers dubbed this the 'Brezhnev doctrine' or what was known in the East as the 'doctrine of limited sovereignty'. In an article in *Pravda* published shortly after the intervention, the interest of the socialist commonwealth was declared to take precedence over the individual interests of constituent states. The article argued that it was the duty of these states to come to the aid of socialism whenever it was threatened. On 6 August *Krasnaya Zvezda* noted that the unity of socialist countries harmonised with the vital interests of each mem-ber, and that the WTO resolutely defended the gains of socialism and the sov-ereignty of the member states. This was hardly new, since before the intervention Brezhnev had declared that the Soviet leadership could not be indifferent to the fate of socialism in other countries. It is interesting, though, that the Soviet leadership felt compelled to spell out both the principle and the warning in unambigious terms, demonstrating clear limits to Soviet tolerance.

It was always unlikely that the Kremlin could have welcomed the changes in Czechoslovakia during the spring of 1968. The demands for the abolition of censorship might have spread, and there were already dissident elements within the bloc who would have seized the chance to embarrass the regime. It was inconceivable that the Kremlin could have turned a blind eye. What is interesting, however, is the fact that the decision to intervene seems to have split the Politburo and been taken only after much effort had been expended in trying to find other means of persuading the Czechs to rein in the reform process. After the intervention the Soviet leadership were faced with outright criticism of their actions not only from Western states but also from Romania, which had not taken part in it. The Brezhnev leadership moved quickly after the Czech crisis to try and maintain a hold over the socialist movement. Ideological conformity was maintained through improving the mechanisms for control, for example, through annual meetings of the East European Party First Secretaries and the CPSU, as well as individual trips by bloc leaders to the Crimea, during which problems were discussed. Meetings of the Political Consultative Committee of the Warsaw Treaty Organisation became more regular, and attention was paid to co-ordinating the foreign polices of the WTO states. Yet, less than two years after the Czech crisis, Moscow was faced with successful political action by workers in Poland that forced the Party First Secretary, Władysław Gomułka, out of power in December 1970.

The reverberations of the Soviet occupation of Czechoslovakia and the termination of Dubček's liberal regime provoked strong dissension in the West. After a visit to Europe in February and March President Nixon embarked on a trip to a number of countries in South and East Asia. On his way back he also visited Romania, a move which aroused strong criticism in the USSR. But the most notable aspect of the trip apart from the apparent desire to improve US links with Romania was a speech Nixon made during a stopover at Guam, when he outlined what became known as the 'Nixon doctrine'. Describing a new approach to defence, he reaffirmed the commitment to those states sheltering under the US nuclear umbrella, but also argued that, in cases of other types of aggression, the US would like the nation directly threatened to assume the primary responsibility of providing manpower for its defence. The implications of this were clear: the US did not want to become involved in any more Vietnams, but would rather build up regional powers against Communism. This had portents for the future which could become much clearer in the next decade.

In the meantime, as Sino-Soviet relations worsened in 1969, it appeared as if Nixon and Secretary of State Henry Kissinger would succeed in their wish to better the relationship with China and put pressure on Moscow – the so-called China card. Between the spring and autumn tension escalated between China and the Soviet Union. A Chinese ambush of a Soviet patrol on an island in the Ussuri river in March led to a retaliatory Soviet action which resulted in over 800 Chinese casualties, whilst the Russians suffered around 60.

Throughout the ensuing months violent clashes continued along the Sino-Soviet border, culminating on 13 August with a major action by Soviet forces near the Dzungarain gate. Moscow also threatened the Chinese with nuclear war. On 11 September, on his way home from the funeral of Ho Chi-Minh, Kosygin held a meeting with Zhou Enlai in Beijing, during which it was agreed that border negotiations would be resumed. This did not resolve tensions, however, and the two sides, whilst not resorting to military means, maintained heated diplomatic exchanges. Indeed, in this very period a huge campaign was launched throughout China to prepare for war, with the Chinese press making it clear that it believed that a war with the USSR was inevitable. This was more than mere propaganda, and whole populations from the border regions with long-established links with the USSR were moved into the central and southern areas of the country.[19] The Chinese Defence Minister, Lin Bao, transferred his staff headquarters to a place near the border. In response, the Soviet leadership increased the number of Soviet troops in the Far Eastern military districts, and by 1970 there were 30 divisions stationed there, with a corresponding increase in Soviet air power in the region.

The massive Chinese campaign against the USSR was of enormous significance for Mao in terms of internal political needs. By the end of the 1960s it was clear to the Chinese leadership that the country was in a worse economic position than at the beginning of the decade. Indeed, the cultural revolution in China had made matters a great deal worse. Mao, in part at least, attempted to divert attention away from the failures of the economy with the threat of an external enemy. The press was used to help cohere national unity. Mao did not want and certainly did not plan for war with the Soviet Union. He knew that China could not win such a war, and that the Chinese army would be destroyed, but external enemies can provide domestic unity.

Whilst Sino-Soviet relations simmered throughout late 1969–70, the Soviet leadership's concerns centred around a fear that China and the United States might form an alliance against it. These fears were inspired by the emergence of China from the isolation imposed by the Cultural Revolution, and by a significant shift in the attitude towards it of the Nixon administration. Even before he was a Presidential candidate Nixon had published an article in *Foreign Affairs* entitled 'Asia after Vietnam'. In this he had written that, in the longer term, a policy which isolated China was irrational, and he advocated that China be brought back into the international community. Once in power Nixon began to take steps to put that very policy into action. In the summer of 1969 the US administration lifted the ban on travel to China for selected professional groups. In December certain US companies were allowed to trade in non-strategic goods, and the Seventh Fleet stopped patrolling the Straits of Taiwan.

The USSR was worried by the prospect of any such *rapprochement*, and in July 1970 the head of the Soviet delegation to the Strategic Arms Limitation Talks (SALT) in Vienna raised the possibility that a Soviet–US alliance could be formed against other nuclear powers – that is, China. It was suggested that if either the USSR or the United States were alerted to a plan for a provocative action or attack from Beijing they would act to prevent it or act jointly in retaliation. This was not taken up by the United States, but was a clear indication of what Moscow hoped for from a détente with Washington.

However, hopes of détente with the United States did not prevent the Russians attempting to take advantage in the Third World. In the autumn of 1970 there was a mini-crisis between the leaders in Washington and Moscow over the Cienfregos naval base. On 16 September a U-2 reconnaissance plane photographed construction of a naval facility at Cajo

Alcatraz in the bay of Cienfuegos on the south coast of Cuba. The base would have had intrinsic value for Soviet missile-carrying submarines, and would have provided certain strategic advantages to the Soviet Union and corresponding disadvantages to the US. The establishment of the base would also have marked a repeal of the limits the United States had imposed on Soviet freedom of action in 1962. This Soviet action was particularly significant precisely because of the background of Soviet–US–Cuban relations in the early 1960s. The Americans claimed that Soviet actions represented a violation of the Kennedy–Khrushchev agreement that ended the Cuban missile crisis. Nixon wanted to make a strong response, but by the time the President and Kissinger returned from Europe to Washington in October Dobrynin was waiting to tell them that there would be no Soviet naval base on Cuba. The United States had successfully compelled the withdrawal of the missiles and restored the political and military status quo. It had deterred a potentially provocative Soviet deployment which, as in 1962, would have altered the balance of strategic military power in the region. Soviet leaders claimed they had been under no obligation to obey unilateral American injunctions against deploying weapons on the territory of a Soviet ally, precisely as the US itself had done in many European countries. Once again, however, Soviet protection of Cuba gave way to broader Soviet interests: in this case, the pursuit of a period of détente with the United States.[20]

The interim assessed

The 1960s saw the two most serious challenges to the Soviet global position since 1945: the Sino-Soviet split, and the rebellion in Czechoslovakia. By 1970, through a massive military build-up east of the Urals and in Mongolia, Moscow had managed to impose itself on China; but this had proved overall to be somewhat counterproductive. Although the Soviet build-up along the border in 1969 did not provoke new Chinese provocations, it was after the Kremlin threatened a nuclear strike that Beijing had actually entered into new negotiations on the problem of the border. Even then, the Kremlin did not mange to compel the Chinese to agree on policy. Rather, Beijing used the period of negotiation to build up its own military strength and seek some form of accommodation with the United States, Japan and Western Europe. The expanded Soviet military presence in the region, and the efforts to intimidate China, had also proved counterproductive in a wider sphere. It had, for example, reinforced Japan's interest in a closer relationship with China, while some in the United States also began to regard China as a counterbalance to increased Soviet global power.

During the 1960s Moscow had also faced a series of challenges to its leadership in Eastern Europe. It had had to resort to military force to ensure that subservience to Moscow was adhered to. The invasion of Czechoslovakia, whilst restoring Communist control, had other, more negative ramifications. The announcement of the 'Brezhnev doctrine' led to Albania's formal withdrawal from the WTO, and certainly slowed the process towards a European détente.

Despite these challenges, however, at the end of the 1960s Moscow could point to a series of achievements. In the short term, at least, there had been a resolution of the problems with both Czechoslovakia and China. A strict regime was established in Czechoslovakia, and the Chinese were at least frightened into negotiations on the issue of the border. Even more importantly, by 1970 the Soviet leadership had managed to achieve a form of strategic nuclear parity with the United States, and could now seriously address the issue of arms control without fear of operating from a position of weakness. This was imperative, given the emphasis which the Brezhnev leadership placed on the need to form a stable and co-operative relationship with both the United States and certain West European states, most notably the Federal Republic of Germany, to achieve preferable terms of trade and the import of high-technology goods.

So, by 1970, the Soviet view of the world was a mixed one. The Kremlin was anxious to court American goodwill for economic reasons, yet the leadership was also ambitious and confident that, buoyed by its advances in strategic nuclear power and the corresponding equalisation of the relationship with the US, it could exert greater influence in the Third World. The interim was over.

Notes

1 John Gooding, *Rulers and Subjects: Government and People in Russia 1801–1991* (London: Arnold, 1996).
2 David Holloway, *The Soviet Union and the Arms Race* (New Haven: Yale University Press, 1983).
3 *Pravda*, February 1965.
4 See Ilya V. Gaiduk, 'The Vietnam War and Soviet-American Relations, 1964–1973: New Russian Evidence', in *The Cold War in Asia*, Woodrow Wilson International Center for Scholars, Washington DC (Winter 1995–6).
5 Gaiduk, 'The Vietnam War'.
6 Gaiduk, 'The Vietnam War'.
7 Stephen S. Kaplan, *Diplomacy of Power: Soviet Armed Forces as a Political Instrument* (Washington: Brookings, 1986).
8 See Alexandre Bennigsen, Paul B. Henze, George K. Tanham, S. Enders Wimbush, *Soviet Strategy and Islam* (New York: St Martin's Press, 1989).
9 Bennigsen *et al.*, *Soviet Strategy and Islam*.

10 Alvin Z. Rubinstein, *Moscow's Third World Strategy* (Princeton, NJ: Princeton University Press, 1988).
11 See Alvin Z. Rubinstein, 'Air Support in the Arab East', in Stephen S. Kaplan, *Soviet Armed Forces*, pp. 468–519.
12 Mark Kramer, 'New Sources on the 1968 Soviet Invasion of Czechoslovakia', *Cold War International History Bulletin*, 2 (Woodrow Wilson International Center for Scholars, Washington DC, Fall 1992).
13 Philip Windsor and Adam Roberts, *Czechoslovakia 1968: Reform and Resistance* (New York: Columbia University Press, 1969).
14 Władystaw Gomułka in *Nowy Kurier* (June 15, 1973), quoted in Stephen S. Kaplan, *Diplomacy of Power*, p. 227.
15 Anthony D'Agnostino, *Soviet Succession Struggles: Kremlinology and the Russian Question from Lenin to Gorbachev* (London: Allen & Unwin, 1988).
16 Windsor and Roberts, *Czechoslovakia 1968*.
17 Zedenek Mlynar, *Night Frost in Prague: The End of Humane Socialism*, trans. Paul Wilson (New York: Karz, 1980).
18 See Jiri Valenta, 'The Bureaucratic Politics Paradigm and the Soviet Invasion of Czechoslovakia', in *Political Science Quarterly*, 94 (spring 1979), and Jiri Valenta, *Soviet Intervention in Czechoslovakia 1968* (Baltimore: John Hopkins Press, 1979).
19 Roy Medvedev, *China and the Superpowers* (Oxford: Blackwell, 1986), pp. 50–51.
20 Raymond L. Garthoff, *Détente and Confrontation: American–Soviet Relations From Nixon to Reagan* (Washington: Brookings Institute, 1985), pp. 76–80.

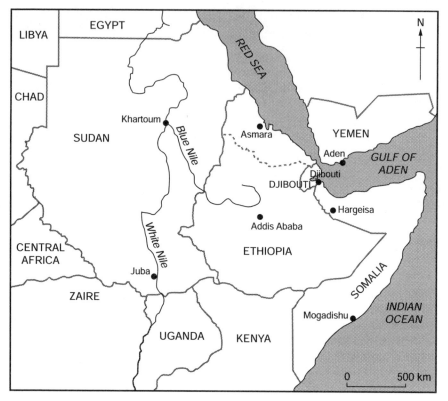

Map 3 The Horn of Africa, 1994

7

The Period of Détente and the Brezhnev Leadership 1970–1980

The late 1960s and 1970s was a time of unprecedented change both in the international system and in the development of an ambitious and expansionist Soviet foreign policy by the Brezhnev regime. These factors had a profound effect on the conduct of Soviet external strategies. A fundamental transformation in global politics took place in this decade, with the relative decline of bipolarity and the emergence of what may be termed nascent multipolarity, specifically with the emergence of China from isolationism. This was important, because the superpower relationship appeared more equal. The determined efforts of the Brezhnev leadership during the 1960s had resulted in a nuclear stalemate with the United States, whereby both powers could inflict nuclear retaliatory strikes upon the homeland of the other. The achievement of a position of approximate military parity with the United States meant that the leadership in the Kremlin was no longer inferior in military arms. A greater degree of confidence became obvious in its actions, particularly in the Third World. This growth in Soviet 'confidence' was aided by the inability of the Americans to secure a military victory in South-East Asia.

The Sino-Soviet schism, however, meant that global politics for those in the Kremlin had taken on a triangular pattern. While China was still inferior to either of the superpowers, it had enormous political and military potential. In terms of population, industrial power and natural resources China had all the factors necessary to be a great power. By 1971 its armed forces were numerically second only to those of the USSR. Beijing was also developing its nuclear stockpile, with sufficient fissionable material for the production of atomic and nuclear weapons. By the 1970s Sino-Soviet relations had deteriorated to such an extent that each side considered the other to be its main enemy. What the Kremlin most feared was that Beijing and Washington would align against it, a fear which was combined with new feelings of equality *vis-à-vis* the United States. This meant that a *rapprochement* with Washington to freeze the Chinese out could be considered.

Changes in the international system were also compounded by domestic turmoil revolving around the state of the Soviet economy, which by 1970 was in a condition of crisis. At the core the problem was one of industrial and economic productivity and how to increase it. One answer which was favoured by Brezhnev and which had historical precedent was to import technology from the industrialised West, particularly from the United States and West Germany. This issue needed to be addressed urgently as popular dissatisfaction with living standards was widespread. As his successors knew at first hand, Khrushchev had in part been removed because he had failed to deliver the goods. Problems for the Brezhnev leadership also emerged when the United States, under President Jimmy Carter, took up the cause of human rights within the USSR. A powerful dissident movement also emerged to question the legitimacy of the Soviet regime. This movement gained encouragement not from the United States, but from the Conference on Security and Co-operation in Europe (CSCE) which was put in place in 1975. Although the Brezhnev leadership succeeded in securing Western recognition of its position in Eastern Europe through a series of agreements on European security, the price was the creation of the CSCE, which kept alive the issue of human rights in the East. There were also continuing and manifest signs of dissatisfaction within Eastern Europe, where some of the ruling regimes were regarded with open hostility.

All of these developments brought about a change in Soviet foreign policy and its appraisal of the external world. Whilst there was little that was new in the recognition that Moscow had to 'relax' tensions with the outside world, the pursuit of peaceful coexistence (or 'détente', as it was known in the West) in the 1970s had several new features. The most obvious of these was that the Soviet leadership sought collaboration with the West across a range of areas: technology, science, trade, crisis avoidance and arms control. This was not just the old attempt to 'use' the West for a breathing space for the Soviet economy, but a wholesale attempt to collaborate with the West on a number of issues. The crisis in Czechoslovakia in 1968 had actually set back the cause of internal economic reform, as it seemed to illustrate that economic innovation could produce momentum for political change. To avoid a wholesale economic restructuring, the Soviet leadership paid far more attention to the import of technologies. The most striking departure, though, was that, unlike in the 1920s or the mid-1950s, the Kremlin leadership was acting from a position of at least partial strength. It did not have to fear arms control because it could no longer be 'frozen' into a position of strategic inferiority through the arms-control process. Therefore, despite its economic weakness, the Soviet leadership displayed a far greater confidence in its dealings with the outside world and in particular in its ability to pursue an expansionist foreign policy in the Third World. During the 1970s it ventured to expand its influence into areas which had hitherto not really been regarded as within its compass. This was most obviously the case with the Soviet engagement in Angola and in the Horn of Africa. The latter area had always interested rulers in Moscow because of its strategic position *vis-à-vis* the Red Sea and Mediterranean. In this expansion of Soviet power, the leadership was profoundly influenced by the alliance with Communist Cuba which urged the Kremlin to assist the cause of revolution in the Third World. By the end of the decade the rapid extension of Soviet interest in revolutionary causes brought about a massive miscalculation of the Soviet global role, when the Brezhnev leadership (or at least parts of it) decided to intervene openly in the politics of Afghanistan with military forces. As a result of Soviet behaviour in the Third World, the Carter administration in Washington terminated the process of détente and declared a new Cold War. A decade which had begun so well for the Soviet leadership in foreign-policy terms ended in political isolation and a military débâcle on its own borders. This chapter examines how Soviet ambition ended in retreat.

The perennial problem: Germany

The détente process really began in the discussions over the status and durability of many of the decisions taken during the Stalin era. In particular, key issues in European security had yet to be resolved. The first problem was still that of Germany. Would there or could there be conditions for the unification of Germany? Would the Federal Republic have access to nuclear weapons? What was the status of Berlin in the longer term? Were the borders of Germany inviolable? Related to these questions was the issue of the relationship between Moscow and the East European regimes and the broader question of the 'legitimacy' of Soviet rule in East and Central Europe. The Brezhnev regime wanted some of these issues resolved; however, the problem was that any settlement would be two-edged. If Brezhnev argued for the status quo in the post-war arrangements in general, he could not then argue that Berlin as a whole should be placed in the Eastern camp. Several steps were taken in 1969 to resolve the issue of the European settlement and the initiative for resolution actually came from within the Federal Republic. The Social Democrats under Willy Brandt, the German Chancellor, abandoned the long-held commitment to a unification of Germany, and instead argued that 'reconciliation' of the two states, not reunification, was the goal. Brandt characterised his thinking as the notion of two German states within one German nation. Before the end of the year, negotiations had opened in Moscow to find ways of concluding a German–Soviet treaty. During the course of the year the Federal Republic also signed up to the Non-Proliferation Treaty, which had been signed by the Soviet Union, the United States, the United Kingdom and 59 other states on 1 July 1968. Under the terms of this treaty nuclear powers agreed not to transfer to any recipient any nuclear weapons or aid a non–nuclear state in the production of nuclear devices. Moscow and Bonn signed a treaty on 12 August 1970 which specifically identified détente as the object of German–Soviet relations. It provided for the mutual renunciation of force and described all borders of all states in Europe as 'inviolable'. For Brezhnev this was a considerable achievement: he had attained or at least seemed to have attained, Soviet post-war goals (apart from the incorporation of Berlin into the GDR) in Europe, that is, recognition of the legitimacy of the Soviet role in Eastern Europe. A second treaty, the Treaty of Warsaw, was signed on 7 December 1970 between the Federal Republic and Poland confirming the Oder–Neisse border as marking the territorial division between the two states.

However, the question of Berlin remained. The four Great Powers began to negotiate on this issue in March 1970, and discussions remained complicated and locked on several issues for well over a year. Part of the problem was that the hardline East German leader Walter Ulbricht tried to impose as a precondition on the discussions that the West Germans recognise the GDR as a sovereign state before discussion on Berlin could even begin. The Russians also refused to countenance the Western request that Western sections of Berlin be recognised as one of the states of West Germany. In addition to these two issues, the perennial question of access to the city of Berlin, which had formed the crisis of 1948, had yet to be resolved. The Western powers wanted the Soviet Union, not the GDR, to guarantee Western access into the city. However, on 3 May 1971 there was considerable movement in all areas of dispute when Ulbricht was removed as First Secretary of the East German Communist Party and replaced by Erich Honecker. (Ulbricht had been a notorious hardliner, unwilling to accept any deviation from the status quo, and was 'persuaded' to resign by the Soviet leadership.) The Final Quadripartite Protocol was signed on 3 September 1971. On 22 December 1972 the two Germanies signed a treaty which entailed mutual recognition. All of this produced a fairly mixed bag of results for the Kremlin. The first was that the status of West Germany's relations with Berlin remained unclear, although the Russians agreed that there were special ties between the two, particularly in the cultural sphere. It was agreed that West Germany would represent West Berlin in all international arrangements. Whilst West Berlin did not became part of the Federal Republic, it was the Soviet Union that was to be responsible for Western access to the city.[1]

All of this appeared to finally achieve a resolution of the Berlin question, whose defusion was a matter of considerable satisfaction to the Kremlin. From this position of the acceptance of the status quo the Soviet leadership also attempted to open up broader issues of security within Europe. The tactic for this was the suggestion for an all-European Treaty on Collective Security, a call familiar to those who had studied Soviet tactics at the Berlin conference of foreign ministers in 1954. Up until the issues of Berlin and Germany had been resolved in 1971–2, the Western powers were less than enthusiastic about these ideas. President Nixon at a summit in Moscow in 1972 gave his endorsement to them; however, he demanded a Soviet commitment to a reduction of Soviet troops and arms on the European continent. Helsinki was selected as the most appropriate place for the European Security Conference, and 35 states met there (all European states, excluding Albania) from July 1973. The Final Act of the Conference on Security and Co-operation in Europe was signed on 1 August 1975, and became known appropriately enough as the Helsinki Declaration. For Brezhnev the value of the declaration was that all of the 35 states involved accepted the territorial status quo and affirmed the non-intervention principle. One principle which was foisted on the Kremlin was what was known as 'Basket Three' of the declaration. This 'basket' affirmed a number of human rights to which all European citizens were entitled, including 'rights' which were clearly unacceptable to the Soviet leadership: they included freedom of thought, conscience and religion, and also affirmed the commitment by governments to improve dissemination of newspapers and journals from other countries. Brezhnev, however, was willing to pay the public price of having to make this commitment in return for securing a détente with the other superpower – the United States; however, the 'Basket Three' was used against the Brezhnev regime by Soviet dissidents.

The central strategic front: The United States

The tidying-up of the outstanding issue in Europe had been carried out alongside a determined effort by the Brezhnev leadership to improve the relationship with the United States. As noted earlier, Brezhnev saw three issues as interlinked and requiring, if not American help, then at least their acquiescence. The first, arms control, required a direct American response. Second, the Russians needed American know-how, and third, Brezhnev wanted to prevent Washington moving closer to the Chinese. This had become increasingly likely as Sino-Soviet relations deteriorated yet further after the border clashes of 1969. During March, Soviet and Chinese forces had engaged each other in skirmishes along the river Ussuri, where there were outstanding disputes over where exactly the border ran. Throughout the summer the Russians attempted to pressurise the Chinese into agreeing to a resolution of the border issues and a stabilisation of relations. By the autumn the Soviet leadership had upped the stakes for the Chinese by letting it be known that they were thinking of a nuclear strike on Chinese territory. All of this, as so often in Russian history, was almost entirely counterproductive, and the Chinese emerged from the isolation imposed by the Cultural Revolution determined to seek new friends and allies.

By the beginning of the decade the White House, too, under the Cold War warrior Richard Nixon, was prepared for a number of reasons to seek a lowering of Cold War tensions with Moscow. Nixon was not above playing the so-called 'China card' to press the Russians into an accommodation. He had many reasons for the turn towards détente, the first, and for him the most compelling, reason being the military and political failure in Vietnam. Nixon's Assistant for National Security Affairs, Henry Kissinger, remained convinced that Moscow could still help extricate the Americans from the quagmire in Indo-China and find some form of honourable peace. Indeed, in return for Soviet restraint throughout the Third World Kissinger was willing to offer credits, technology and endorsement of the European Security Conference. This was linkage, that is, the strategy adopted by Nixon and Kissinger to make positive trade relations with Moscow conditional upon Soviet good behaviour in the Third World.

In the meantime, there was the issue of nuclear arms. The high point of Soviet–American relations in the post-war period was the Moscow summit meeting in May 1972 at which the Strategic Arms Limitation Treaty (SALT 1) agreement was signed. Discussion in Soviet newspapers just before the summit displayed a recognition that the 'new' and equal nuclear strategic balance might be upset in one of two ways. The first was that one side could achieve a superiority in the number of offensive missiles. (Here the Soviet leadership appeared to fear that, although Moscow had been the first to test ICBMs, the Americans had very quickly equalled and then overtaken Soviet ballistic missile technology.) A second way the Kremlin feared that the nuclear balance might be overturned was through the creation of efficient ballistic missile defences which could provide one side with an advantage. In particular, the Soviet press indicated that the deployment of an American anti-ballistic defence system could undermine mutual deterrence by rendering a Soviet attack less efficient. In 1970 Moscow had proposed that a treaty be concluded on ballistic missile defence systems alone, but Washington had insisted that offensive missiles be included in any agreement. The subsequent SALT agreement, and the parallel Anti Ballistic Missile (ABM) Treaty, appeared to solve both American concerns over ICBM deployment and Soviet concerns over an arms race in defensive systems.

Brezhnev and Nixon also signed a trade agreement and set out principles to govern superpower behaviour in the Basic Principles Agreement.[2] The Soviet leadership had insisted on this document, and set great store by the terms of the agreement, which was enshrined on the basis of equality, reciprocity, mutual accommodation and mutual benefit. In the official commentaries in the Soviet press which evaluated the outcome of the summit for Russia it was noticeable that the Basic Principles Agreement was ranked first in importance.[3] In many ways this was understandable, as the Soviet leaders considered that they had at last caught up, equalised with and perhaps overtaken the capitalist states. At the time of the Cuban missile crisis Khrushchev had lamented the fact that Kennedy had treated Moscow 'unequally'. The situation in 1972 was rather different in terms of strategic arms talks, although the Kremlin greatly resented the American attitude over trade, especially in 1973 when under the Jackson–Vanik amendment the Congress tied trade to Soviet behaviour over the emigration of Jews from the USSR.

It is also interesting that, during the period of the talks over SALT 1, the Brezhnev leadership attempted to negotiate an official agreement on superpower behaviour in the event of a third party (probably China) using nuclear weapons to provoke a war. By June 1973 at least some if not all of Soviet concerns were addressed when the two superpowers signed an agreement on the prevention of nuclear war.[4] The Soviet leadership had hoped to get an agreement on no first-use of nuclear weapons with the United States, but the Americans remained reluctant to agree to that principle. At a meeting at Camp David in June 1973, Nixon assured Brezhnev that the Americans would not enter into an agreement inconsistent with the prevention of nuclear war with either Japan or China. The Soviet leadership appeared satisfied with that promise as it embarked upon a massive expansion of its influence in the Third World.

The Third World

Thus far, the story of the 1970s for Soviet foreign policy was a mixed one. Success had been achieved in strategic nuclear arms talks, the Americans had been humiliated in Vietnam and the Soviet military and naval forces appeared stronger than ever. The Soviet leadership had not, however, succeeded in gaining the full range of economic benefits they had sought from the 'new' relationship with Washington. Indeed, by 1974 there were some within the Kremlin who believed that the détente process had not brought Moscow substantial rewards, and urged Brezhnev not to negotiate the SALT 2 treaty. Alongside this rather pessimistic assessment of the relationship with Washington, however, there was also a belief that the trend of global politics was moving irrevocably in favour of Soviet power. This was most apparent in assessments of the balance of power in the Third World.

During the mid- to late 1970s the Soviet Union made significant attempts to expand its power abroad outside the European sphere, especially in the Middle East and in Africa. Before the 1970s the Kremlin had remained relatively cautious over expansion in non-contiguous areas, but this caution was now abandoned. The interesting question is why the Brezhnev leadership abandoned traditional restraint. Several reasons have been identified.[5] The first is that Soviet expansionism in the Third World was a reaction to weakness on the part of the United States in the wake of the defeat in Vietnam. In particular, the Kremlin believed that the military failure in South East Asia had compelled the American leadership to seek a process of détente and a *rapprochement* of sorts with Moscow. The Soviet Union, it was felt, could now exert power and authority globally without having to fear it would always 'lose' to superior American military power. This belief in relative American weakness was underlined by the achievement of Soviet strategic parity and the growth in Soviet conventional and naval forces. Throughout the late 1960s the USSR had invested in a wholesale expansion of the Soviet navy, the development of a fleet of long-distance transport planes and enlarged training facilities. The Admiral of the Fleet, Sergei Gorshkov, who had overseen this development of the Soviet Navy, argued that Moscow now needed facilities in all the main oceans if the Soviet Union was to be a global power. Opportunities and a perceived American weakness were combined with an evolving military strength and confidence on the Soviet side which set the scene for a period of wholesale expansion.

Some experts have pointed also to the impact that significant changes in elite politics can have on the making of foreign policy.[6] Phases of expansionism in Soviet foreign policy are associated with the rise of a new leadership or leader, and foreign-policy activity in new geographic spheres can legitimise the claim to rule. The Brezhnev agenda in the 1960s was to build on the consolidation of the previous decade and export the Soviet model of development into the Third World. This desire to promote the Soviet model was reinforced by certain institutional changes. Alongside the consolidation of Brezhnev's position the International Department of the CPSU Central Committee began to gain ground at the expense of the Foreign Ministry. This in itself was important, because although the Foreign Ministry concentrated on the more traditional arenas of foreign policy such as the relationship with the Atlantic Alliance states, the International Department had a far greater expertise in Third World affairs and an inclination to act in this area. This interest in the Third World was also to be found in analysis produced by another part of the Soviet bureaucracy – the KGB. Reports produced by the KGB from 1970 on put forward the view that some of the regimes in Southern Africa were searching for international allies. It was noted with interest by the KGB that both the United States and China sought influence in the region. By 1975 a series of opportunities arose for Moscow as a result of the collapse of the Portuguese empire.

Angola

In April 1974 a military coup was staged against the Caetano regime in Portugal signalling the end of the empire. The new leader in Lisbon, General Antonio de Spinola, set a date of 11 November 1975 as the date for Angolan independence from Portugal. The situation within Angola, however, was quite complex. Three liberation movements quickly emerged to compete for power in the expectation of the Portuguese withdrawal. The first of these was the Union for the Total National Liberation of Angola (UNITA) which was led by Jonas Savimbi. This grouping had a power base along the frontier with Namibia in the south. A second group was the Front for the National Liberation of Angola (FNLA) which was headed by Holden Roberto. This group received support from Zaire, and it had received some aid from Washington during the Kennedy Administration. Most important of all, though, as far as Moscow was concerned, was the interest of China in the area. In 1973 Beijing had begun to supply arms and to help in the training of FNLA recruits in Zaire. A third group which wanted to compete for power was the Popular Movement for the Liberation of Angola (MPLA). This group was led by the Marxist poet Agnostino Neto, and received its primary support from the Soviet Union, Cuba and Yugoslavia; the USSR had begun to support it in 1958. The MPLA, however, had several weaknesses. It was beset with factionalism and was probably, at a national level, the least popular of the three movements. Indeed, in mid-1975, when UNITA and the FNLA joined forces, it appeared as if the MPLA would be completely marginalised. It was at this point that Soviet and, more particularly, Cuban influence proved decisive.

Early in 1975 the Organisation of African Unity (OAU) sent a mission into Angola to appraise the political conditions within the country and see which of the three movements would be best suited to take power after the withdrawal of Portugal. After investigations, the OAU called upon all three groups to rule in a coalition government. It also declared a principle of non-intervention by great powers in the affairs of Angola, hoping through this combination of coalition politics to avoid civil war and Great-Power interference. There was little hope of this. Angola's neighbours had already staked out claims within the country. President Mobutu of Zaire armed the FNLA and argued that such action was necessary to keep Moscow and its brand of Communism out of the region. Mobutu, though, had another, more prosaic ambition, which was to gain access to the oil rich provinces in Angola. Meanwhile, President Kenneth Kaunda of Zambia had formed connections with UNITA, and he too hoped to protect strategic interests in Angola. Meanwhile, the regime in South Africa had made it clear that it would exert influence, through military means if necessary, in Angola. In addition to interference from immediate neighbours, in July 1974 the American President Gerald Ford had actually sanctioned a plan developed by the CIA for 14 million dollars' worth of arms for the FNLA and UNITA to counter Soviet ambitions in the region.

By 1975 the Soviet objective in Angola was to support the MPLA and use it as a counterweight not only to the potential influence of Washington, but also to balance Chinese influence. Indeed, the leadership in Moscow appeared to have been more fearful of the extension of Chinese influence on the African continent than that of Washinton. The engagement by the Chinese through Zaire in the training of the FNLA was perceived by Moscow as a decision to expand its influence. When in March 1975 the MPLA applied for aid from Moscow to help in the fight against the Chinese-backed FNLA, the Kremlin, urged on by Fidel Castro, obliged. Indeed, it has become clear that it was Castro who took the initiative when it came to sup-plying the MPLA. Before he had even secured Moscow's agreement, Castro had made Cuban armed support available to the MPLA. This placed Moscow in an embarrassing position. If the Kremlin did not support the MPLA, then Castro and Angola would turn into a battleground between Chinese Communism and Cuban Communism. Moscow could be left out of the bat-tle for Africa.

Yet the Soviet leadership did not want to antagonise the OAU or be seen to be breaking the principle of non-intervention, so a back door into Angola had to be found. The Kremlin used the Cubans to deliver arms through the port of Brazzaville into the hands of the MPLA. Soviet involvement escalated further in August 1975 when it appeared likely that the South African Army would intervene in Angola. As it turned out, it did intervene in the autumn. In November, in a bid to shore up the MPLA fur-ther, the number of Cuban troops 'assisting' the MPLA rose from around 12,000 to 19,000. Despite this, the MPLA controlled only about half of the country, South African forces were still in place, and the FNLA and UNITA had set up a rival government. The MPLA had survived thanks to Soviet–Cuban assistance, but it was not strong enough completely to eradi-cate its opponents (indeed, the MPLA itself remained racked by internal feuding). Soviet/Cuban supplies of both men and material assistance were necessary to keep the MPLA in power.

The Soviet leadership had, through its engagement in Angola, achieved some foreign-policy objectives. Soviet prestige was enhanced in black Africa. Specifically, the aid supplied to the MPLA was perceived within the country as strengthening the struggle against white minority imperialism. (This view was reinforced in the autumn of 1975, when the South African Army inter-vened in the Angolan conflict.) The close links with the MPLA also provided the Soviet Navy with bases in Angola, which meant that the West African Patrol was no longer dependent on bases at Conakry, but could go as far south as Luanda. Perhaps most satisfactory of all, however, was the failure of China and its allies in the FNLA to exert decisive influence in the conflict. The Soviet leadership also appeared to have gambled successfully that after the defeat in Vietnam they would not encounter direct opposition from the United States in Africa. This was an important (and, as it turned out, erro-neous) perception; but, in the mid- to late 1970s the Soviet leadership also sought to extend its influence throughout the Horn of Africa.

Ethiopia and Somalia

While, in the short term, it appeared as if the Soviet leadership had benefited from its involvement in Angola, the 'adventure' there had vividly illustrated a problem – the volatility of African politics. The MPLA had not proved capable of imposing unity on the country, and civil war continued to rage. Angola had to be constantly supplied with arms and munitions to keep the MPLA in power. This would in the longer term prove to be a heavy burden; in the meantime in the Horn of Africa, the Soviet leadership actually found itself for a time supporting both sides in a civil war between Ethiopia and Somalia.

The five areas that made up the Horn of Africa were Ethiopia, Eritrea, Somalia, the Djibali Republic and Sudan. The Russian ambition in the Red Sea region was an established one. As far back as the time of Peter the Great in the seventeenth century, Russian leaders had displayed an interest in establishing ports throughout the Mediterranean and the Red Sea. Yet, apart from Ethiopia, the Red Sea area had traditionally been dominated by Britain, France and Italy. After the defeat of Italy in the Second World War the United States had assumed the dominant role in the region. Washington concluded a defence agreement with Ethiopia and established a communications relay centre at Kagnew in Eritrea. This, in the immediate post-war period, was vital to American naval communications. After 1973, however, Kagnew lost its importance for the United States, as it became possible to use communications centres on ships at sea. In the wake of this technological advance, the Nixon administration cut aid to Ethiopia.

The Brezhnev leadership had actually displayed an interest in gaining a foothold in the Horn of Africa during the 1960s. Not only was Moscow interested in the strategic location of the Horn of Africa, which gave it an important vantage position *vis-à-vis* the Middle East, but it saw the region as one in which traditional Western influence could be usurped by the forces of anti-imperialism. Under the Emperor Haile Selassie Ethiopia had traditionally followed a strong pro-Western policy. In 1953 it had signed a mutual defence agreement with the United States, but in 1974 a military takeover in Addis Ababa by the Provisional Military Administrative Council (PMAC) or Derg overthrew the government, and a Marxist regime eventually seized power. Despite his ambition in the region Brezhnev was slow to take advantage of the situation, as he feared antagonising Somalia, which was a Soviet ally. Since 1969, when General Mohammed Siad Barre had staged a military coup in Somalia, he had turned the country into a Soviet ally, allowing Moscow access to the port of Berbera. Somalia and Ethiopia were at this point engaged in a dispute over the Ogaden, and Brezhnev was reluctant to antagonise the Somalis. In spring 1977, however, the new leader of Ethiopia, Mengistu Haile Mariam, was invited to Moscow, and a military aid agreement was concluded. (He had only emerged as leader after a series of bloody power struggles within Ethiopia.) Mengistu professed a deep attachment to Marxism–Leninism and within a year announced that Ethiopian ties with the United States would be severed. Somewhat optimistically, the Soviet leadership had hoped that this new *rapprochement* with Ethiopia would not affect its longer-standing alliance with Somalia. Indeed, it had only been in 1974 that Moscow had concluded a Treaty of Friendship and Mutual Co-operation with Somalia. Mengistu, however, repeatedly used the 'China card' to ensure a continued supply of Soviet arms and goods into the country, threatening to turn to Beijing for support. In a bid to reconcile the differences between Ethiopia and Somalia, the Kremlin actually suggested that Ethiopia and Somalia might wish to join with South Yemen and form a new Marxist Federation in the Horn of Africa. Somalia objected, however. Moscow had attempted to remain even-handed between the two states, but in the summer of 1977 a bitter bloody dispute erupted when Somalia attacked Ethiopia. Officially the Somali government claimed that the action was an irregular one, staged by guerrillas. At first, Moscow vacillated over which country to support and did make attempts to try and bring the two to a settlement. Despite a sizeable military presence in Somalia, Moscow refused to back it at the complete expense of Ethiopia, whereupon Somalia expelled all Soviet military advisers and denied the Soviet Union the use of bases and facilities. Moscow appears to have calculated that Ethiopia would, in the longer term, prove to be a more fruitful ally, providing Soviet forces with access to the ports of Assaba and Massawa. Ethiopia, too, was a significant gain in terms of the size of its population and influence in black African politics. In July Mengistu urgently requested Soviet aid, and in August Moscow decided to accede to these requests. In November–December 1977 a massive Soviet airlift operation was made into Ethiopia.[7] By March 1978, with Soviet and Cuban backing, Ethiopian forces (and 16,000 Cuban soldiers) had expelled Somali troops out of the Ogaden desert. Somalia was roundly defeated, and once again Moscow appeared to have made a significant inroad into African politics, with influence in the second largest country on the continent.

Eritrea as well as Somalia, however, became a casualty of the shift in Soviet politics. At the end of the Second World War Eritrea had been taken away from Italy and placed under the administration of Ethiopia and its Emperor, Haile Selassie. Moscow had held that Eritrea should be independent, mainly because at this point the Ethiopians were pro-Western. Under an agreement of 1952 the United Nations and Eritrea had agreed on independence. The Eritrean Liberation Front (ELF) formed later in the decade when it appeared that Ethiopia would renege on the promise of independence. In response to the threat of a secessionist movement, Haile Selassie in 1962 declared unilaterally that Eritrea should and would form the fourteenth Province of Ethiopia. Throughout all of this, the ELF engaged in endless skirmishes with Ethiopian troops. The Emperor proved adept at preventing substantial exter-

nal assistance reaching ELF. In a bid to isolate the Eritreans, Ethiopia normalised relations with China and improved relations with the USSR. It
appeared as if Eritrea had been outmanoeuvred by the Ethiopians. This was
compounded in 1972, when civil war broke out between ELF and a rival
group, the Eritrean People's Liberation Front (EPLF). However, when the
Emperor was toppled in Ethiopia in 1974, it appeared as if Eritrea might
break free.

The degree to which the Soviet Union actually aided the ELF is still a
matter of controversy. Before the revolution in Ethiopia, and the subsequent
rapprochement with Moscow, the Soviet Union had a vested interest in aiding
the struggle against a Western-backed Ethiopia; after Mengistu's seizure of
power and his public adoption of a pro-Soviet stance, however, it had good
strategic reasons to reinforce his policy on Eritrea. Not least, Moscow did not
want to see an independent Eritrea which could form links with Western
states. It was Soviet assistance in 1977 that allowed the Ethiopians not only to
defeat the Somali forces but stymie the Eritrean bid for independence.

In all Moscow's African adventures a large part of what attracted the
Brezhnev leadership to staking out new areas of influence was, of course, the
acquisition of new military facilities from which to pursue the superpower
competition with Washington. The calculation was made by those in the
Kremlin that the contest in the Third World would not and should not affect
the détente process. In short, the Kremlin professed the belief that détente
was a 'divisible' process. Competition in the Third World would not interfere
with the central planks of détente, trade and arms control.

However, the NATO powers, especially the United States, did demonstrate
concern over the growth of Soviet and Cuban military engagement in the
Horn of Africa. During the supply of troops and materials to Ethiopia in the
autumn of 1977 the United States issued public protests over Soviet behaviour. In January 1978 President Jimmy Carter called for a conference to be
convened in Washington on the Horn of Africa which could arrange a negotiated settlement to the war in Ogaden, and in late February Carter sought to
limit the conflict further. A delegation was sent to warn Mengistu of the danger of Ethiopian troops actually crossing into Somalia. Carter called for a
retreat from the Ogaden of Somali troops, and the withdrawal of Soviet and
Cuban forces from Ethiopia. Cyrus Vance, the American Secretary of State,
warned that Soviet involvement in the crisis would affect the détente relationship. He argued that Soviet actions would affect the negotiations for a
SALT 2 agreement. The later comment by Brzezinski that, 'SALT died in the
sands of the Ogaden', demonstrated that Soviet notions that activity in the
Third World would not affect either arms control or trade were erroneous.

The Soviet leadership had counted on American reluctance to engage
militarily in the Third World after the defeat in Vietnam. It was felt that
Washington, especially Congress, would not wish to be embroiled in other

Third World conflicts. Whilst the United States might disapprove of the growth of Communism in Africa, it would not intervene directly but would, as Moscow did, use proxies or allies. Moscow feared in particular that Washington would act in concert with China to retard Soviet progress. (It should be noted that the leadership in the Kremlin also feared a China acting unilaterally.) As the cases of Ethiopia and Angola demonstrate, a substantial part of Soviet Third World strategies was dictated by a fear that China would develop its own socialist model in the Third World. Nowhere was this more apparent than in South East Asia.

Vietnam

During 1976 hopes had been harboured amongst the Soviet leadership that relations with China might improve. During the year the two great leaders of China in the post-war period had died, Zhou Enlai and Mao. This had invoked a power struggle amongst the rest of the leadership. In fact, the Chinese initially seemed utterly preoccupied with infighting. The Kremlin hoped that a more 'moderate' and amenable group might emerge. It appeared at first that this might occur when Hua Guofeng and Deng Xiaoping assumed control in Beijing; however, there was little change in Sino-Soviet relations. Attempts on the part of the Soviet leadership to negotiate on issues such as the outstanding border areas proved futile. Indeed, in a short period of time the two Communist giants were close to war over South East Asia.

After the American withdrawal in 1975, a newly unified Vietnam developed close ties with the Soviet Union. This was officially announced with the signing of a Treaty of Friendship and Mutual Co-operation between the two states in late 1978 which contained a mutual security guarantee that, should one state be attacked, the other would immediately take measures to remove the threat. This became an important commitment as throughout the late 1970s relations between Vietnam and Cambodia deteriorated. Cambodia had became an ally of Beijing. In December 1976 forces from Vietnam invaded Cambodia in support of a Communist uprising against the dictator Pol Pot. By January a government was set up in Cambodia which was pro-Vietnam. In response, China invaded Vietnam. To those in the Kremlin this appeared to be at the instigation of Washington. Shortly before the invasion, Washington and Beijing had normalised relations. Deng Xiaoping had also just visited Washington on a state visit. Despite Moscow's concerns that a Sino-American axis was opening up, or, indeed, because of them, Moscow avoided retaliation. China, too, stepped back from the brink of war and terminated its military involvement in North Vietnam. War had been avoided, but Sino-Soviet relations under the new regime in China had not provided the window of opportunity that Moscow had hoped for after the death of Mao.

Indeed, from a Soviet perspective the United States was more than willing to play the China Card to restrain the Kremlin.

By the end of the decade, the Carter Administration decided that the détente process had been counterproductive. Jimmy Carter was placed under enormous pressure to end détente. Those on the right wing argued that the period of détente had proved disastrous in foreign-policy terms for Washington. The United States had not reaped benefits from the opening to Moscow. Indeed, it appeared that after the defeat in Vietnam and the consummate loss of prestige and power for the United States, the leadership in the Kremlin had merely taken advantage of American difficulties and successfully increased its involvement throughout the Third World. In 1979 Soviet actions in the Middle East seemed to confirm this.

The Middle East

Although the Soviet leadership had ventured into the Horn of Africa and Southern African politics in the mid-1970s, the Middle East had been a region where, since the end of the Stalin period, the Soviet leadership had sought a greater role. Throughout the 1950s and 1960s the Kremlin had tried to establish reliable allies amongst the Middle Eastern Arab states. The position of the Soviet Union had, however, been anything but stable. In the autumn of 1970 conflict had erupted between Syria (a Soviet ally) and Jordon. Syrian tanks crossed the Jordanian border on 18 and 19 September. Washington reacted by placing its troops on alert, and Israel proposed a counter-offensive. For Syria the situation looked bleak, and the USSR retreated. During the 1970s Moscow also suffered another blow which was inflicted by an erstwhile friend – Egypt. On 15 March 1976 President Anwar Sadat terminated the Treaty of Friendship and Co-operation between Moscow and Cairo. Sadat had proved to be an ardent pro-Westerner and had actually expelled Soviet troops and military advisers in 1972–3. He had also approached Israel directly for negotiations on a settlement of the Egyptian–Israeli problem. Indeed, it was the actions of Sadat that opened the way for the signing of the Camp David Accords of 1978 and the Egypt–Israeli Peace Treaty of March 1979. This process was overseen by the American President, Jimmy Carter, and for the Soviet leadership it marked a low point in its standing in Middle Eastern politics. A Soviet presence in a key strategic area had been ejected and replaced with an American one. The American success in weaning Egypt away from its Soviet patron was a blow to the prestige of the leadership in Moscow. It also confirmed the long-held view within the Kremlin that the spirit of détente did not extend into Third World affairs. In a statement made in 1992 a former Soviet policy adviser, Victor Israelian, commented, 'The Soviet leadership, particularly Brezhnev, had no strategy, no political line. What was our line, to strengthen our relations with the United States or to strengthen our relations with the Arabs and the progressive forces? The two principles were contradictory. We never recognised this.'[8] This, however, is history with hindsight, and was not the Soviet position during the 1970s. Although American statesmen hoped that the détente process would restrain Soviet behaviour in the Third World, this was not accepted or acted upon by the Brezhnev leadership. Indeed, the opposite was true: as a result of a new-found confidence in foreign affairs, the Soviet leadership felt that it could and should act to promote socialism in the Third World. (As we noted earlier, though, the Soviet leadership sometimes had to be nudged on by Castro.) The situation in Egypt after 1973 was a blow precisely because of the expectation of success. It is against this backdrop of the 'failure' of the Soviet Union to maintain its position in the Middle East that the twin crises of 1978–9 in Iran and Afghanistan should be viewed.

In 1978 Iran was in turmoil and in revolution. The Shah, who had been placed in power by Washington during the 1950s, was forced out. Moscow at first welcomed his fall as a setback for Western influence in the region, and the Soviet Union was one of the first countries to recognise the new regime of Ayatollah Khomeini in February 1979; however, the situation in Iran deteriorated sharply when the Shah was admitted onto American soil to receive medical treatment. A group of radical extremists seized the US Embassy in Tehran and held 50 hostages captive, complicating the position of the Soviet leadership. In the United Nations the Soviet representative deplored the actions of the extremists but did not support the motion to impose economic sanctions on Iran. The Soviet leadership expected that, over time, the expulsion of the Shah would allow Communism in Iran to gain ground; but it was also expected that the United States would attempt to compensate for its lost position in the region through a presence in Afghanistan, which had itself undergone a revolution in 1978.

Afghanistan

The Soviet Union had started supplying arms to the Communist group in Afghanistan during the 1950s. This group was led by Mohammed Daoud, who was Prime Minister from 1953 to 1963, and who, following a coup against the King in 1973, became President of the Afghan Republic. Daoud needed arms, as he was engaged in a border dispute with Pakistan. The Americans, who were allied to Islamabad, refused to assist him, and he turned to Moscow for support. The Soviet leadership, willing to help neutralise American influence in the area, cultivated its relations with the ruling clique and, by the mid-1960s, two pro-Soviet factions had emerged: the Khalq group, led by Mohammed Taraki, and the Parcham group, led by Babrak

Karmal. These factions united into the People's Democratic Party of Afghanistan, or PDPA, in 1965, split in 1967, but under Soviet pressure united again in 1977. In April 1978 an anti-Daoud Communist coup took place in Afghanistan. The PDPA seized power, and the Kremlin stepped up its aid to it. In December 1978 the Soviet Union and the Afghan government signed a Treaty of Friendship: although the Soviet leadership had reservations about the leaders of the Afghan Communist Party, it felt compelled to help them build socialism in the country, and a raft of Soviet military and political advisers were put in to Kabul to help the regime establish itself. But many policies of the new regime were ill-considered. In particular, from the point of view of many Afghans, particularly in non-urban areas, the decrees on land reform and the status of women seemed unnecessary and anti-Islamic. A series of rural uprisings took place in late 1978.[9] When a serious rebellion broke out against the Communist regime in the Western provinces of the country, the Kremlin hesitated. Some blame for the rebellion was placed on the leadership in Kabul, who were regarded as unsophisticated and lacking a grasp of Leninist thought. When the Afghan President Taraki was murdered by his deputy, Hafisullah Amin, in the autumn of 1979, the Soviet leadership worried that Amin might turn out to be another Sadat. Specifically, the KGB believed that the Americans would welcome an opportunity to establish their intelligence monitoring equipment in Afghanistan after they had lost their stations in Northern Iran.

By October 1979 the Soviet leadership were actively considering intervention on the side of the Communist regime in Afghanistan. Interestingly, the force behind this planning was the Defence Minister, Dmitri Ustinov. In this he was backed by the head of the KGB, Yuri Andropov. The position of the KGB had been greatly strengthened in the later Brezhnev period. In April 1973 Andropov had been promoted to became a full voting member of the Politburo, giving the KGB a greater input in the decision-making process. The KGB itself had tried over the summer to either murder Amin or at least remove him alive from power. None of these attempts had succeeded. Both Andropov and Ustinov were acutely aware that, with an ailing Brezhnev still in power, the question of who would succeed him was liable to be determined at least in part by those who appeared dynamic in response to the developing crisis on the Soviet southern border. Brezhnev himself was unwilling to alienate two of his most powerful supporters by opposing their advocacy of the military option in Afghanistan.[10] By late November, after Amin had demanded the replacement of the Soviet Ambassador to Kabul, Ustinov and Andropov made their recommendations to the Politburo.

Ustinov and Andropov were aided in their representations to colleagues by the significant downturn which had occurred in Soviet-American relations during the preceding 12 months. Despite the fact that Carter and Brezhnev had actually signed the SALT 2 Treaty in June at a summit in Vienna, relations were still uneasy. Congress looked unlikely to ratify the SALT 2 Treaty anyway and, from a Soviet perspective, the NATO decision taken in 1979 to deploy a new class of intermediate nuclear forces in Western Europe (the Cruise and Pershing missiles) was immensely provocative. These missiles, although intermediate, would actually have the capability to hit Moscow. Some Soviet decision-makers were therefore convinced that, regardless of the intervention by Soviet forces in Afghanistan, the détente process was already dead. However, there were still powerful opponents ranged against the Ustinov/Andropov strategy in Afghanistan. Not least, Kosygin was vocal in his opposition, as indeed was Andrei Brutents, the head of the Central Committee International Department who had prepared papers opposing a military solution to the emerging crisis in Afghanistan. As it turned out, these papers were not even presented to the Politburo. Ustinov and Andropov proved adept at ensuring that an ailing Brezhnev received only the information that was 'required', and that the decision was taken quickly.[11]

On 8 December 1979 Brezhnev and Gromyko held a meeting with Ustinov and Andropov and discussed the strategic situation in Afghanistan and the region in general. Andropov and Ustinov warned that there was a possibility that, in the light of the NATO decision to deploy new intermediate forces in Europe, the Americans might also deploy such weapons in Afghanistan and aim them at targets in Kazakhstan and Siberia. Ustinov's plan to deploy 750,000 troops in Afghanistan to ensure the toppling of Amin's regime and to guard the borders of Afghanistan was approved by Brezhnev. On 12 December the Politburo approved the plan. (Kosygin was absent from the discussions.) Within two days a team from the Soviet General Staff commanded by Marshal Akhromeyev was on site for the operation from bases in Uzbekistan on the border with Afghanistan.

The operation to invade began on Christmas day. On 27 December Soviet paratroopers and KGB agents attacked Amin's palace and, although meeting with resistance, killed Amin and his advisers. Babrak Karmal was selected to preserve a pro-Soviet government in the capital. By January, when Andropov visited Afghanistan, he recognised that Soviet troops would be in the country for an indefinite period. At this stage the USSR had already deployed over 85,000 troops in a bid to secure Communist control of the country. Even at this early stage the Soviet leadership were already looking at ways to withdraw troops, but lacked an overall exit strategy. This ambiguity about the length and aim of the Soviet occupation grew when it became apparent that the Red Army could not quell the Islamic resistance movement within Afghanistan. Indeed, rather than subduing resistance, the Soviet intervention boosted it. The use of repression and terror against civilian groups was entirely counterproductive: resistance which had been almost entirely local in character became national and focused around the Islamic resistance movement, the Mujahideen (Holy Warriors). The introduction of Soviet forces *en masse* was the only instance of a sustained foreign occupation in Afghanistan during the modern period, and although Afghan society had been characterised by ethnic and tribal divisions, Soviet intervention provoked bloody resistance. It should be noted that Soviet armed forces had very little experience of dealing with insurgency or developing counter-insurgency strategies: whilst they had studied counter-insurgency, their actual military involvement in any counter-insurgency operations had been primarily indirect, through surrogate forces, as in Angola or in Ethiopia, for example. The Soviet armed forces had been trained for global war, not small war.[12] This in part explains the initial difficulties in Afghanistan after invasion. Military difficulties were compounded by the unexpected and forceful American reaction to the Soviet intervention in the affairs of another state. For many in Washington the intervention proved that the Kremlin was dedicated to an expansion of its influence throughout the region. Moscow's actions also provoked widespread condemnation from many other states, such as Syria, Saudi Arabia, Pakistan and China, which were affronted by Soviet boldness in attempting to dictate the future of this Third World State. Sino-Soviet relations, in particular, deteriorated still further after the intervention.

From an American perspective, the Soviet intervention in Afghanistan represented a qualitative and quantitative escalation in the Third World strategies of the Kremlin. Although during 1979 Jimmy Carter had sought to make political capital out of news 'leaked' by Senator Frank Church of Idaho that the Soviet leadership was still maintaining a 'brigade' of soldiers on Cuba,[13] the intervention in Afghanistan was of a significantly different order. This was the first time in the post-1945 period that Soviet troops had been used openly to interfere in the affairs of another non-WTO state, albeit a state right on the Soviet periphery. After hearing of the invasion President Carter urged a prompt withdrawal of Soviet forces and ordered that an immediate series of punitive measures be taken against the Soviet Union, including a ban on grain sales and hi-tech exports, and a boycott by American athletes of the 1980s Olympics which were to be held in Moscow.[14] There was little chance after this that the SALT 2 agreement would be ratified. On 2 January the American ambassador, Thomas Watson, was recalled from Moscow, and on 3 January Carter asked the Senate to postpone consideration of SALT 2, declaring that in the wake of the intervention the détente process was dead.[15] On 23 January he publicly unveiled the 'Carter Doctrine' for the defence of the Persian Gulf area, which promised American military force in the event of a Soviet attack on the region.

The death of détente was not just about Soviet behaviour in Afghanistan, however. Ronald Reagan, who succeeded Carter as American President, is often credited with pursuing a 'tough' strategy *vis-à-vis* Moscow. Indeed, as we will see in Chapter 8, he did indeed invoke a new anti-Soviet mood in Western capitals, but Carter had already been operating strategies to place maximum pressure upon the Brezhnev leadership. This was apparent in his stance on human rights which, in tandem with internal political developments, had a profound impact upon the leadership in the Kremlin.

To most observers, the Soviet Union under Brezhnev appeared to have reached the pinnacle of power. It was beyond question a military superpower, had attained nuclear equality with the United States and in the decade of the 1970s had increased its global reach though Africa into Asia and the Middle East. It had 5 million men under arms, and every year defence expenditure increased by some 4 per cent. But these very figures give some clue as to a grave problem. The Soviet Union by 1980 was spending more on defence than the United States, despite having less than half its GNP. By November 1978 even Brezhnev was worried enough to admit that the economic situation was serious enough to present a threat to political stability within the USSR.[16] The continuing decline in growth rates was the major indicator of the problem. An annual growth rate of 5 per cent had halved in the decade between the late 1960s and 1970s. Future productivity looked in doubt as the Kremlin also confronted a problem of the supply of labour. A surplus population no longer existed, except in Central Asia, which would have allowed for an expansion of the work force. In addition to the problems of the economy, Brezhnev also faced the growth of a dissident movement which had gathered around the figures of Andrei Sakharov and Alexander Solzhenitsyn. Sakharov was a physicist who had helped develop the Soviet hydrogen bomb and who had first shot to public prominence because of his outspoken criticisms of the Soviet regime and its indifference to the dangers of nuclear weaponry. From the late 1960s onwards he publicly placed the issue of human rights on the Soviet agenda. In an open letter to the Brezhnev regime in 1970 he argued for democratisation. He left the Communist Party and advocated a Western-style democratic path for Russia. Solzhenitsyn, too, was committed to the cause of human rights. When his famous work *The Gulag Archipelago* was published in Paris in 1973 it openly exposed the maltreatment of political prisoners within the Soviet system. In 1974 he was expelled from the USSR, and in June 1980 Sakharov was sent into internal exile in the closed city of Gorky. Although these were the two most famous cases of dissidents and their treatment at the hands of the Soviet authorities, there were literally thousands of others. Religious dissidents were surpressed, including Baptists, Catholics and Jews. Here, though, it is worth noting that Jews were treated as a special case and, throughout the 1970s, because of pressure from the United States, over 200,000 left the USSR to start a new life abroad. Carter's constant championing of human rights, however, was a major problem and a continual source of embarrassment for the Soviet leadership. The rights that the dissidents demanded – freedom of speech, assembly, fair trials and freedom of movement as could be found in Western democracies – were not actually permitted under the Soviet system. Therefore the claim to these rights necessarily questioned the regime itself. (It should be noted, however, that a new Soviet constitution formulated and published in 1977 did, at least in theory, provide Soviet citizens with the rights of free speech, freedom of the press and assembly.) American encouragement of the dissident movement within the Soviet Union was greatly resented by the Kremlin which declared it to be interference in the internal affairs of another country. Carter's insistence that trade and aid be linked to the treatment of minority groups such as the Jews within the Soviet Union was unacceptable to a Soviet leadership, which was riven with infighting over who was to succeed Brezhnev. By the beginning of 1979, therefore, a combination of factors had already led to the death of the détente process as far as Moscow was concerned.

Conclusions

The détente process did not reward the Soviet Union as the Brezhnev leadership had hoped. There had been early disappointment with the lack of economic and technological agreements signed with Washington, and in particular, in 1973, with the United States' tying of the Soviet application for 'most-favoured-nation' (MFN) status with a requirement that Soviet restraints on emigration be eased as a condition for granting MFN. However, the Soviet leadership was interested in arms control to relieve its economic burden, and the signing of SALT I in 1972 was a considerable achievement, as were the Great-Power agreements over Berlin and Poland signed earlier in the decade. At least in Europe, some outstanding issues had been resolved to the satisfaction of the USSR.

It was in the Third World, however, that superpower détente was really tested and failed. Soviet ambition, based upon the demands of the military in tandem with the competition with China and the United States, led Brezhnev to seek to achieve long-standing Soviet geopolitical ambitions in the Horn of Africa. The Kremlin, buoyed by the achievement of strategic nuclear parity, sought to take advantage of a United States weakened, or at least so it seemed, by defeat in Asia. Even if the intervention in Afghanistan in 1979 could be regarded as defensive because it was a state on the border of the Soviet Union, intervention in Ethiopia could not be so justified. This was about ambition. What was so odd about this expansion of Soviet power and Soviet ambition was that it was set against a backdrop of irrevocable economic decline which mandated trade and aid from the West. This mismatch between Soviet ambition and capabilities was striking. Little thought appears to have been given to the connection between the considerable burden of defence expenditure in making these commitments to Third World states and the growing economic crisis at home. It appears that an elderly and ill Brezhnev was influenced by a combination of powerful institutional ambition from within the military and the KGB. 'Success' in the Third World, or at least in some parts of it, stood at odds with the inability to reform the domestic political system. This legacy of Third World engagement and decline at home would prove a dubious and difficult one for his successors. The Soviet Union under Brezhnev had assumed a global role: his successors were left with the problem of how to pay for this ambition.

Notes

1 For the Soviet call for European security to be based on the territorial status quo, see *Pravda*, 17 April 1975; *Pravda*, 27 April 1973.

2 *Pravda*, 22 July 1973.

3 *Izvestiya*, 22 June 1972.

4 *Izvestiya*, 24 June 1973.

5 Odd Arne Westad, 'Moscow and the Angolan Crisis, 1974–1976; A New Pattern of Intervention', in *Cold War International History Project* (Woodrow Wilson International Center for Scholars, Washington, DC, winter 1996/7), pp. 21–7.

6 T. H. Rigby, *The Changing Soviet System: Mono-Organisational Socialism from its Origins to Gorbachev's Restructuring* (Aldershot: Edward Elgar, 1990).

7 Ermias Abebe, 'The Horn, The Cold War, And Documents From the Former East-Bloc; An Ethiopian View', in *Cold War International History Project* (Washington, DC: Woodrow Wilson International Center for Scholars), pp. 40–44.

8 Victor Israelian, quoted in Richard Ned Lebow and Janice Gross Stein, *We All Lost the Cold War* (Princeton, NJ: Princeton University Press, 1994), p. 149.

9 Amin Saikal and Wiliam Maley, 'Introduction', in Amin Saikal and William Maley (eds), *The Soviet Withdrawal from Afghanistan* (Cambridge: Cambridge University Press, 1989), p. 5.

10 Martin McCauley (ed). *The Soviet Union After Brezhnev* (London: Heinemann, 1983), pp. 18–19.

11 For a full discussion of the decision-making process within the Soviet elite, see Odd Arne Westad, 'Concerning the Situation in "A" New Russian Evidence on the Soviet Intervention in Afghanistan', in *Cold War International History Project Bulletin*, pp. 127–9.

12 For an official Soviet military account of the war in Afghanistan, see Colonel A. Khorunzhii, in *Kommunist vooruzhenykh sil*, 24 (1984), pp. 76–79.

13 See Raymond L. Garthoff, *Détente and Confrontation: American–Soviet Relations from Nixon to Reagan* (Washington, DC: Brookings Institute, 1985), pp. 828–9.

14 Joseph L. Nogee and Robert H. Donaldson, *Soviet Foreign Policy Since World War II* (Oxford: Pergamon Press, 1984), p. 289.

15 For an explanation of the American view of Soviet behaviour during the later 1970s, see Raymond L. Garthoff, *Détente and Confrontation*, Chs 26 and 27.

16 See John Gooding, *Rulers and Subjects: Government and People in Russia 1801–1991* (London: Edward Arnold, 1996), pp. 274–5.

8

The Second Cold War 1980–1985

The years of the early 1980s have been characterised as a period of the Second Cold War.[1] Tension between the United States and the Soviet Union had mounted, fuelled in particular by the determination of the first Reagan administration to pursue Cold War policies. Relations were characterised by a spiralling arms race and renewed competition in the Third World, most notably in Afghanistan. When Brezhnev died in November 1982 his successors faced a series of problems. For the last 18 months of his life he had been a feeble and incompetent leader, little able to deal with the growing crisis within the economy or the international isolation of the Soviet Union in the wake of the intervention in Afghanistan. To compound Soviet problems the Kremlin also had to deal with the formation and popularity of the Solidarity movement in Poland.

By 1980 the Polish problem seemed almost as severe as the one which the Kremlin had had to confront in Hungary during the uprisings of 1956. During 1980 an independent trade union – Solidarity – had led a series of mass strikes against the government in Warsaw. The situation was regarded with particular trepidation by the Soviet leadership because Solidarity had allied itself with the Catholic Church in Poland. The increased authority of the Church and its defiant stance against the Communist government had created difficulties for Moscow in Catholic Lithuania. In addition, Moscow had to face rumours throughout Eastern Europe that the Soviet leadership had been involved, through Bulgaria, in an assassination attempt on Pope John Paul II in May 1981. By August 1981, the Polish Party had actually held a democratic Party Congress in the sense that the USSR had not known since the 1920s; and with the removal of the Chief of Police, Moczar, from leadership, Moscow suspected that Poland was moving away from Communism.[2] In December 1981, the Polish General Secretary, Wojciech Jaruzelski, who was also the Prime Minister as well as First Secretary of the Communist Party, staged a military coup. The alternative faced by the Polish leadership was that Warsaw Pact forces would invade to 'correct' the Polish Communists. During December 1980 the Russians had actually set up field hospitals throughout Poland and were even at that stage reputed to be on the verge of invasion. The military coup in Warsaw in December 1981 had gone some way to restoring Soviet confidence in the Polish Communists, but the imposition of martial law in Poland had not helped Soviet relations with the Western powers.

The Kremlin in this period was faced with the Reagan administration in Washington, which was determined to wage a second Cold War on the Soviet Union. When Brezhnev died it appeared as if his successor, Yuri Andropov, might be capable of energising the leadership and moving some way towards reform of both the economy and the international environment. This was a rather ironic expectation, as not only had Andropov been head of the KGB when it had expelled Solzhenitsyn, but he had actually been Soviet Ambassador to Hungary at the time of the military intervention in 1956. Andropov was 68 when he became General Secretary, and was suffering from kidney disease. Despite all this, he did have some credentials to suggest that change was possible. He was untouched by the scandal and corruption which had marked Brezhnev's later years and, indeed, had even launched the investigation into allegations of corruption against Brezhnev's family. Not the least of these was the allegation that Brezhnev had promoted members of his own family to leading positions in both the Party and government. Brezhnev's son Yuri had become a senior figure in the Foreign Trade Ministry and was also a candidate member of the Central Committee,[3] while Brezhnev's son-in-law was promoted rapidly from lieutenant to Colonel-General and had actually been appointed as first deputy minister.[4] However it was the rather bizarre affairs of 'Boris the gypsy' which had really aroused attention. Brezhnev's daughter, Galina, had been having an affair with an actor with the Bolshoi theatre, but who had become well known for acting with a troupe of gypsies – hence the 'Boris the gypsy' tag. He was said to be at the centre of an illegal trade in diamonds, and the affair attracted much attention in the Western press and within the Soviet elite,[5] and Andropov appears to have seized on the allegations of corruption to strengthen his political position *vis-à-vis* Brezhnev.[6] At the end of his short period in power, Andropov had succeeded in sacking one-fifth of all the Province-level secretaries in the provinces, most of these having been appointed by Brezhnev.

Andropov had been a strong supporter of Khrushchev's 'destalinisation' efforts, and it was Khrushchev who had promoted him to Secretaryship of the Central Committee in 1962.[7] In his position (before he became head of the KGB) in the Central Committee apparatus, he had gathered around him a number of men regarded as 'progressives', including Georgiy Arbartov, Aleksander Bovin (who had for many years been a commentator for the leading newspaper *Izvestiya*), Georgiy Shakhnazarov and Mikhail Gorbachev.[8] Andropov had met Gorbachev for the first time in April 1969, when he had visited the Stavropol region of which Gorbachev was then the First Secretary.

In addition to making a number of personnel changes, Andropov initiated a drive for discipline in the workplace, punishing absenteeism, alcohol abuse and shoddy production. It was not unknown for the police to round up absent workers from shops and bars. However, if the structural problems of the Soviet economy were to be addressed, the economic system really needed a radical overhaul, not tinkering with. Andropov never really had the time to initiate grander or radical schemes. However, in his final weeks he did signal his desire to continue with a reform programme, indicating that he wished Mikhail Gorbachev to stand in for him. However, this idea found little favour with the rest of the Politburo and on Andropov's death, an old Brezhnevite, Konstantin Chernenko, was appointed to the position of General Secretary. He himself was 72 years old and ill with heart disease. The state of the Soviet leaders in these years personified a system in decay. Throughout this period, the leadership did not embark on new foreign policy initiatives: indeed, the most marked characteristic of the short Andropov and Brezhnev periods was the attempt to renew the détente process despite the obvious lack of interest displayed by the Reagan Administration in this idea.

Renewing détente

By the early 1980s American diplomats were clear that détente was dead. US foreign policy was focused rather on how to obtain the release of the hostages been held in Tehran, co-ordinating a coherent response to the Soviet invasion of Afghanistan and rearming the Western alliance.[9] The Soviet leadership, however, wanted to keep détente alive. On 13 January 1981 Brezhnev argued that the events in Afghanistan were not the real cause of increased tension between Washington and Moscow. He argued, rather, that this was a pretext,[10] and indeed Soviet commentators claimed that the Americans had been shifting away from détente since 1977. They cited the shelving of the SALT 2 agreement as evidence of this, and argued that, for most of his Presidency, Carter had been practising containment.[11] Despite all of this the Soviet leadership in public at least remained committed to the process of détente. This was an interesting assessment of American policy. By placing the blame on the Carter Administration for the breakdown in détente, Moscow hoped to open the way for a significant improvement in relations with the new President in the American White House. At a plenary session of the Central Committee in June the Politburo decided to continue to pursue peaceful coexistence, although it still remained deeply critical of American policies.

Just how hopeful the Soviet leadership really was as to the possibilities for the resuscitation of détente with the United States is a moot point. Not least after the intervention in Afghanistan, the Kremlin did have to come to terms with the reality of US sanctions. Some, most notably the ban on the sale or export of hi-tech goods, created a series of problems and mandated a read-justment in economic and trading relations. Trade had to be redirected away from the United States and avenues opened up to other Western states. At the 26th Party Congress in February 1981, Brezhnev analysed the international environment in pessimistic terms. He spoke of the years since the 25th Party Congress in 1976 as 'stormy', and said that 'dark clouds' had begun to darken the international horizon. He called for a moratorium on the introduction of new atomic-theatre weapons into Europe, and argued for the creation of zones of peace.

In reality this meant a greater emphasis on relations with the West Germans and other West European states. Already during the years of the 1970s an International Information Department had been set up and attached to the Central Committee. The remit of this department was to influence trends in public opinion within Western Europe, but most specifically within West Germany. The new department was headed by Valentin Falin, a former ambassador to Bonn.[12] Earlier, Brezhnev had established a good relationship with Chancellor Schmidt, and this had been useful as an avenue to the West; indeed, West Germany was regarded within the Kremlin as a potential back channel to exert influence, particularly over NATO issues. The Kremlin had not failed to note that many of the West European states had actually proved unwilling to translate disapproval at Soviet actions in Afghanistan into extensive trade embargoes that might prove damaging to their own economies. The West Germans in particular, even after the invasion of Afghanistan, had maintained links with the Brezhnev leadership: Brezhnev's visit to Bonn in November 1981 was actually his last to a Western capital.

As well as seeking to make up for the loss of trade with Washington there were other sound reasons for the Soviet leadership in the 1980s to seek friends in the capitals of Western states, and especially in Bonn. Not least, hopes were harboured within the Kremlin that, in addition to using the West Europeans to compensate for the loss in trade with the United States, there was room for manipulation of intra-bloc tensions over nuclear and military issues. The Soviet leadership had been acutely aware of the intra-NATO debates over nuclear issues since the decision taken by NATO in 1977 to deploy new nuclear medium-range weapons in Europe to offset the perceived threat from Soviet SS-20s. In 1978, while on a visit to Bonn, Brezhnev had appeared to accept the need to accept certain limits on Soviet medium-range missiles deployed within the European theatre. At that stage, though, he had not envisaged having to counter a new generation of American-produced forward-based systems which could reach Soviet targets. By October 1979, when this threat had become apparent, Moscow came up with an offer to restrain future Soviet deployments in Eastern Europe of the SS-20s. However, any restraint in future deployments was made conditional on the cancellation of the new NATO programme. This was unacceptable to the West, as the new missiles were perceived as crucial to alliance solidarity and cohesion. By early December NATO had decided to go ahead with what became known as the 'duel track' decision. This meant that although NATO *would* deploy the weapons it would also continue to *negotiate* on the deployment of the 108 new Pershing 1A missiles and the 464 new ground-launched Cruise missiles. At this point Moscow withdrew its offer to negotiate on intermediate-range missiles, and hopes of talks late in 1980 were suspended when President Carter was defeated in the November American presidential elections. He was replaced by the Republican Ronald Reagan.

The Reagan Administration conducted its own defence assessment and a review of American-theatre nuclear policy. The Administration's first defence guidance plan focused heavily on the need and requirements for the conduct of a protracted nuclear exchange with the Soviet Union, leading to concern in Moscow over what might form the content of an initial phase of nuclear war, and to a reversal in Soviet thinking on nuclear issues. It had been held during the 1970s that the threshold for a future nuclear war or exchange would probably be quite high. But given American rhetoric, Soviet anxieties were so profound that, in 1981, a KGB nuclear alert was declared. This was the year of the so-called 'war scare'.

In terms of the European theatre, the Reagan review concluded that the projected deployment of new intermediate missiles by NATO was a mere token, constituting a barely adequate response to the Soviet deployment of the SS-20s. The NATO allies in Europe had by this stage a series of conflicting pressures to deal with. Whilst the West Europeans had actually pressed for the deployment of new missiles to build confidence, governments had now to contend with a growing peace movement agitating for an early resumption of negotiations on the new weapon-systems. Moscow continued to put pressure on the West Germans with a powerful propaganda campaign, arguing that the deployment of new systems would upset strategic nuclear parity. It also raised the possibility that, with an augmentation of theatre capabilities, the Reagan Administration was considering limited nuclear strikes from Europe. The deployment of new missiles into West Germany, the Kremlin argued, also raised the spectre of the destruction of *Ostpolitik*.

When the Intermediate Nuclear Forces (INF) talks finally did begin in November 1981 to discuss the issue of theatre nuclear systems in Europe, the American and the Soviet delegations were poles apart. The Soviet position was unambiguous: that within the European theatre Eastern and Western intermediate-range systems were 'symmetrical'. The American delegation, however, disagreed, and claimed that the Kremlin actually enjoyed something in the region of a 6:1 advantage in intermediate systems. The American position was that British and French nuclear systems should not and would not be included in the negotiations over INF. The crux of the negotiating difficulties over INF was therefore what systems should actually be included in the discussions. President Reagan confirmed the American position on 18 November, in what became known as the 'zero option'. Under this rubric he proposed that America would not deploy its new intermediate missiles if, in return, Moscow promised to dismantle all SS-4s, SS-5s and SS-20s in the European theatre. The Soviet counter-position was one which proposed an allowance for East and West of 300 systems, including the British and French systems, but which allowed the Western alliance to choose which systems would be reduced. The Soviet proposal, although made when Brezhnev was still leader, was confirmed in a speech by Andropov shortly after he took over as General Secretary in December.[13]

The immediate reaction from the US and its Western allies to the Soviet offer was a straightforward rejection. But it was not universally endorsed, and some West European leaders called upon Reagan to demonstrate a greater flexibility in the negotiations rather than just advancing the zero option.[14] In the United Kingdom, for example, leaders of the opposition parties, James Callaghan and Dr David Owen, called for the UK and France to have seats at the Geneva INF talks to look at the issues. Intriguingly, the Soviet leadership hoped to exploit these differences of opinion amongst Western politicians. It was noted in earlier chapters that in the period since NATO was founded in 1949 Moscow had attempted to 'mould' public opinion in the West through a plethora of initiatives designed to undercut support for nuclear and military strategies within the Atlantic alliance. A number of what may be termed 'front organisations' were established, most notably the World Peace Council, to ensure that anti-nuclear platforms received attention. In Moscow the International Department had control of these organisations and was responsible for their activities in Western Europe. As noted earlier in this chapter, the International Information Department was established in 1978 to make Soviet propaganda more effective. During the late 1970s and early 1980s, this department was heavily involved in the very many public demonstrations against the neutron bomb. By 1979 the World Peace Council had decided to broaden its activities to include demonstrations against the NATO dual-track decision to try and prohibit the actual deployment of the new weapons systems. The 'World Parliaments of Peoples for Peace', convened in Sofia in the autumn of 1980, demonstrated against the NATO decision. By 1983 the Soviet press was reporting that the peace movement had 150,000 activists in West Germany, and that 87 per cent of the population opposed the stationing of new missiles. The peace movements, however, never provided the Kremlin with the benefits it sought; even though there was considerable opposition within Western Europe to the deployment of the new Cruise and Pershing 1A missiles, NATO held firm, and by the end of 1983, once the missiles were in place, the peace movement went into a rather rapid decline. The Soviet negotiators walked out of the talks in Geneva, and the Kremlin quickly moved to deploy SS-12 and SS-23 operational-tactical missiles in Czechoslovakia and East Germany. More SS-20 bases were constructed during 1984 than in any other year.

Despite the fact that Andropov, like Brezhnev, continued to advocate a continuation of détente, there was little real prospect of renewed co-operation with Washington. In March 1983 Ronald Reagan described the Soviet Union as the 'evil empire' and its leaders as the focus of all evil. Shortly afterwards, he stunned the world with a call for the development of a Stars Wars initiative – that is, the construction of satellite-based ballistic missile defences to provide a 'hard' cover for the United States against a Soviet nuclear attack. Some American officials admitted that this was an attempt to go back to the days in which the United States had enjoyed a 'territorial invulnerability', before the USSR had achieved strategic equivalence in 1969. For the Soviet leadership this was a body blow, indicating not only that the Americans were attempting to build a position of military preponderance, including a first-strike nuclear capability, but that one of the central achievements of the détente period – the Anti-Ballistic Missile (ABM) Treaty – would be rendered redundant.

The SDI initiative faced the Soviet Union with the prospect of a new challenge which it was economically incapable of meeting. It was not so much that the leadership believed (at least initially) that the SDI might work or prove foolproof; but the evidence of American technological superiority in mounting such a programme was testament to the strength of capitalism. By 1984, when it was apparent to the Soviet leadership that Reagan was serious in pursuing the programme and, in addition, was upgrading American nuclear counter-force capabilities, the Soviet leadership was in no doubt that a new round of the arms race in ballistic missile defences was underway. To counter American developments, the Soviet Union was faced with the option of having to develop offensive means of neutralising or outflanking the American capability, or simply investing in defensive systems. The Politburo actually agreed to initiate a parallel venture to SDI – the so-called Red Star programme. In response to the March announcement there was a considerable change in the tone of Soviet pronouncements. In April Andropov accused the Americans of seeking military superiority and of not taking the issues of peace and war seriously. By September in a formal declaration as General Secretary, Andropov characterised the struggle between socialism and imperialism as an ever-deepening one. He declared that the Soviet Union would respond as necessary to the American actions and accused the Reagan Administration of an ambition to dominate the world. By this stage though Andropov was too ill to appear in public, and for the first time his statement was read out on television and radio.

Soviet–American relations had thus already worsened considerably when on 1 September 1983 a Korean airliner, KAL 007, went off its established course and flew deep into Soviet airspace in the East. It was then shot down, amid claims from Soviet officials that the aircraft was a 'spyplane', collecting data for the United States, an accusation vigorously denied by the Reagan Administration. There were 269 people killed in the incident, and the Soviet actions were widely condemned, while Washington banned Soviet Aeroflot flights into the United States. Soviet leaders resented the fact that airspace had been violated and that Washington had reacted so sharply, and were deeply suspicious when Reagan used the incident to increase American defence spending. During the crisis, Andropov was advised by his intelligence services that President Reagan might order a nuclear strike on the USSR, and they argued that a planned NATO exercise due to start on 2 November could be used as cover. In response the Soviet leader ordered Soviet nuclear forces to a heightened degree of readiness. Unlike the Cuban missile crisis of 1962, the public were not made aware of the possibility of nuclear exchanges, but it seems that the Soviet side did believe that in 1983 there was a real possibility of war. There were other ramifications of this worsening of Soviet–American relations, not least diminishing hope of a resolution of the war in Afghanistan.

Afghanistan

At Brezhnev's funeral in November 1982 Andropov had given the impression of some flexibility over Soviet strategies towards Afghanistan. Three weeks afterwards the Soviet leadership approved a draft from the United Nations for a negotiated withdrawal of troops from Afghanistan. As early as January 1981 Moscow had pushed Kabul into accepting the United Nations as an intermediary in the negotiations with Pakistan which had been the most obvious supporter of the Afghan resistance movement. The first round of informal discussions had begun in the summer of 1982 and during the course of these talks consensus had been reached on some elements of a settlement, including agreement over the withdrawal of all foreign forces. All this was in stark contrast to the Soviet reaction to a plan put forward by Lord Carrington, the British Foreign Secretary during 1980–1. The Carrington plan had provided for the withdrawal of Soviet troops in exchange for guarantees of neutrality for Afghanistan and the creation of multilateral peace-keeping forces. Through the EEC he had pushed for an international treaty to provide for the neutralisation of Afghanistan, and although it had not been considered acceptable by the Soviet leadership, it was hoped in 1982 that the UN plan would be more successful. However, when the UN draft had been sent to Gromyko in October 1982 he had not responded, although Andropov appeared to indicate a far more positive stance towards a negotiated withdrawal.[15] Hans Dietrich Genscher, the West German foreign minister, came away from his first meeting with Andropov convinced that the new Soviet leader was searching for a way to leave Afghanistan. Of course, Andropov had been one of the Politburo who had most eagerly endorsed the military intervention in Afghanistan, but after three years of war he appeared ready for withdrawal. By early 1983 there were admissions in the Soviet press that there were casualties in the war in Afghanistan, and in April the UN-sponsored talks in Geneva produced a draft agreement. This year was the only one in which Soviet troops were not augmented in Afghanistan. In 1981 and 1982 an additional 10,000 troops were placed either into combat or onto the border.

Progress on a settlement for Afghanistan, however, stalled in the summer of 1983. In addition to the problems at Geneva over the INF negotiations and the KAL-007 incident, Soviet leaders believed that Reagan was engineering a downfall of the regime in Kabul. Alongside the general deterioration in Soviet–American relations, the USSR demonstrated no further interest in UN-mediated negotiations throughout the next 18 months. Indeed, while the Soviet leadership proved intransigent over political issues the military escalated its efforts to 'win' the war itself. The total number of Soviet forces was again increased in 1984 by 10,000, and there were by this stage approximately 155,000 troops engaged in the conflict. The Soviet military began to use a mix of large conventional forces and small specialist forces to engage in guerrilla-type operations, with tactics including increased attacks on civilians (concentrating on civilian targets in areas of strong resistance) and a far greater reliance on Soviet as opposed to native forces. New Soviet tactics also included the establishment of security outposts manned by Soviet troops. The general levels of destruction rose as crops were destroyed, animals killed and homes demolished.

From 1980 onwards the Soviet Government became increasingly worried about possible 'spillover' from Afghanistan into the Soviet Central Asian republics, and concerned that the USSR's Muslim problem was being exacerbated by outside forces. This concern was not actually inspired by the war in Afghanistan or the revolution in Iran, as the revival of Islamic radicalism in the non-Slavic republics had been a continuing source of concern for the leadership in Moscow. Until 1980, however, most Soviet commentators, at least in public, had discounted the possibility of Central Asia becoming 'contaminated'. However, after the revolution in Iran and the problems encountered in the Afghan war, the fear grew that foreign powers, the United States in particular, might exploit unrest. Over the previous decade there had been a revival in the activities of underground Islamic organisations.

During the 1980s there was much speculation in the West that the Soviet leadership had suffered a shock during the original intervention into Afghanistan at the reaction of Central Asian troops (those drawn from Uzbekistan, Kirghistan, Tajikistan and Turkmenistan) who were on service in the region. Rumours were widespread that these troops had demonstrated loyalty to the army but had been somewhat beguiled by the struggle of their Muslim brethren, rumours which had been compounded when in March 1980 many of the troops were withdrawn. The explanation for their withdrawal was rather more prosaic, however. For security reasons, the original intervention force had been drawn from the Turkman military district on the border of Afghanistan, and local reservists had been called up. Reservists were only ever called up for 90 days at a time. The reservists originally called up had served their time by March 1980. So there appeared little hard evidence that these troops were actually unreliable.

Nevertheless, a concern remained over the loyalty of troops from Central Asia in the Afghan conflict. Suspicion was compounded by a demographic problem which affected the Soviet Union generally. By the early 1980s, the non-Slavic groups were registering striking population growth. The percentage of Muslims within the Soviet population had grown from 11.6 in 1959 to 16.5 by 1979. In the Central Asian republics, the population had grown from 6.2 per cent to 9.9 per cent of the total Soviet population. This growth meant that while Russia itself suffered manpower shortages and labour shortages, there were large labour surpluses in Central Asia.[16] Within the Red Army this had particular repercussions, in that the officer corps was drawn predominantly from within the Russian republics, while the bulk of troops from Central Asia and the other non-Russian republics, on the whole, made up the lower orders and the less technical arms of the military service. On one side this led to allegations of discrimination against non-Russian troops, but on the other it also led some Russians to believe that the Central Asian troops were not trustworthy and not capable of leadership. Indeed, there is evidence that some civilian Russians resented the fact that troops from the Muslim republics might not be contributing fully to the conflict in Asia, while young Russians were actually serving and being killed in action in what was a predominantly Muslim war.[17] In addition to these internal problems, the continuing presence of Soviet troops in Afghanistan continued to sour relations not only with the United States, but also with China.

China

In the early 1980s China had begun to demonstrate signs of an opening to Moscow. The Kremlin responded positively, hoping that an opening to China could weaken the Sino-American axis which had developed during the 1970s. For the first time since Brezhnev had attempted to create a *rapprochement* in 1964, an improvement in Sino-Soviet relations seemed possible. The Soviet invasion of Afghanistan, however, had stalled any *rapprochement*. In January 1980 the Chinese declared that the invasion meant that any negotiations would be inappropriate. In March 1981 Moscow proposed to the Chinese a series of measures to build confidence. Although the Chinese rebuffed the proposal, a series of meetings did take place between officials of the Soviet and Chinese foreign ministries. By September 1981 Moscow had proposed the resumption of negotiations on the outstanding issues of the border. Soviet initiatives were renewed in March 1982 at Tashkent. Brezhnev announced that the USSR wished to negotiate on issues of the border, but indicated clearly that he would not make concessions on the situation in Afghanistan. In this speech he did concede, however, that the People's Republic was socialist too, reversing a long-held tenet of Soviet thinking about China. Although the Chinese rejected the approach in public, contacts continued between Beijing and Moscow and overall Soviet trade with China increased. Brezhnev's funeral in November 1982 provided an opportunity for the highest public demonstration of Sino-Soviet relations when the then Chinese Foreign Minister, Huang Hua, attended. In the aftermath of the funeral, Moscow announced that discussions would take place over the outstanding disagreements on the border. Andropov continued the strategy which had developed since 1980 of seeking a *rapprochement* with Beijing, but without making major concessions either on the border or on the issue of Soviet troops in Afghanistan. In part first Brezhnev and then Andropov pursued a strategy of *rapprochement* because of the worsening of relations with Washington and, after 1983, because of the American military build-up. By the early 1980s the Soviet leadership was convinced that Sino-American forces were attempting to encircle the USSR. There was every incentive to try and 'break down' the Sino-American *rapprochement* and reverse the trends of the 1970s.

In addition, the Soviet leadership was also influenced by the growing relationship between Washington and Tokyo. Moscow was anxious about the growing industrial and military power of Japan and what appeared to be its inevitable anchorage in an alliance with the United States. This development provided a greater degree of urgency to the necessity of certain strategic developments such as the securing of the Sea of Okhostk for the deployment of Soviet SLBMs.

When Andropov died in March 1984 practically all his foreign policy initiatives had ended in failure. There was little progress on the Polish issue; more Soviet troops were in Afghanistan, but with little prospect of victory; and he had failed to forestall the SDI programme. Indeed, rearmament in the United States was advancing rapidly. Andropov had also not succeeded in preventing the deployment of new theatre forces in Western Europe. He had been seriously ill during the last 6 months of his time in office, and his subordinates had spent much of the time bickering and plotting for the succession. When Andropov actually died, because the state of his health had been kept secret there was widespread shock at the announcement. Andropov's preferred choice for General Secretary was Mikhail Gorbachev who, during the period of Andropov's illness, had already taken over several major functions. Archie Brown notes that when Andropov was lying in state Gorbachev was the only top leader to be shown on TV sitting with his family.[18] However, Gorbachev did not make a bid for the leadership and Andropov was succeeded by Konstantin Chernenko. This appointment amazed Western observers of Soviet affairs, as it had been predicted that either Gorbachev or Romanov would succeed Andropov.[19]

Chernenko

Chernenko, the son of a Russian peasant, had been born in 1911. He began work as a farm hand, and joined the Party in 1931. Chernenko had met Brezhnev in Moldavia in the early 1950s and was regarded as a close associate of his. By 1976, under Brezhnev's patronage, he was a Central Committee Secretary, and by 1978 he was a full member of the Politburo. During the 1970s he had fully supported Brezhnev's strategy of détente. His short period in office, however, was characterised by an overwhelming conservatism. The only change in the composition of the Politburo came with the death of Marshal Ustinov in December 1984, and even then, such was the atrophy at the top, Ustinov was not replaced for weeks.

Chernenko appears to have been chosen as leader basically to end the period of anti-corruption initiated by Andropov. He had used the campaign as a lever to get Brezhnevites out of office. The choice of Chernenko allowed many top officials to keep their posts and end the anti-corruption campaign. However, it appears that there was a general contempt felt for the ageing Chernenko, and it was noticeable that when he was appointed General Secretary he was not accorded the usual courtesy of a standing ovation. Indeed, foreign visitors to the Kremlin reported that he was treated with contempt even by his own officials, who often paid no attention at all when he spoke.[20] Even so, in the period of Chernenko's leadership the number of Soviet missiles in East Germany was increased, Soviet troops increased in Afghanistan and Soviet athletes were withdrawn from the Olympic Games of 1984, none of which resulted in any improvement of relations with Washington. In December 1984 Chernenko had a stroke, and by January he was so ill that he was hospitalised. Gorbachev appears to have led the Politburo while the infirm Chernenko spent an increasing amount of time away from the public gaze.

Conclusions

In the period from 1980 to 1985 the Soviet Union was paralysed in many of its actions because of the infirm and ageing nature of the leadership. In the last years of Brezhnev's life, and under Andropov and Chernenko, a group of elderly and ill men attempted to respond to the challenges posed not only by a newly resurgent United States but by the obvious problems of the economy. Their response to the external world was to repeat the commitment to détente, but, once that had failed to transpire, to fall back upon policies of military escalation in Afghanistan and in the deployment of new nuclear systems into Eastern Europe. The only real shift in Soviet foreign policy during the early 1980s was in the attempt to stabilise relations with China. Even that initiative, though, appears to have been a pragmatic opening to assuage Sino-American relations.

The politics of the Soviet Union during the early 1980s were dominated by the question of the leadership and the battle between those within the Kremlin who saw clearly that the USSR needed radical solutions to the series of economic ills besetting it, and those who sought to hang onto the established ways of ruling. However, by 1985, when Chernenko died, there was a consensus that a younger ruler should be appointed to oversee a regeneration of Soviet fortunes both at home and abroad.

Notes

1 Fred Halliday, *The Making of the Second Cold War* (London: Verso, 1983).

2 Karen Dawisha, *Eastern Europe, Gorbachev and Reform: The Great Challenge* (Cambridge: Cambridge University Press, 1988), p. 198.

3 See John Gooding, *Rulers and Subjects: Government and Peoples in Russia 1801–1991* (London: Edward Arnold, 1996), p. 284. The Western press speculated at the time that Andropov enjoyed sipping Scotch and enjoyed the records of Glenn Miller. Gooding notes, however, that the suggestions that Andropov enjoyed jazz and collected icons were probably concoctions of the KGB.

4 John Keep, *Last of the Empire: A History of the Soviet Union* (Oxford: Oxford University Press, 1995), p. 211.

5 Anthony D'Agnostino, *Soviet Succession Struggles: Kremlinology and the Russian Question from Lenin to Gorbachev* (London: Allen & Unwin, 1988), p. 212.

6 Myron Rush, 'Succeeding Brezhnev', in *Problems of Communism*, 32 (January–February 1983).

7 Archie Brown, 'Andropov: Discipline and Reform?' in *Problems of Communism*, 32 (January–February 1983).

8 Archie Brown, 'Andropov'. See also Mikhail Gorbachev, *Memoirs* (London: Transworld, 1996), p. 10.

9 Raymond Garthoff, *Détente and Confrontation: American–Soviet Relations From Nixon to Reagan* (Washington, DC: Brookings Institute, 1985), p. 991.

10 *Pravda*, 14 January 1981.

11 Garthoff, *Détente and Confrontation*, p. 994.

12 Edwina Moreton, 'The German Factor', in Edwina Moreton and Gerald Segal (eds), *Soviet Strategy Towards Western Europe* (London: George Allen & Unwin,

1985), p. 131. See also Robbin F. Laird and Susan L. Clark, *The USSR and the Western Alliance* (London: Allen & Unwin, 1990).

13 *Pravda*, 22 December 1982.

14 Jane Sharpe, 'Arms Control Strategies', in Moreton and Segal (eds), *Soviet Strategy*, p. 276.

15 Michael McGwire, *Perestroika and Soviet National Security* (Washington, DC: Brookings Institute, 1991).

16 'The All Union Census of 1979 in the USSR', in *Radio Liberty Research Bulletin* (September 1980).

17 Geoffrey Jukes, 'The Soviet Armed Forces and the Afghan War', in Amin Saikal and William Maley (eds), *The Soviet Withdrawal from Afghanistan* (Cambridge: Cambridge University Press, 1989), p. 88.

18 Archie Brown, *The Gorbachev Factor* (Oxford: Oxford University Press, 1996), p. 51.

19 See Jerry F. Hough, 'Andropov's First Year', and Vadim Medish, 'A Ramonov in the Kremlin?' in *Problems of Communism*, 32/6 (1983).

20 Robert Service, *A History of Twentieth-Century Russia* (London: Allen Lane 1997). See also Anthony D'Agnostino, *Soviet Succession Struggles*, p. 220.

9
Decline and the End of the Soviet Union
1985–1991

The view from the Kremlin

By the time Mikhail Gorbachev came to power in 1985, the view from the Kremlin presented a dismal picture of Russia's place in the world. After the military intervention in Afghanistan, détente had irretrievably broken down with the United States. Indeed the post-invasion period had found Moscow isolated and condemned even by its allies in the Third World. There had been no quick victory in Afghanistan, and Soviet troops remained bogged down in what had turned out to be the Kremlin's very own Vietnam. This pessimistic picture of the external environment was compounded by political and economic stagnation at home. The weak economic foundations of the Soviet Union had finally brought into doubt the viability of any massive foreign-policy commitments in aid of global socialism. In comparison to the economic plight of the USSR, Ronald Reagan had embarked upon an unprecedented spree in American defence and promised the reinvigoration of the United States as a global power. Despite or at least in part because of this, the new General Secretary, Mikhail Gorbachev, initiated a programme of radical change designed to transform both the internal and external fortunes of the USSR.

In domestic terms, the key innovation was a *perestroika* (reconstruction) of both the economy and the political system. Reform had at its core a policy of *glasnost* (openness), which meant that a greater transparency and accountability was aimed for in the way the Soviet Union was governed. Gorbachev, like Khrushchev before him, aimed to establish a new relationship between governors and governed. The Gorbachev agenda was also to reinvigorate the Soviet economy and reconstruct external relations with the outside world. For Gorbachev, these two were interlinked: in many ways the success of the former would determine the credibility of the latter. The new Soviet leader espoused the notion that 'organic ties between each state's foreign and domestic politics become particularly close and practically meaningful at crucial moments. A change in domestic policy inevitably leads to changes in attitude towards international issues.'[1] Specifically, Gorbachev stressed his desire to return to the détente of the 1970s, when international tensions had been eased and peaceful co-operation with the West had brought at least some benefits in trade.[2]

The new generation

It is worth recalling the words of Archie Brown, that 'the changes in the Soviet Union have been so great that it is easy to forget what the unreformed Soviet system was like and how modest were the expectations of significant innovation when Gorbachev succeeded Konstantin Chernenko as top Soviet leader in March 1985.'[3] With the advantage of hindsight, it now seems incredible that Mikhail Gorbachev even attempted a *perestroika* to reconstruct Soviet society and the economic system. To quote one historian, 'Did he not realise that genuine reform of the political and economic system would irrevocably damage the Communist Party itself and its grip on the Soviet Union?'[4] This was a problem, of course, although one that was not seen clearly at the time. Any 'democratic' political innovation necessarily challenged the monopoly of the Communist Party and was in essence a questioning of the Communist right to rule.

Yet Gorbachev did not set out to destroy the USSR. Indeed, the new General Secretary was a product of the Soviet system. As he told a group of his former Moscow State University classmates in 1990, he had grown up with socialism and it would have been unthinkable for him to reject it. His father, he pointed out, had been a Party member, and one of his grandfathers had been a Bolshevik who had headed a collective farm. All of this was true, yet Gorbachev had qualities which marked him out as noticeably different from his predecessors. He had been born in 1931, and represented a different generation to that of Brezhnev and Andropov. He had not served in the Great Patriotic War of 1941–5, the first post-war leader not to have done so (even though we know now that Brezhnev's war record was probably not as heroic as he had led the Soviet people to believe). Most notably of all, though, Gorbachev was born and grew up in a region, the Stavropol Province north of the Caucasus, which had a long tradition of independence from the centre and a history of resistance to central dictate. Not least, this region had avoided the imposition of serfdom. It was only in the 1930s that it had been subjected to the terrors of collectivisation. During the terrors of that decade one of Gorbachev's grandfathers had actually been sent into exile in Siberia. The new General Secretary knew at first hand what the Stalinist system could do to an individual family. Indeed, Gorbachev records that, while a student at Moscow State University, he and his peers would turn Stalin's picture to the wall while discussing political issues. Yet even if Gorbachev had a less than conformist family background, he had prospered under the Soviet system. Stalin had died while he was still a student, and although he was basically from a peasant background, during the Khrushchev years he had transformed himself into a middle-class and educated professional. Moreover, although he had begun his career while destalinisation was under way, he had prospered during the political stagnation of the Brezhnev years. By 1978 he had risen through the ranks to become Central Committee Secretary for agriculture, and by 1979 had became a full member of the Politburo. There was therefore little in his political past to indicate that in 1985–9 he would actually preside over the dismantling of the entire Soviet system.

Indeed, Gorbachev's first initiatives were very much along the lines which had been adopted and implemented by Andropov, what might be termed traditional Party methods. The slogan 'acceleration', for example, was adopted for reviving the economy. An anti-alcohol campaign was initiated to deal with social problems and stimulate levels of worker production. There was also a move to cut the burden of defence spending. Mikhail Gorbachev appreciated that the disproportionate amount spent on Soviet defence, some 25 per cent of GNP, frustrated any real attempt at domestic reform. Such spending distorted the economy and meant that its civilian sector suffered, and the USSR lagged behind the advanced nations in terms of technological innovation. This emphasis on satisfying the economic needs of the military also meant, as far as Gorbachev was concerned, that the conservative military-industrial complex carried far too much weight within the political system, which the new Soviet leader perceived as a hindrance to his plans for reform of the economic and political systems. For the first two years there was little that was truly radical in the domestic arena. It was in the sphere of foreign policy that Gorbachev first sported his credentials as a radical leader.

Restructuring the international environment: new thinking

In foreign policy Gorbachev moved rapidly to seize the initiative and gain control. A series of key appointments in foreign policy were made, sweeping away the 'old guard'. Most notable of these was the appointment of Eduard Shevardnadze in the summer of 1985 as a full member of the Politburo and Soviet Foreign Minister in succession to the 'old hand', Andrei Gromyko.[5] Shevardnadze was not a career diplomat, but he was a politician and a moderniser. His leadership of the Ministry of Foreign Affairs meant that it became more responsive to Gorbachev's agenda and allowed the General Secretary to become the decisive figure in the making of Soviet foreign policy. Another indication of Gorbachev's determination to have 'new blood' in the foreign-policy sector came with the replacement of another Brezhnevite, Boris

Ponomarev, by Anatoly Dobrynin as Head of the International Department of the Central Committee in 1986.

The central problem in foreign policy was identified by Gorbachev as the Cold War and the ceaseless competition with the United States. It is worth remembering that during the period of the first Reagan Administration both the Chernenko and Andropov regimes had chosen very traditional ways of responding to Reagan, leaving the arms control talks in Geneva and intensifying efforts in the Third World, most obviously and disastrously in Afghanistan, to extend Soviet influence. It was Gorbachev, because of his domestic agenda, who chose to alter the terms on which Moscow would respond to the Cold War. Advised early in his term as General Secretary to simply ride out the second Reagan Administration, as Archie Brown has pointed out, Gorbachev chose not to. He and the new political thinking in foreign policy can in part be attributed to the influence of 'intellectuals' and academics within the Soviet establishment. Even under Brezhnev some academics had propounded radical new ideas about international relations; in particular, some had long argued for a reappraisal not only of the Soviet–American relationship, but also of the failure of the Soviet Union to transplant socialism to certain parts of the Third World, most notably to Africa. Some of these ideas were actually very similar to concepts which had been gaining ground in Western circles studying international relations. These were most clearly seen in ideas about the integration of the global economy, the growth of financial interdependence and the need for international co-operation on arms control. Soviet analysts also recognised that the most economically prosperous states were those which were fully integrated into a worldwide flow of goods and services.[6] Although Soviet scholars such as Georgi Shakhnazorov had previously noted that certain problems existed in terms of the Soviet global position, it took the boldness of the new regime under Gorbachev to bring these ideas into the mainstream of thinking about the Soviet place in the world.

A public enunciation of the New Thinking in Soviet foreign policy was made at the first superpower summit meeting in November 1985. The keynote of Gorbachev's speech was that the Soviet Union acknowledged both the notion of global interdependence and the 'reality' that the USSR could not exempt itself from the world but was inextricably tied to it and had therefore to accept some responsibility for the present international order.

Gorbachev also served notice of a new anti-nuclear and pro-environmental agenda with a speech at the 27th Party Congress in 1986 openly calling for 'New Thinking' in foreign affairs.[7] Although he did not yet set out a coherent foreign policy programme (indeed, the speech was notable in many respects for its insistence that there was a general and deepening crisis of capitalism), it did introduce several new ideas. The theme of 'mutual security' was raised, and again the claim was made that the Soviet leadership recognised that any rational form of security was interdependent. Whilst the Stalinist notion of the 'inevitability of war' had already been abandoned with the proclamation of peaceful coexistence in Khrushchev's proclamations of 1956, it had been envisaged, as we have seen in previous chapters, that 'peaceful coexistence' would be accompanied by a corresponding heightening of the class struggle in the Third World. Gorbachev's emphasis on 'interdependence', universal values and the individual interests of humans *per se* was quite new. This new thinking modified the Marxist–Leninist belief in the inevitability of an enduring struggle between two opposing blocs. Above all, though, it posed the revolutionary question of whether such a struggle was even worth waging. The renunciation of the belief that the two systems need not endlessly struggle meant that international relations was no longer a zero-sum game. In essence, Gorbachev noted that the notion of a two-bloc system was no longer relevant. Rather, he argued that the tension between socialism and capitalism which had become a reality should give way to a recognition of the interdependence of countries and classes. In practical terms this meant that wars of national liberation and other struggles were now seen in a new light. Most of all, though, the Leninist tenet that there could not be 'peace' without the establishment of global socialism was rejected. Instead Gorbachev inverted that view. Peace, not war, he argued, was the necessary precondition for the growth of socialism; hence revolutionary struggle was marginalised. This reinterpretation of Marxist–Leninist thinking meant that the Kremlin no longer had to support all anti-capitalist movements. The practical consequences of this are discussed below.

The new Party Programme of 1986 affirmed that a nuclear war would yield neither victors nor vanquished. This view was not entirely new: in 1977 at a speech in Tula Brezhnev had declared that it was impossible to win a nuclear war, although he had gone on to add that the imperialists in particular could not hope to win a nuclear war. Thinking about nuclear war had been modified again in 1981 when Brezhnev stated that no party could hope to win a nuclear exchange. Soviet academics believed that this idea, although it had taken time to take hold, had actually gained its greatest resonance by the nuclear disaster at Chernobyl.[8] On 26 April 1986 a reactor exploded at this nuclear power plant not far from Kiev, and the world's worst nuclear disaster ensued. This had been critical in hastening a gradual redefinition of nuclear war as nuclear catastrophe and this encouraged the leadership to elevate war prevention to a formal position in military doctrine. Whereas Soviet military doctrine had previously been defined as a system of views on the preparation and waging of war, under Gorbachev war prevention was proclaimed as the highest objective. The question for the new leadership as formulated by Gorbachev was the apocalyptic phrase 'to be or not to be'. This was radical: never before had a Soviet leader taken the stance that capitalism and communism had a joint responsibility for the safety of the world. If these were the ideas behind the new political thinking, they had practical application in every sphere of foreign policy activity.

Mutual security: the relationship with the United States

During the first phase of his leadership Gorbachev was preoccupied by the central strategic relationship with the United States. Some argued that initially Soviet foreign policy had moved away from its 'obsession' with its relations with the United States. In this vein at the 27th Party Conference the new leader pronounced that the Soviet state would not confine its foreign relations solely to the relationship with the United States. Gorbachev informed his officials in the Foreign Ministry that the world should no longer be seen just through the prism of 'US–Soviet relations'.[9] In particular, it seemed that Gorbachev was interested in diversifying his foreign policy agenda to take account of the growth of new power centres, most obviously the rise of Japan and the European Community. These centres, while weak in military terms, could challenge the United States both technologically and economically, reinforcing his belief that positive relationships with economic centres was the key to the Soviet future. Despite this rhetoric, however, it soon became apparent that the relationship with Washington remained key to Gorbachev's evolving foreign policy strategies. The United States was too important a power to be relegated to second place behind Japan.

Indeed, despite all of Reagan's rhetoric about the 'evil empire,' he and Gorbachev shared one common belief: the idea that nuclear weapons should and could be eradicated. Part of what had attracted the American President to the SDI programme in 1983 was the belief that it might eventually allow for a wholesale elimination of nuclear weapons. Gorbachev had been profoundly affected by the Chernobyl disaster of 1986, and this distaste for nuclear weapons was notable at the meeting in Reykjavik in October 1986. It is worth noting that the Soviet planning document for the summit was prepared by Marshal Sergei Akromeev, the Chief of the General Staff.[10] Although within two years the Soviet military were to develop a very bitter relationship with the General Secretary, at this point his relationship with the military was a positive one.

The Reykjavik summit, much to the surprise of observers, came close to achieving a wide-ranging agreement on the eradication of an extensive array of nuclear weapons. However, the sticking-point proved to be Reagan's insistence that the SDI programme would not and could not be abandoned. Gorbachev insisted that the Americans had to agree that all work on SDI be confined to the laboratory, in line with the agreements over defensive systems enshrined in the ABM Treaty of 1972. Despite this sticking-point, both leaders agreed quite happily that nuclear weapons should be eliminated; and despite the failure of the Reykjavik summit to achieve concrete proposals, both leaders believed that there had been a breakthrough in the superpower dialogue. In a later speech made in Murmansk Gorbachev argued that Reykjavik had indeed represented a breakthrough; although adding, in time-honoured Soviet fashion, that the so-called 'Atlanticists' in the United States might attempt to block any arms control agreement.[11]

Despite this note of scepticism, the relationship with Washington improved steadily throughout 1987, not least because Gorbachev made it clear that from the start of his time in office he had been determined to end Soviet involvement in Afghanistan. It is worth noting that the Soviet military opposed any such withdrawal, but Gorbachev regarded the war as costly and damaging to broader Soviet interests. In this context, one of the by-products of the new policy of *glasnost* had been a growth in public agitation over the issue of numbers of the war dead in the Afghan War, and in particular there was immense public concern over the return of soldiers' bodies to the USSR. The treatment of veterans from the war in Afghanistan also engendered an unprecedented public debate over government behaviour. Most notably, the shortage of wheelchairs within the USSR for those disabled in combat entered the realm of public debate.[12] Whatever the internal problems over the war, Soviet assurances that it was to withdraw did much to improve the relationship with the United States further. By the time of the Washington summit in December 1987 the ground was almost prepared for a breakthrough in arms control. There was still wrangling, however, over the place of the SDI initiative in any arms control agreement. During the preparatory visit by Secretary of State George Shultz to the Kremlin in October, Soviet and American officials remained divided over whether American adherence to the ABM Treaty of 1972 would remain a sticking-point. Gorbachev continued to insist right up to the last minute that the United States had to observe the letter of the ABM Treaty for at least 10 years.[13] The breakthrough came finally on the issue of intermediate nuclear weapons (INF) in Europe. Most notably, this involved the removal of both the Soviet SS-20 missiles and the NATO Cruise and Pershing missiles from European soil.

Gorbachev made a number of concessions in order to achieve this agreement in intermediate missiles. Contrary to his original position, he eventually conceded that the SDI programme would not be linked to the issue of INF, and he also conceded that, at least in this round, the British and French nuclear arsenals would not be included. These concessions opened the way for the signing of the Intermediate Nuclear Force Treaty in Washington in November 1987,[14] under which an entire class of nuclear weapons was eliminated. What was interesting was that the process which led to the INF Agreement represented a considerable deviation in Soviet negotiating tactics on arms control. The Soviet leadership had always up until this point refused to accept certain Western conditions, such as on-site intrusive verification regimes. Gorbachev signalled a willingness to allow Western observers into the USSR to 'verify' Soviet adherence to the Treaty. Another sea-change came over the question of what the USSR was prepared to concede. Previous Soviet leaderships had been adamant that they could not and would not tolerate any agreement that was asymmetric – that is, they would not give up more arms than the West – but under the INF Agreement Moscow agreed to destroy almost four times as many warheads as the US. These turnabouts in Soviet behaviour were connected to a sophisticated political and military agenda which Gorbachev hoped to pursue via Western powers.

Restructuring the relationship with Western Europe

A central plank of New Thinking was the emphasis upon a more positive relationship with Western Europe. Gorbachev made this a key feature of his regime. At first this 'pro-Western' agenda aroused an enormous degree of suspicion in Western European capitals. Many feared that this 'charm offensive', as it was termed, was designed over a longer period to 'disengage' or weaken American military and political influence in Europe. This was appreciated by the civilian analysts who had come to dominate the policy-making circles around the new Soviet leader. Henry Trofimenko, the head of the Foreign Policy Department of the USA and Canada Institute in Moscow, stated, for example, that 'there is this accusation that the Soviet Union was driving a wedge between Western Europe and the USA. But for the past 40 or 35 years we were driving the wedge between Western Europe and ourselves, you see. We were pushing Europe further from us … We were frightening Europe….' What occurred under Gorbachev was that Soviet analysts appreciated more fully the roots of the Western alliance, particularly the commitment of the United States to the defence of Western Europe, and they accepted its durability. Acceptance of a greater unity in the West was expressed as part of the new vision of interdependence. It was recognised that Moscow's actions could cause scepticism among some of the pragmatic Western partners, and that more account should be taken of 'West European conditions'.

Gorbachev accepted too that the post-Second-World-War disposition of massive Soviet and Warsaw Pact conventional forces throughout Eastern Europe and in the Western theatres of the USSR actually constituted a threat to West European states and marred progress towards better East–West relations. Apparently influenced on this issue by the British Prime Minster, Mrs Thatcher, he determined that Moscow would have to alter its military stance on the European continent. This meant a reduction in the size of Soviet forces and a movement away from the post-1945 reliance on an 'offensive' military doctrine, which also, of course, quite conveniently fitted with the need to cut the costs of Soviet military expenditure.

A historic change in Soviet military doctrine was signalled in an announcement by Gorbachev at the United Nations on 7 December 1988 of a unilateral troop cut in Soviet conventional forces of some 500,000 men, accounting for approximately 10 per cent of the Soviet military budget.[15] Subsequent statements indicated that 200,000 of the 500,000 troops would come from the Far East, 60,000 from the southern region, including those withdrawn from Afghanistan, and the remaining 240,000 from the European theatre.[16]

One of the most important aspects of the December 1988 announcement was the fact that it directly addressed what had been the highly sensitive issue of Soviet capability to launch a surprise attack and invade Western Europe. Five thousands troops, including assault landing formations and river-crossing units which, to NATO, seemed designed for offensive operations in West Germany, were withdrawn from the Soviet front line. Bridging equipment too was to be withdrawn. All of this conformed to Gorbachev's demands that the armed forces take account of a new notion of 'reasonable sufficiency'. In February 1987 he had argued that the Soviet armed forces would 'not make a single step in excess of the demands and requirements of sensible sufficient defence',[17] a notion adopted by the Warsaw Pact at a meeting in Berlin in May 1987, which declared that the USSR sought only armed forces and armaments which would strictly comply with the limits of 'sufficiency for defence'. This was expressed through the notion of 'reasonable sufficiency'. While this was obviously driven by Gorbachev's political agenda to restructure political relations with the West European states, it aroused controversy at home. Marshal Kulikov, the Commander-in-Chief of the Warsaw Pact Forces, disagreed openly with Gorbachev's definition of 'sufficiency'; in this period he was still defining sufficiency as 'lower levels of parity', and maintained that parity existed between East and West. This was disputed by civilian analysts such as Sergei Karaganov of the Soviet USA and Canada Institute who, along with Gorbachev, had come to believe that the USSR simply could no longer afford to be reactive to Western military deployments. Indeed, they argued that an action–reaction process had been employed by the West as a deliberate device to exhaust the USSR economically through a race in both conventional and nuclear arms. In the civilian view, Moscow should in the future determine its own force levels according to its own criteria and priorities. From this perspective, the criterion of 'reasonable sufficiency' could permit asymmetric reductions. More dramatically, it was argued that this should even allow for unilateral Soviet reductions. Civilian analysts suggested that if the Soviet Union could escape a massive commitment of resources to defence it could also reject the notion of having forces capable of achieving victory in several independent theatres of military operations at the same time. At a meeting of the Ministry of Foreign Affairs in May 1986, Gorbachev himself publicly rejected the idea that the USSR could be as strong as any possible coalition of opposing states. Civilian analysts supported this position by arguing that the possibility of war in Europe was virtually nil. This was obviously at odds with the outlook of the Soviet military establishment, who argued that the possibility of aggression against the WTO states remained a reality. In a speech at the May Day parade in 1987 General Yazov argued that there was still a threat from the West which had to be met. Military misgiving at Gorbachev's cuts was expressed through the resignations of many career officers, including Marshal Akhromeev, the Chief of the General Staff, on the very day of Gorbachev's speech at the United Nations. He was replaced by Marshal Mikhail Moiseev.

Despite the misgivings of the military, these changes did indeed, as Gorbachev had hoped, pave the way for a radical overhaul of the Soviet relationship with many of the West European states. Improved relations with Western Europe were pursued within the framework of the so-called 'Common European Home'. This idea was actually borrowed from Brezhnev, but appropriately, it was raised by Gorbachev in Paris in 1985. He also took up an idea of De Gaulle's that Europe should be defined as the geographic area which stretched 'from the Atlantic to the Urals'. The Soviet leader called for an end to the schism of Europe. On 10 April 1987, while on a visit to Czechoslovakia he stated that Moscow was firmly opposed to any division of the continent. At least in part what worried the leadership in the Kremlin was the prospect of greater West European economic integration during 1992. This raised the prospect of yet another division on the continent. In order to avoid isolation from the benefits of the European Community (EC), in June 1988 Comecon signed a first agreement with the EC and, led by Hungary, some East European countries signed deals with Brussels which provided them with associate status with the EC. This type of latitude in the behaviour of East European states would have been unthinkable under Brezhnev.

The German problem: from the Brezhnev doctrine to the Sinatra doctrine

If Gorbachev was serious in his discussions and public backing for a common European home that stretched from the Atlantic to the Urals, where did that leave the issue of Germany – or rather, the two Germanies? The continued division of Germany had been a central plank of Soviet European policy after 1949. Although there had been the occasional show of support from the Kremlin for a neutral and unified Germany, Soviet leaders had remained wedded to the notion of division. There is little evidence that Gorbachev intended that Germany should be reunited. Indeed, while the Soviet leader was willing to contemplate the notion that a unified Germany might come about, in conversation with the West German President, Richard von Weiszacker, he placed a timescale of about 100 years on such an eventuality. It is also significant that he appeared to see the reunification of Germany as occurring only after the division of Europe had been resolved. Soviet–West German relations were in fact characterised by a fair degree of mistrust, not helped by the fact that, in 1986, Chancellor Kohl had compared Gorbachev to Goebbels. How, then, did German unification take place?

Primarily, we must go back to the UN speech of December 1988 to understand what occurred in Germany. As well as serving notice that Soviet military doctrine and force dispositions would change throughout Eastern Europe, Gorbachev signalled a sea change in the Soviet view of its relationship with East and Central Europe. Repeating a statement that he had made in 1987 at the Nineteenth Party Conference, he reiterated the view that each 'country had freedom of choice'. This declaration had to be taken in conjunction with the notice that Soviet troops would be withdrawn from Eastern Europe. Eight weeks later, while visiting Kiev, Gorbachev followed his UN announcement up with a further pronouncement that the relationship between Moscow and the East European states would be conducted on the basis of 'equality' and non-intervention. In other words, the Brezhnev doctrine was dead. Indeed, one of Gorbachev's more flamboyant spokesmen, Gennadi Gerasimov, declared that the Brezhnev doctrine had been replaced by the so-called Sinatra doctrine, based apparently on the Frank Sinatra song 'I Did It My Way'.

In part at least, relinquishing control in Europe stemmed from Gorbachev's domestic needs. Maintaining Eastern Europe under military occupation was no longer of any great advantage to Moscow. Although the Soviet military hierarchy might have disagreed, the political leadership believed that the Kremlin no longer needed a military 'buffer' from Western Europe. Moreover, from an economic perspective the states of East and Central Europe had become a considerable drain on the Kremlin. The acquisition of aid from the United States and other Western states assumed primary importance, and Gorbachev gambled that the prestige and political benefits he might gain from 'freeing' Eastern Europe would persuade the West to support his broader economic objectives, thus outweighing the potential disadvantages of military withdrawal. It should also be noted that he found some of the more 'conservative' leaders in Eastern Europe, with their refusal to innovate political and economic changes, somewhat embarrassing and certainly frustrating. However, it should be reiterated that Gorbachev did not intend that Germany should be reunified. By late 1989, though, the situation in East Germany was beyond his control.

The transformation of the regimes in Hungary and Poland, and in particular the opening of the Hungarian/Austrian border, meant that a flood of East German refugees were swarming into Hungary and then into Austria. In 1969 the Hungarians had signed an agreement with the GDR that prevented East Germans from leaving for a third country. In September 1989 the Hungarians asked how the USSR would respond if this agreement, which was clearly futile was scrapped. By the time that Gorbachev arrived in the GDR to celebrate the fiftieth anniversary of the creation of the state on October 6, over 45,000 East Germans had already left. On 18 October the hardline East German leader Erich Honecker stepped down and was replaced by Egon Krenz. The situation in East Germany was so precarious that when Krenz asked Gorbachev for advice, he was told that he should open the border in order to stabilise the situation. The Berlin wall was opened and actually fell in November 1989.

In 1990 Gorbachev proclaimed that it was up to the Germans to determine the nature and speed of their future. Gorbachev's views were subject to intense criticism within the USSR, and many voiced the view that both he and Shevardnadze had given away post-war gains. However, both the General Secretary and his Foreign Minister made massive efforts to forestall unification and the possible entry of a newly united Germany into NATO. Gorbachev stressed again and again for an international audience that the two Germanies were a historic fact, as well as trying to keep the notion of four-power control of Germany, by the Soviets, Americans, French and British, at the front of the agenda.

Moscow was adamant that NATO membership for a united Germany would be unacceptable. Valentin Falin, the head of the Central Committee International Department, argued that a German neutrality guaranteed by the other 33 Helsinki signatories would be the best solution. Shevardnadze tried to find a way around the problem. Initially he suggested joint German membership of both NATO and WTO, and then suggested putting the question in the context of a much broader restructuring of European security on the CSCE model. In Shevardnadze's speech to the so-called two-plus-four foreign ministers in May he went out of his way to stress the dangers of unification, and as an alternative offered this idea of a 'greater Europe' security mechanism which would implement the two-plus-four mechanism (that is, the two Germanies and the four Great Powers of the US, the USSR, Britain and France). Conservatives within the Kremlin, such as Igor Ligachev, protested at the inability of the Soviet leadership to retard a unified Germany. In a speech in 1990 he argued that while the commonwealth of socialist states was falling apart, the NATO alliance was being strengthened at the expense of the USSR.

However, by 1989–90 there was little that the Soviet leadership could do to forestall the integration of the two Germanies as one state into the NATO alliance. It is true that under an old-style Soviet regime the troops stationed throughout East and Central Europe might have been used to stem the rise of nationalism and anti-Communism, but under the Gorbachev regime such actions, at least on European soil, were unthinkable. Not least, this was because the United States had thrown its influence behind the idea that the new Germany should join NATO. All Gorbachev was left with was haggling over the price of Soviet acceptance of this reality. What he did achieve was to heighten the financial costs of German unification by demanding from Chancellor Kohl 12 billion deutschmarks, plus a further 3 billion in credits to cover the costs of the relocation of Soviet troops out of Germany. The final deal over Germany demonstrated clearly that the Soviet leadership had little to bargain with. Indeed, it could be argued that the West bought the freedom of Germany. But for the Soviet leadership it was an ironic turn to be selling the fruits of victory in the Second World War. They could no longer afford or maintain a vigorous foreign policy; and nowhere was this more apparent than in the Soviet withdrawal from its Third World commitments.

Cost–benefit analysis: leaving the Third World

The Reagan doctrine discussed in Chapter 8 presented a military challenge to the USSR in the Third World to 'roll back' Communism. In February 1989 the USSR withdrew its troops from Afghanistan and cut back its support for a number of other Third-World allies such as Cuba, Vietnam and Nicaragua. Moscow also pressed for political solutions to long-standing regional crises in Central America, Africa, Indo-China and the Middle East.

The costs of empire had grown burdensome. An *Izvestiya* report stated that the developing world owed Moscow 85 billion roubles, whilst some estimates put the costs of the Afghan war at 60 billion roubles from 1979 to 1989. The returns were not obvious and, indeed, Soviet Third World strategies had, on the whole, turned out to be almost wholly unproductive. Soviet refusal to accept linkage had resulted at least in part in the decline of the détente process. Many Soviet academics in the 1970s had already come to the conclusion that Soviet Third World policy was a failure; it took the Gorbachev regime, however, to make that view both official and explicit. Shevardnadze openly commented that countries such as Ethiopia were not expected to follow a socialist path, and that therefore Moscow should cut its losses and not waste valuable resources on Third World states.

The standard Western view is that US support for the Mujahideen played a decisive role in the Soviet withdrawal from Afghanistan. In particular, many analysts believe that the supply to them of Stinger anti-aircraft missiles in 1986 was a critical turning-point. This view, however, has been challenged as overly simplistic, and some analysts claim that actually the decision to withdraw was taken long before the US deployment. At the 27th Party Congress in 1986, for example, Gorbachev expressed the view that the war in Afghanistan was, for the USSR, a 'bleeding wound'. The Stingers were also less deadly and militarily decisive than has been claimed. The Soviet military were still able to operate their helicopters and remained overall in charge of the major cities and roads. However, after 1987 the effects of *glasnost* did come into operation. The issue of the war dead became a political one: Mark Urban's much-quoted contention, that the West did not win the Twentieth Century Great Game – Gorbachev simply decided that he was not playing any more – not with Soviet soldiers at least, appears apposite. The Soviet leader therefore accepted the American strategy of linkage.

One result of Gorbachev's reforms was to marginalise the issue and importance of Third World revolutions. As noted above, it had been clear to Gorbachev that Soviet activism in the Third World had damaged its relationship with the United States. The 1986 party programme barely mentioned the Third World, although Gorbachev was careful to stress the need to find solutions to the problems of the Third World and specifically the issue of debt. Central to the new thinking was an effort to remove the overtly ideological component in Soviet policy. The most dramatic manifestation of this was the renunciation of a policy seeking to expand socialism, and stressing instead the principle of non-intervention. Speaking in Havana in April 1989, Gorbachev argued that 'we are resolutely opposed to any theories and doctrines justifying the export of revolution or counter-revolution'.[18] In a major speech to the Supreme Soviet in October 1989, Shevardnadze stated that the intervention in Afghanistan had violated the norm of proper behaviour.[19] Under Gorbachev the USSR decreased its economic support for Communist Governments and movements throughout the Third World. Pragmatism, as demonstrated over Afghanistan, became the key theme of Soviet foreign policy. Withdrawal from Afghanistan was part of a larger pattern of retreat. In Angola, Cambodia, Namibia and Nicaragua there was a downgrading of Soviet influence, whilst Moscow made overtures to a different set of states, such as South Africa, Brazil, Thailand and Japan, all of which had more to offer the USSR in economic and trading terms. Most notably of all, though, the downgrading of ideological influences in the making of foreign policy was seen clearly in the Sino-Soviet relationship.

China

In what became known as the Vladivostock speech of 28 July 1986, Gorbachev made it clear that the Soviet Union was not simply a European state but also saw itself as an Asian and an Asian–Pacific one. He described Vladivostock as the 'wide open window on the East'. The Soviet strategy in the region was to restore political and economic relations with China and establish a presence by consolidating relations with a series of key states. The relationship with China had steadily improved throughout the 1980s as both countries had embarked upon ambitious reform programmes. As early as 1982 Brezhnev had indicated that the USSR would have welcomed a better relationship with Beijing. In a speech at Tashkent it had appeared as if Brezhnev was seeking to reopen a new era of relations, but the Chinese had pointed out three key issues which would forestall any such thing. These were the large Soviet forces on the border, the Soviet forces in Afghanistan and the presence of Vietnamese forces in Cambodia. Once Gorbachev had signalled that Soviet troops would leave, Afghanistan had gone some way to improve relations, and the situation was further improved with the removal of 200,000 Soviet troops from Mongolia and Central Asia in February 1989. By May 1989 relations were so improved that Gorbachev was able to visit the Chinese capital. Part at least of the transformation of the relationship had occurred because of the insistence of the Soviet regime that relations should be conducted on a state-to-state basis rather than a party-to-party one. This allowed Gorbachev to sidestep neatly the perennial problem of which state actually led the global Communist movement.

Despite this thoroughgoing shift in the Soviet approach to the Asia–Pacific region, Gorbachev's initiatives were received with a great deal of mistrust and hostility. Of all the developed countries, Japan remained less than impressed by the new Soviet leader, and in particular made the outstanding issue of the Kurile islands (the ownership of which had been disputed since 1945 when the Russians had failed to gain a place in the post-war settlement of Japan) the litmus test of how far the Soviet leadership was actually prepared to go under the guise of New Thinking, demanding that the Kremlin rethink its post-1945 occupation of these four islands. This was not easy for Gorbachev; if he conceded this issue he would leave the leadership in Moscow open to a whole host of claims resulting from past Soviet and particularly Stalinist behaviour. In the Pacific area and Siberia the legacy of Stalin's labour camps was likely to be opened up, and Gorbachev was unwilling for the moment to unleash that particular Pandora's box.

The power of history

Whilst the issue of the Kurile islands was one that, at least in the short to medium term, Gorbachev had to side step, there was under the rubric of *glasnost* a far greater 'openness' over what had been sealed historical controversies. Stephen Cohen has argued that one of the tests of a reform-minded Soviet leadership was its willingness to come to terms with the historical legacy of Stalinism, and has pointed out that history, or interpretations of historical incidents, were used by those who opposed reform in the Soviet system to justify the regime. Most notably, after 1953 the Stalinist past was depicted as a series of great victories, particularly over Germany in 1945.[20] *Glasnost*, however, demanded unprecedented steps in this direction.

The regime in Moscow did demonstrate a willingness to examine at least some aspects of the past. One issue was the extent to which the Soviet Union had been responsible for the outbreak of Cold War in 1945, and how far the traditional Soviet version which held that the Cold War had been launched by Churchill's Fulton speech in March 1946 was accurate. More critically, the debate centred around Soviet behaviour during 1939, the 'real' facts of the Nazi–Soviet pact, and the secret protocol allowing for the annexation of the Baltic states. Other key issues discussed were the murder of Polish soldiers in the Katyn forest and the invasion of Czechoslovakia in 1968.

This 'unlocking' of Soviet and East European history was crucial to the Soviet relationship with states such as Poland and Czechoslovakia, and was to prove fatal to the Warsaw Pact once it was combined with the acceptance of diversity within the Communist movement. Gorbachev at first appeared reluctant to accept that East and Central European states might imitate the USSR in its move to democratisation. Archie Brown claims that the initial preference was for like-minded leaders to emerge in Central and East European states, certainly not that the regimes would be overthrown. Indeed, Gorbachev was highly critical of those Central and East European leaders unwilling to embrace political and economic changes that he himself had already endorsed in the USSR. However, by 1989 the unlinking of security and ideology had advanced far enough to allow each state to redefine its own destiny. Proletarian internationalism gave way to a new concept of socialist sovereignty based on equal rights between states. Whilst Gorbachev might have wished to manage the process of change within East and Central Europe in tandem with sympathetic leaderships, he was simply overtaken by events on the ground.

By the time 1989 came, Gorbachev was actually in no position to hold back the process of change in East and Central Europe. After the Czech revolution of 1989 and a demand from Prague that the Kremlin apologise for the events of 1968, the Soviet leadership prevaricated. It argued that it had not welcomed the opportunity of dismantling the Stalinist system in 1968, but still refused to confirm the nature of the intervention. Soviet politicians, authors and writers demanded that the 'truth' should be told. But it took until December 1989 for Gorbachev, shortly before a summit meeting with the US President George Bush, to denounce the Soviet intervention in Czechoslovakia in 1968. His caution in commenting on the events was at least in part determined by the likely knock-on effects throughout the Soviet bloc. (This had, of course, been part of the reason why the Soviet authorities had been so keen to surpress rebellion in Poland in 1981 and in Czechoslovakia in 1968.) Once again, though, there was little that

Gorbachev could have done to halt the process of change throughout Eastern Europe. He was proved right, however, as both Khrushchev and Brezhnev before him had feared; any process of reform in Eastern Europe would have profound effects in the Soviet Union itself. Once the details of the Nazi–Soviet Pact were made public there was little to prevent the opening up of the issue of how the non-Russian republics had been forced into the Soviet Union: the so-called 'national question'.

Perestroika: the national question and the unravelling of the Soviet Union

The first warning signs that *perestroika, glasnost* and the liberation of the East and Central states would have a profound impact on the USSR came from Kazakhstan, but it was in Eastern Europe and specifically in the Baltic Republics that Gorbachev was confronted with the most serious challenge to the continued existence of the USSR. Although it might not have seemed to be the case, there was an intimate connection between Gorbachev's treatment of Eastern Europe, *glasnost* on historical issues and the very future of the USSR itself. Robert Conquest has argued that it was evident that a democratic Soviet Union was a contradiction in terms.[21] The Soviet constitution gave the right of secession, however theoretically, to Union republics. The last thing that Gorbachev wanted after the 'loss' of Eastern Europe, as his enemies depicted it, was the 'loss' of any of the Union republics, and during 1989 he mounted a rearguard action to persuade them to stay within the Soviet orbit. In September 1989 a Central Committee plenum meeting disagreed on the issue of the national question: Gorbachev was regarded as not having gone far enough to satisfy the Baltic demands for independence by liberals, but on the other hand was seen as having been too soft on the republics by the hardliners. In April 1990 he introduced a law on secession, providing for the need for a two-thirds proportion of the electorate within a republic to vote for secession, a five-year transition period, and recognition of the legislature of the USSR. In this way he tried to slow the whole process of independence down and buy time for economic and political changes to convince populations in the republics that they wanted to opt in, not opt out.

One of the enduring criticisms of Gorbachev was his inability to deal with the national question. His sternest critics within nationalist circles in Russia were harsh in their condemnation of his inability to deal with the republics and hold the Soviet federation together. In particular he was condemned for his lack of 'force'. In part these criticisms led to the so-called 'turn to the right' by Gorbachev during the period between October 1990 and March 1991. It is necessary to examine why Gorbachev was under such political pressure by 1990 that both he and his reform programme appeared under imminent threat, and why he was forced to step back from the most radical of his economic reforms. We have already noted the rise of the 'nationalities' issue, but he also had to face pressure from other groups in society who were dissatisfied with the nature of the reform process.

One of the many ironies of the period from 1985 to 1989 was that, despite the massive transformation of both Soviet foreign and domestic policies, Gorbachev's popularity was on the wane. There were good reasons for this. What he had attempted was in essence a revolution from above. This was bound to cause disruption and damage to many of the vested interests which had dominated Soviet life. T. H. Rigby has argued that, on the whole, revolutions 'from above' are accompanied by an intensification of state control and a centralisation of power. The Gorbachev reform programme, however, was one which depended on a loosening of control, an amelioration of the command economy and the creation of a political system based on voluntarism.[22] This notion of voluntarism was a central issue by 1988–9, as the economic reforms initiated by Gorbachev were almost universally perceived in a negative light. The move towards an economy based on market mechanisms and private enterprise came to be seen by radical reformers as half-hearted and by Soviet consumers as still inadequate to meet growing demand. Industrial efficiency also suffered as administrative changes, severe staff cuts and low morale over the changes made in the economy began to hit home. It is no exaggeration to say that by 1989 there was a level of mass dissatisfaction with Gorbachev that boded ill for his political fortunes. A further source of aggravation was the anti-alcohol campaign, a prohibition which was not only unpopular but which caused a sharp fall in state revenue from sales of liquor.

Dissatisfaction at the lower levels of society was mirrored by a level of dissatisfaction within the major elite groupings in the USSR, with the notable exception of the creative and professional intelligentsia. The most obvious example of this was within the party apparatus. *Glasnost* had cost Communist Party officials the right to constantly direct and supervise all public activities. The power of the Party was further confounded in 1988 when Gorbachev drastically cut the Party apparatus, particularly at the higher levels, and refused it the right to issue directives to economic agencies. This change was essential if market mechanisms were ever to take hold, but it had the effect of undercutting the Party's political authority. The introduction of a degree of pluralism into political elections also meant that Party officials under Gorbachev's reforms had to face the prospect of democratic elections and run the risk of not being selected by voters. Many Party officials were angry at the decline in their authority. By July 1989 the practical implications of the erosion of Party power and the power of *glasnost* was apparent when a large miners' strike took place in Siberia and Donbass. In the old days of the Brezhnev regime, this type of strike would immediately have been broken with a series of repressive actions, an information blackout and some (unpublished) concessions. Such action was no longer possible; the miners were able to organise, protest and gain publicity, representing to conservatives all that was threatening in Gorbachev's reform programmes.

It appears that Gorbachev himself did not recognise the gravity of the crisis until the miners' strike in mid 1989. A reform commission was hurriedly set up, led by a liberal economist, Leonid Abalkin, who informed Gorbachev that there was no option but to move fully towards a market economy. By October 1989 the commission announced that the introduction of a full market economy would occur over a six-year period. This might have seemed rather slow, but the rest of the report was radical in its recommendation of the introduction of stock exchanges and the creation of commercial companies. These latter notions were too radical for many of the more conservative-minded in the leadership. Under the Prime Minister, Nickolai Ryzhkov, the conservatives worked out a rather different programme, postponing any major economic changes for the next few years. Gorbachev himself did not fully agree with either programme. It appeared that he was trying to keep all his options open, but he gave the appearance of vacillation and a leadership in drift. By March 1990 he received yet another document from Abalkin, urging him not to delay in economic reform. Another special commission was set up to find a new way forward. When the commission finally presented its findings, it recommended a massive jump of some 50 per cent in retail prices, news which led to near-panic amongst shoppers. Although the price rise did not go through, this débâcle led to robust criticism of the reformers at the 28th Party Congress. In the meantime the more radical-minded of the economic reformers had gathered around the figure of Boris Yeltsin. The radicals proposed so-called 'shock therapy' for the USSR, with an economic programme that was to be rammed home in 400 days.

Neither economic programme appeared likely to work, and by the summer both Gorbachev and Yeltsin had agreed to work together on economic plans. By 1 September, they had produced a massive document outlining a programme of reform for the entire Soviet economy. Yet once again, just as the programme was to be submitted, Gorbachev drew back and allowed the conservatives to think up an alternative. Leading reformers resigned, and popular discontent mounted further. In particular, at this point we see a fusion of popular discontent over the state of the economy as well as increasing attacks on Gorbachev and Shevardnadze for the foreign-policy agenda that had allowed Germany to be reunited. The position of Gorbachev himself appeared precarious, so much so that on 7 November 1990, at anniversary celebrations to mark the Revolution, two shots were fired at him. If this was the face of public protest against the Soviet leader, there were also groups within the elite working against him.

On 20 December the Foreign Minister, Eduard Shevardnadze, resigned. In a sensational and public attack on Gorbachev, he argued that no-one, including Gorbachev, had come to his aid when he had been attacked by the conservatives for 'betraying Soviet interests abroad', and alleged that a dictatorship was pending within the Soviet elite. It was not clear if he meant that Gorbachev himself was moving back to the 'right' or whether he believed that the Soviet leader would be ousted and replaced by a figure who would steer the USSR back to a dictatorship, reversing the reform process. Gorbachev himself, although furious with this attack, still vacillated over the future. In the meantime the USSR itself fell apart. The demand for freedom continued in the Baltic states, while in Moscow 100,000 people turned out in Red Square to demand that Gorbachev resign his post as leader of the USSR. In scenes which bizarrely echoed the Revolution of 1917, the people of Leningrad set about organising themselves to defend their newly acquired democracy. Yeltsin emerged as the clear rival to Gorbachev's position. He backed the demands of the Balts, and in March he challenged Gorbachev by running for the position of Russian President. In June he was duly elected with 57 per cent of the vote. The Gorbachev candidate, Vadim Bakatin, who represented the Gorbachev party of Democratic Socialism, garnered a miserable 3.5 per cent of the vote. In the first truly representative elections since 1917, Yeltsin's vision of the future was endorsed. His job description as President of Russia matched that of the Soviet leader.[23]

The August coup

It has been argued that, by the summer of 1991, Gorbachev had moved back towards the left as a result of the challenge to his authority. Specifically, he made an attempt to reformulate relations between Russia and the other non-Russian republics of the USSR through a new union treaty involving a number of concessions towards them. Most notably, this stipulated that membership of any future union with Russia had to be voluntary. 'Nine plus one', as it came to be known, aroused anger in the conservative camp, which alleged that the draft violated the Soviet constitution. Critics argued that the Soviet President had sanctioned the very break-up of the Soviet Union itself, and argued that the Union Treaty should not and could not be signed. Conservatives were also alarmed when shortly after Yeltsin had been sworn in as Russian President on 10 July 1991 he issued a decree prohibiting all activities of the Communist Party. The Party was finished.

Yet, ironies of ironies, the conservatives still could not make up their minds if Gorbachev might yet turn out to be on their side and whether he could be recruited back into their camp as an ally against Yeltsin. Part of those who formed the conservative clique decided to take action to 'save' the USSR and perhaps Gorbachev. The leading conspirators were key members of the Soviet establishment and, in some cases, his old friends. They included

Valentin Pavlov, the Prime Minister, Dimitrii Yazov, the Minister of Defence, Kriuchkov, the Minister of State Security, Genadii Yanaev, the Vice-President and Boris Pugo, the Interior Minister; and they appear to have plotted to 'persuade' Gorbachev to renege on the Union Treaty and reverse the move towards the market.

The Union Treaty was due to be signed on 20 August. On the morning of the 19 August tanks rolled into central Moscow. The media announced a state of emergency and the formation of a State Emergency Committee. Conveniently for the plotters, the Soviet President was on holiday in the Crimea (thus almost providing a neat historical parallel with the ousting of Khrushchev, who had also been in the Crimea when he was actually removed from power). Gorbachev, however, refused to take part in the coup, or counter-coup. It remained unclear what the plotters intended: the KGB placed Gorbachev and his family under house arrest pending developments in Moscow. It was Yeltsin who proved to be the hero of the day, mobilising opposition to the coup and calling for a general strike. Military units refused to storm the Russian White House, and the plot quickly ran out of steam. The major consequence, however, was that the position of Gorbachev as President of the Soviet Union had been fatally undermined.

Postscript: the Russia question, Yeltsin and the forces of Russian nationalism

In 1991 the Soviet Union ceased to exist. On 20 November 1991 the Supreme Soviet of the USSR failed to get enough votes to pass the state budget, and the USSR faced bankruptcy. Russia offered to take over the responsibility for budgets and the payments of Soviet officials. On 1 December a further blow was dealt to the Soviet state when Ukraine declared its independence. Without Ukraine, there was no Soviet Union left. On 25 December Gorbachev handed over the control keys of the Soviet arsenal to Yeltsin. The man who had started the reform process was an isolated and deeply unpopular figure, while Russia itself was left with borders that resembled those of Tsarist Russia.

Since 1991 and its transformation from the heart of the USSR to the capital of Russia, Moscow has seen a set of circumstances emerge to challenge its position as a serious power on the European continent. The political and economic systems within Russia itself are still undergoing massive changes, and there is still little indication that the move towards a democratic, market-driven system will be successful. The new political elites within Russia are beset with factionalism over the pace and direction of reform. In foreign policy, this domestic turmoil has resulted in an often-contested agenda, with liberals and nationalists arguing over what degree of co-operation should be sought with the West. The last few years have seen a complete collapse of the Soviet position in East and Central Europe and a concomitant decline in Moscow's influence. The inability of the Kremlin to prohibit the expansion of NATO into the heart of Europe has revealed the extent of Moscow's impotence, and has raised the question of where Russia's geographic borders begin and end.

Gorbachev's successor Boris Yeltsin's response to the break-up of the USSR appeared at first to be a pragmatic acceptance of a new and reduced role for Russia. In 1991 and 1992 he placed emphasis on articulating a vision of what constituted the national interest of Russia. Among the foreign policy elite a vigorous debate took place which had something in common with the nineteenth-century debate between the 'Slavophiles' and the 'Westerners'. Initially, a pro-Western stance was adopted, in the manner established by Gorbachev. Indeed, Yeltsin appeared to believe that the maintenance of good relations with the West would bring Moscow economic benefits. Contacts with Western leaders was an evident priority within the Kremlin, and during 1991–2 the new Russian leader visited Germany, France, the UK, Italy, the United States and Canada; in other words, all the G-7 states apart from Japan. Some of the Russian elite, such as Yigor Gaudier, argued that an alignment with the advanced industrial nations could help Russia prosper both economically and politically. Of the pro-Westerners, Andrei Kozyrev, the Foreign Minister, was the most notable. He had been a consistent supporter of Gorbachev and initially, under Yeltsin, he was given wide-ranging powers in foreign policy. In early 1992 Kozyrev asked the European Community to assist Russia in becoming a 'normal' state, while the June 1992 summit between Russia and the United States was notable for its promises of greater collaboration. Kozyrev argued that at least part of the problems that had dogged the 'Soviet Union' had sprung from the fact that it had been on the 'wrong' side of the Cold War.

A series of measures were taken by Yeltsin to reassure the West of Russia's good intentions. Moscow agreed to abide by the START Treaty, signed in July 1991; whilst in January 1992 Yeltsin announced that Russian nuclear weapons would no longer target Western cities. In May 1992 Russia endorsed the position of the United Nations when, in a bid to resolve the ethnic conflict that had broken out in former Yugoslavia, it imposed economic sanctions. In January 1993 Yeltsin and President Clinton signed the START 2 Treaty in the Kremlin. Yet in 1992 this 'honeymoon' in Russian–Western relations was already under a cloud. Not least, it was threatened because of the internal opposition which was gathering against both Yeltsin and Kozyrev. Their pro-Western stance was openly questioned by so-called 'Eurasianists', such as Sergi Stankevich, who argued that the 'near abroad' (Russians living in the former Soviet republics) should be the central preoccupation of the Kremlin, and that foreign policy in the post-Soviet era should focus on the problems with immediate neighbours, such as Ukraine.

There was also an institutional problem. The changes of 1990–1 had made it unclear as to where foreign policy should be actually made. Did the power to make policy reside with the Foreign Ministry, the Ministry of Defence or Parliament? Foreign policy became immersed in the struggle between Yeltsin and his parliamentary opponents, who claimed that his pro-Western stance was affecting Russia's economic interests. In particular, Yeltsin came under attack in late 1992 for the forging of links with Western international organisations such as the International Monetary Fund (IMF). Opponents claimed that he was allowing the IMF to treat Russia as a Third World state. Furthermore, when some policies advocated by international organisations such as the deregulation of prices in January 1992 appeared to cause an immediate worsening of the economic situation, this damaged the position of liberals such as Kozyrev. Nationalism grew as economic hardship continued.

This was not really surprising. At other key points in Russian history, the pragmatic need for advanced technologies and collaboration with the West has always been recognised, while the fact that increased collaboration with the West can lead to increased external influence has been resented and has often dampened enthusiasm for these contacts. In late 1993 a reaction against the pro-Western policy was most clearly manifested in the relative success of Vladimir Zhirinovsky's Liberal Democratic Party in the elections. His neo-Fascist party did not win enough votes to form the largest bloc in Parliament, but it represented the growth of nationalism within Russia and perhaps a reversion to a neo-imperialist foreign policy.

For scholars of history it appears that Russia has reverted to a position similar in some respects to that of 1917. There are question marks over how the state will move forward both politically and economically, and a debate is in progress over where Russia's foreign policy interests lie. Should Russia turn inwards, or should it attempt some form of integration with the West? There are also questions, however, over whether Russia itself can survive the challenges from its various non-Russian regions. What had begun as an agenda under Gorbachev to reinvigorate the USSR has ended with a question mark over the continued existence of Russia itself.

Notes

1 Archie Brown, *The Gorbachev Factor* (Oxford: Oxford University Press, 1996).
2 Archie Brown, *The Gorbachev Factor*.
3 For the first speech by Gorbachev as leader, see *Report of the Plenary Session of the CPSU Central Committee* (11 March 1985). Reported in *Pravda*, 12 March 1985. See also Archie Brown, *The Gorbachev Factor*, p. 1.
4 John Gooding, *Rulers and Subjects: Government and People in Russia 1801–1996* (London: Edward Arnold, 1996).
5 *Pravda*, 2 July 1985.

6 See Allen Lynch, *The Soviet Study of International Relations* (Cambridge: Cambridge University Press, 1987).

7 *Pravda*, 26 March 1986.

8 Steven Kull, *Burying Lenin: The Revolution in Soviet Ideology and Foreign Policy* (Boulder, Colo.: Westview, 1992), p. 18.

9 On this issue see Brown, *The Gorbachev Factor*, p. 230–1.

10 *Pravda*, 26 November 1987.

11 Murmansk speech, *Izvestiya*, 2 October 1987.

12 *Pravda*, 14 October 1987; *Pravda*, 25 November 1987. See also *Moscow News*, 13 December 1987.

13 *Pravda*, 24 October 1987.

14 *Pravda*, 26 November 1987.

15 *Pravda*, 8 December 1988.

16 Mike McGwire, *Perestroika and Soviet National Security* (Washington, DC; Brookings Institute, 1991), p. 324.

17 McGwire, *Perestroika*.

18 Kull, *Burying Lenin*, p. 88.

19 Kull, *Burying Lenin*, p. 89.

20 Stephen F. Cohen, *Rethinking the Soviet Experience: Politics and History since 1917* (Oxford: Oxford University Press, 1986), p. 150.

21 Cited in Brown, *The Gorbachev Factor*, p. 252.

22 T. H. Rigby, *The Changing Soviet System: Mono-Organisational Socialism from its Origins to Gorbachev's Restructuring* (Aldershot: Edward Elgar, 1990).

23 For an authoritative account of the twists and turns in Gorbachev's political furtunes in the period 1989–1991, see John Keep, *Last of the Empires: A History of the Soviet Union* (Oxford: Oxford University Press, 1996).

Conclusions
Russia and the World in the
Twentieth Century

As Eric Hobsbawm has suggested, for most of the twentieth century Russia's relations with the world were seen through the lens of the Soviet experiment. Yet what had begun in 1917 as a bid to change the world ended in the failure of the Soviet Union, the Russian Empire which it had inherited and expanded, and the Communist Party which had ruled both. Russia, however, failed to imprint itself as it had hoped on the world, and ended not even with a nuclear bang – as so many had feared – but with a nationalist whimper. From start to finish, however, the story of the Russian/Soviet state and the outside world was and remains a fascinating and complex one, with many lessons still to teach us.

Although the call of the Bolsheviks in 1917 was to 'smash' the old world and build a new one,[1] in foreign policy terms the Soviet state did not start 'fresh' in 1917. It had inherited many of its characteristics from the Tsarist Russian Empire: the tradition of autocracy, a suspicion of the West, and the tendency of the elite to view Russia's 'natural' role as one of territorial expansion. It is, of course, obvious that although the Tsar was overthrown in 1917 the geographic position of Russia remained the same: a gigantic country, that not only straddled the heart of the European continent, but which also led to the shores of the Pacific and sought power in the East. In terms made popular by the geopoliticians of the early twentieth century, Russia seemed poised to inhabit the 'world island', the Eurasian landmass, whose dominance meant world domination. However, the location of the country also made it vulnerable. As Ken Booth has written, the history of Russia has read like the 'who's who of invasion'.[2] Although initially the Bolsheviks took little notice of the need for secure borders, this very quickly became as much a priority for them as it had been for their predecessors. Indeed, throughout the decades of the 1920s and 1930s the new leadership in Moscow had as its primary mission the search for 'secure borders'. It could be argued that insecurity because of 'geographic' position was a defining characteristic of both Russia and the Soviet Union. These feelings of vulnerability were compounded by the hostile relations which developed between Moscow and other states. Throughout the nineteenth century Russia had been perceived both as a necessary counter-weight and a threat to the European balance of power. Western perceptions of threat from Russia were reinforced in 1917, when the Bolsheviks under Lenin made clear their opposition to the continuation of a capitalist European state system and vowed to take the Revolution beyond Soviet borders. In terms of a framework of ideas that informed Bolshevik thinking, Marxism–Leninism mandated the destruction of the old system. Bolshevik hopes of radical transformation outside of Russia were disappointed as Marxism–Leninism failed to take a grip either in Western capitals or among Western populations. This failure did not mitigate suspicion. The very attempt by the Bolsheviks to transform the state system created a legacy of mistrust and distance between Russia and the outside world. In this sense, 'ideology' was and remained important throughout the entire Soviet period. The very creation of the Soviet state along Marxist–Leninist lines was a challenge to other states outside it, not least because the USSR created an alternative model. In addition, the continued and prolonged attempts by Moscow to orchestrate some form of international Communist movement engendered mistrust among Western politicians. In some respects the period after the First World War witnessed the birth of competing models for global politics. In the years 1917–19 the American President, Woodrow Wilson, and Lenin, the new leader of Russia, enunciated very different views of the world, one was based on liberalism and the other based on Marxism and authoritarianism.[3] The continued struggle of these ideas and systems was a defining one for Russia, particularly after 1945 when, with the fragmentation of the old imperial powers in Europe, a bipolar world emerged.

Perhaps, though, the greatest paradox in this tale about the Soviet experience and the outside world was that the propagation of a radical new economic and political global system was based on a remarkably fragile political and economic system at home. There was never a robust economic and political system within the USSR to ensure the survival of Communism at home, let alone its success abroad. We have seen throughout the early parts of this book how the Bolsheviks had to impose militarily their 'vision' of society onto parts of Russia that were unwilling to share the dream. The very existence of the civil war showed that the Soviet regime was at the very least a contested one right from its inception. The use of the military instrument throughout the decade after the Revolution to subdue areas contiguous to Russia such as Ukraine and Belorussia points to an enterprise based not on voluntarism but on force.

This 'forced' incorporation of minority peoples into the Soviet Union provided the regime with problems from the beginning. Even though Stalin might have claimed that the nationalities issue had been resolved, this was far from the case. Resistance in certain regions during the late 1920s and 1930s to the process of collectivisation was testament to the dislike of the dictate of the centre. Indeed, the support by ethnic peoples such as the Ukrainians for the foreign invading force of Germans in 1941 was evidence of this 'structural' weakness. Although Stalin ultimately proved successful in forging a 'consensus' over the survival of the Soviet state during the war years, this did not occur without the enforced movement of 'suspect' peoples, such as the Chechens, away from their homelands. This regime was not, therefore, one based on consensus. It was an unwilling one.

What do I mean by this? Simply that, as the book has continually demonstrated, leaders in the Kremlin were constantly and rightly worried by the periodic rebellions which took place against Soviet rule. There was a sense that the rule of the centre was always fragile and support for it was grudging. Relations with external powers were affected by the concern over how secure the rule of the centre actually was: any prospect of external intervention within the USSR itself might ignite rebellion or disaffection.

The protection of the principle of non-intervention therefore became a cardinal principle in Soviet affairs. This 'defensiveness' characterised not only the inter-war period but also the post-1945 period. As tensions associated with the period of Cold War escalated, successive American Presidents sought to 'exploit' internal weaknesses within the USSR, in a bid to manipulate the Kremlin's foreign policy agenda. Most noticeable of these was the creation of the Marshall Plan in 1947 and the strategy of linkage pursued by President Nixon and Secretary of State Kissinger during the early and middle years of the 1970s. An attempt was made in Washington to 'link' the provision of economic and technological benefits to Moscow with the Kremlin's treatment of dissidents and ethnic minorities, most notably the Jewish community. The lack of 'voluntarism' within the Soviet system made it vulnerable to such an approach, although Moscow remained determined up until 1985 to rebuff any such attempt. Yet the leaders in the Kremlin needed Western technological expertise to develop the Soviet Union's own industrial base. Post-Revolution backwardness mandated a *rapprochement* with Germany in the 1920s and a massive domestic effort to reorganise industrial and agricultural resources. In the post-1945 period the sheer economic and technological strength of the United States provided a constant problem for the Soviet leadership of how to compete not just in the military and nuclear spheres but also in the provision of goods for its own peoples. The military and nuclear dimension of the Cold War years mandated a massive input of resources into the military-industrial complex. Yet, at the same time, but most markedly after the death of Stalin in 1953, Soviet leaders remained increasingly vulnerable to the complaint that they were failing to deliver 'the goods' for consumers.

The rejection of the use of terror to maintain order had been at least in part adopted by the Khrushchev leadership through the process of destalinisation.

This demonstrated an acute awareness amongst the leadership of the need for a 'compact' of some sort with the people. How to manage the external competition with the West, receive technological aid and provide for economic stability at home was a perennial problem. Reform of the political and economic system was sporadically attempted in the post-1945 period, most notably under Khrushchev, but it always struggled with the tradition of autocracy. Moshe Lewin has argued that Soviet history can be understood as 'a two-act play, replayed several times with different sets and casts'.[4] These two acts, he argues, represent the different Soviet experiences: of autocracy and intolerance, and of pluralism and a degree of idealism. The former ideas, rather than the latter, dominated most of the period between 1917 and 1985. Only really right at the beginning of the Soviet experience had there been any indication that a liberal outlook might triumph. This interlude, though, did provide reformers, in the post-Stalin period, with the notion that the original ideas of the Revolution were worth reinventing under the guise of 'proper socialism'. Reform attempts, however, always provoked the possibility of loss of control and stability.

This problem of stability was most vividly expressed in the relationship with the East European states which had been subdued at the end of the Second World War. The nature of the forced imposition of Communist governments in various guises meant that the Kremlin always faced the possibility of rebellion. As we have seen, this was vividly illustrated in East Germany in 1953, in Hungary in 1956, in Czechoslovakia in 1968 and in Poland in 1980. It is now clear that a great deal of effort was expended by the Kremlin on how to best manage relations within the bloc. In addition to the problem of potential rebellion at home, the leadership had a similar challenge on the periphery of the USSR. Rebellion in East or Central Europe rendered the Soviet leadership vulnerable. We now know,[5] as Chapter 6 demonstrated, that much of Brezhnev's thinking over the crisis in Prague during 1968 was governed by the fear that 'rebellion' there might 'spill over' into the USSR itself. The Soviet response to such fears was almost invariably the use of the military instrument. This says much about the nature of Soviet thinking about the military, but also a great deal about the nature of the alliance system in the East. The creation of the WTO in 1955 was, in theory, meant to mirror the establishment of NATO in the West. While it was in reality no such thing, the WTO became seen by the Kremlin as the most reliable instrument for the control of the East.

Although it was perceived in the West as an instrument for use against the NATO countries, ironically but not surprisingly the only use it was actually put to was within the Eastern alliance. As it turned out, despite Western rearmament Moscow's military forces for most of the Cold War period were more about internal suppression than about external aggression. This necessity of a strong military for the regime was emphasised in the post-war years, and led to the elevation of the military leadership in the bureaucratic politics of policy-making within the Kremlin. The dominance of the military in foreign-policy making reached its apogee in the late 1970s with the influence of Marshal Ustinov and the backing of military leaders for the decision to intervene militarily in Afghanistan in 1979.

It is quite interesting, however, that although the sheer size of the Soviet military and its nuclear capacity led to the idea that the Soviet Union was a superpower, it was only ever a one-dimensional great power. Despite the bellicosity of the Khrushchev years, Soviet strength was an illusion, albeit one that was carefully cultivated by the Kremlin. The Soviet Union never developed the economic basis nor the political system needed to compete effectively. What conclusions can be drawn from this?

The Cold War was not a competition of equals: rather, it was an unequal struggle between one strong regime, the United States, and one fragile regime, the Soviet Union. Materially, geopolitically and ideologically the United States was the strongest state in the world for much of the twentieth century. Though resource-rich, the USSR was materially, politically and militarily inferior throughout the period. In all of this, as indicated earlier, there remains the problem of ideology, perhaps the most difficult aspect of the Soviet experience to assess.[6] Some international relations' textbooks argue that ideology had little part to play in the Cold War or, indeed, in the formulation of Soviet foreign policy. While it is true that, after 1922, the Soviet leadership seemed happily to abandon the notion of the export of global revolution in favour of defence, it was not quite that simple. Marxism–Leninism justified the very existence of the Soviet state. Without it there could be no reason for the state's existence, and certainly no reason why the Party and the leadership should continue to wield the absolute power that they did. Part of what legitimised the Soviet state and its conduct abroad was the propagation of another way in politics and society and economics. If the Soviet model failed to compete with capitalism either at home or abroad, the leadership itself was doomed. While this was masked in the period of Stalinism, it became increasingly apparent in the post-1945 period.

In addition to this ideological competition with capitalism, though, the Soviet global role was further complicated by the emergence of alternative centres of Communism or socialism after 1949. This was most obvious in the relationship with China, but also, to a lesser extent, in the conduct of foreign affairs between Moscow and the leaderships of Yugoslavia and Cuba. Tito was at least in part responsible for the hard line adopted by the Cominform after 1947, while Fidel Castro appears to have been active in drawing the Kremlin into a more active engagement in the Third World. While Mao's victory in China was initially welcomed by the Soviet leadership as a welcome addition to the global camp of socialism, the new Communist leader in Beijing quickly proved to be a rather problematic partner.

The Soviet leadership, despite both Khrushchev's and Brezhnev's 'adventurism' in certain regions of the Third World, remained inherently cautious in its dealings with the United States. Throughout the 1950s and 1960s Mao's foreign-policy agenda threatened to lead the Communist camp into a series of military confrontations with Washington. This engendered much ambivalence within the Kremlin. On the one hand, Moscow could not be seen to be following rather than leading Beijing in confronting capitalism; but on the other, confrontation with the United States might reveal that the Soviet Union actually had rather few 'nuclear clothes'. Only when the Soviet leadership did achieve strategic nuclear parity by around 1970 was the Soviet leadership willing to follow a policy of wholesale expansion into the Third World; and even then it was careful on the whole to use proxy forces rather than be seen to be intervening directly. Indeed, by this stage much of Soviet activity in the Third World was an attempt to mitigate not only the growth of American power, but that of Moscow's erstwhile ally, China. In all of this, apart from the fact that the Communist world was very far from monolithic, one of the most intriguing questions is: why did a Soviet leadership acutely aware of its own internal fragility operate such a strategy?

There are several explanations. Obviously, expansionism into the Third World could bring benefits: resources, military bases, enhanced prestige (perhaps) and the chance to export the Soviet model of development. It also carried risks. The most obvious was that Soviet behaviour could offend the United States and destroy any hope of obtaining a viable trading relationship. The second was that any such expansion would prove expensive and a drain on resources, and the third was that the leadership might fail to successfully impose its economic and political model and as a consequence suffer a degree of humiliation. By the early 1980s, as the book has demonstrated, all three risks had materialised.

What is apparent in the story of 'Russia and the World' is that despite its inherent caution, the leadership was prepared to take certain risks in pursuit of an agenda of expansion. Those in the Kremlin, very much like those men who had been in power in Moscow before them, saw Russia as having a natural role to play certainly in Eastern Europe but also in the Middle East. Part of this at least did arise from the securing of the approaches to both Russia and the USSR, and it was also about denying potential opponents opportunities to obtain footholds on the periphery. In this respect very little had changed between the times of Imperial Russia and the Soviet state. However, what was more important was that those in the Kremlin did have a Great-Power mentality, believing that the Soviet Union had a global role to fulfil and global interests to protect. Moscow could not allow the United States, or indeed China, to take advantage of it.

Throughout the period there is the problem of who formulated Soviet foreign policy. As noted above, because of the legacy of autocracy the making of foreign policy was always the preserve of the few within the walls of the Kremlin, who were engaged in a perennial contest for individual power. This raised throughout the Soviet period the question of *kto-kogo* (who is prevailing over whom),[7] and it was the question that preoccupied Sovietologists throughout most of the post-war period. We now know that intense struggles between key individuals over the making and course of foreign policy took place. In some cases this was the result of genuine differences over policy direction, as in the 1930s, for example, between Litvinov and Molotov over policy towards Nazi Germany. But policy divisions also came about within the ruling circle as a result of bureaucratic politics. Quite often, for example, representatives of the military would press for the use of the military instrument in a bid to enhance their bureaucratic position, reputation or budget. Equally, individuals used the arena of foreign policy to build positions of support. For example, Stalin's desire to enhance his own political power shaped Soviet foreign policy towards China during the middle years of the 1920s, as he and Trotsky took up opposite positions on how much support should be extended to the revolutionary forces in China. Equally, Yuri Andropov's advocacy of a military invasion of Afghanistan in 1979 was at least inspired by his belief that, as Brezhnev ailed, a dynamic action would strengthen his position in the leadership contest. Apart from a period in which Stalin did maintain supreme control of policy-making, individuals had on the whole to build a consensus within the leadership over foreign policy activities.

What, however, does emerge from any story of foreign policy is the importance of individual leaders and their ability to 'lead'. As Robert Service has written; 'Lenin, Stalin, Khrushchev and Gorbachev have gripped the world's imagination. Even losers in the struggles of Soviet politics, such as Trotsky and Bukharin, have acquired an enduring reputation.'[8] Partly this derived from the emphasis in Russian history on the role of a strong leader. Stalin was the most notable example of this, but each period of history was associated with a leader with particular qualities and agendas. Yet Soviet foreign policy was not just about a collection of notables developing policy in the splendid isolation of the Kremlin. We have seen that it was quite often the case that the leadership was reactive to a series of problems both internal and external against the backdrop of economic weakness and the problem of how best to rule.

Although the Soviet Union is defunct, certain themes and ideas can be teased out from a study of Russia's recent past. One is that, given the tradition of autocracy and leadership, it will not prove and has not proved easy to plant democracy on Russian soil. It will remain the case that the making of foreign policy will be the preserve of a political elite (albeit one that now has a Parliament to answer to) who will, when expediency demands, use foreign policy issues to enhance internal positions and build coalitions. In this respect the old study of 'Sovietology' will have to be replaced by 'Russianology' to answer the question of 'who is prevailing over whom'.

Because the Soviet Union is now defunct, Marxism–Leninism is dead and buried, and it would appear that the issue of ideology need no longer concern those who study contemporary Russian foreign policy. Yet there is an ongoing tussle over the ideas that should and will inform foreign-policy behaviour. In this struggle, nationalist sentiment or what might be termed Greater Russian nationalism appears to be the predominant characteristic. The more ambitious and militaristic elements of such nationalism compete with ideas espoused by men such the former Foreign Minister Andrei Kozyrev, who seek to substitute a more liberal and pro-Western approach. In the debates over the Russian role in post-Cold-War Yugoslavia, both traits were patently obvious and, indeed, remain so.

Whether Russia can move towards democracy remains the key question in political terms. If it does not do so, then in foreign-policy terms the future is problematic for those states who share borders with it. This is important, as although Russia is no longer a global power it is a European one. It is here, perhaps, that at the end of the twentieth century we can witness developments that take us back to 1917. Russia has now reverted in geographic terms to its position at the time of the Revolution. The 'temporary' expansion of its borders into East and Central Europe is no more, and its foray into the Third World is a bitter and expensive historical lesson. Yet it is worth remembering that the borders of Russia have never been fixed for more than 50 years,[9] and that some leaders in Moscow dispute the retreat from certain parts of Europe, most notably from the Baltic area. The expansion of the NATO alliance to include member states from East and Central Europe is a sensitive and controversial issue with Russia. The extension of what are essentially Western institutions into the East means that Russia is once more on the defensive and on the edge of Europe. It has returned to its past.

Notes

1 Paul Dukes, *A History of Russia c. 882–1996* (3rd edn, London: Macmillan, 1998), p. 208.
2 Ken Booth, 'Soviet Defence Policy', in J. Baylis, K. Booth, J. Garnett and P. Williams, *Contemporary Strategy, Theories and Policies* (Beckenham, Kent: Croom Helm, 1975).
3 See, on this point, Vendulka Kubalkova and Albert Cruikshank, *Marxism and International Relations* (Oxford: Oxford University Press, 1989).
4 Moshe Lewin, *Political Under Currents in Soviet Economic Debates: From Bukharin to the Modern Reformers* (London: Pluto, 1975), quoted in John Gooding, *Rulers and Subjects: Government and People in Russia, 1801–1991* (London: Edward Arnold, 1996).

5   This phrase is from John Lewis Gaddis, *We Now Know: Rethinking Cold War History* (Oxford: Oxford University Press, 1997).

6   Vernon V. Aspaturian, *Process and Power in Soviet Foreign Policy* (Boston: Little, Brown, 1971).

7   Joseph L. Nogee and Robert H. Donaldson, *Soviet Foreign Policy Since World War II* (Oxford: Pergamon Press, 1984), p. 42.

8   Robert Service, *A History of Twentieth-Century Russia* (London: Allen Lane, 1997), p. xxvii.

9   Paul Dukes, *A History of Russia c. 882–1996.*

Select Bibliography

Abel, Elie, *The Missile Crisis* (New York: Bantam, 1966).

Adomeit, Hannes, *Soviet Risk-Taking and Crisis Behaviour: A Theoretical and Empirical Analysis* (London: Allen & Unwin, 1982).

Ascherson, Neal, *The Polish August* (Harmonsworth: Penguin Books, 1981).

Aspaturian, Vernon V., *Process and Power in Soviet Foreign Policy* (Boston: Little, Brown, 1971).

Barghoorn, Frederick C., *Détente and the Democratic Movement in the USSR* (New York: Free Press, 1976).

Bennigsen, Alexandre, Henze, Paul B., Tanham, George K. and Wimbush, S. Enders, *Soviet Strategy and Islam* (New York: St Martin's Press, 1989).

Beschloss, Michael R. and Talbott, Strobe, *At the Highest Levels: The Inside Story of the End of the Cold War* (Boston: Little, Brown, 1993).

Bialer, Seweryn (ed.), *The Domestic Context of Soviet Foreign Policy* (Boulder, Colo.: Westview, 1980).

Borisov, O. B., and Koloskov, B. T., *Soviet–Chinese Relations, 1945–1970*, ed. Vladimir Petrov (Bloomington, Ind.: Indiana University Press, 1975).

Brown, Archie, *The Gorbachev Factor* (Oxford: Oxford University Press, 1996).

Brzezinski, Zbigniew K., *The Soviet Bloc, Unity and Conflict* (Cambridge, Mass.: Harvard University Press, 1971).

Brezhnev, L. I., *Selected Speeches and Writings of Foreign Affairs* (New York: Pergamon Press, 1979).

Bruce, Franklin (ed.), *The Essential Stalin: Major Theoretical Writings, 1905–52* (Garden City, NY: Anchor Books, 1972).

Bullock, Alan, *Hitler and Stalin: Parallel Lives* (London: HarperCollins, 1991).

Bezymensky, L., 'The Secret Protocols of 1939 as a Problem of Soviet Historiography', in G. Gorodetsky (ed.), *Soviet Foreign Policy, 1917–1991* (London: Frank Cass, 1994).

Carew Hunt, R. N., *The Theory and Practice of Communism: An Introduction* (New York: Macmillan, 1957).

Carr, E. H., *A History of Soviet Russia* (London: Penguin, 1950–78).

Churchill, Winston S., *The Second World War*. Vol. 1, *The Gathering Storm*; Vol. 2, *Their Finest Hour*; Vol. 3, *The Grand Alliance*; Vol. 4, *The Hinge of Fate*; Vol. 5, *Closing the Ring*; Vol. 6, *Triumph and Tragedy* (Boston: Houghton Mifflin, 1948–53).

Cohen, Stephen F., *Rethinking the Soviet Experience: Politics and History since 1917* (Oxford: Oxford University Press, 1985).

Cohen, Stephen F., *Bukharin and the Bolshevik Revolution: A Political Biography 1888–1938* (New York: Vintage Books, 1975).

Conquest, Robert, *Stalin: Breaker of Nations* (London: Weidenfeld & Nicolson, 1991).

Craig Nation, R., *Black Earth, Red Star: A History of Soviet Security Policy* (New York: Cornell University Press, 1992).

D'Agnostino, Anthony, *Soviet Succession Struggles: Kremlinology and the Russian Question from Lenin to Gorbachev* (London: Allen & Unwin, 1988).

Dallin, Alexander, *The Soviet Union at the United Nations* (New York: Praeger, 1962).

Dallin, Alexander, 'Soviet Foreign Policy and Domestic Politics: A Framework for Analysis', in *Journal of International Affairs*, 23 (1966).

Dallin, David J., *Soviet Foreign Policy after Stalin* (Philadelphia: Lippincott, 1961).

Deutscher, Isaac, *Stalin: A Political Biography* (New York: Oxford University Press, 1949).

Dinerstein, Herbert S., *War and the Soviet Union, Nuclear Weapons and the Revolution in Soviet Military and Political Thinking* (New York: Frederick A. Praeger, 1959).

Donaldson, Robert H. (ed.), *The Soviet Union in the Third World: Successes and Failures* (Boulder, Colo.: Westview, 1980).

Edmonds, Robin, *Soviet Foreign Policy, 1962–1973: The Paradox of Superpower* (New York: Oxford University Press, 1975).

Fischer, Louis, *The Road to Yalta: Soviet Foreign Relations 1941–1945* (New York: Harper & Row, 1972).

Filtzer, Donald, *The Khrushchev Era: De-Stalinization and the Limits of Reform in the USSR, 1953–1964* (London: Macmillan, 1993).

Freedman, Robert O., *Soviet Policy toward the Middle East Since 1970* (New York: Praeger, 1978).

Fukuyama, Francis, 'The End of History?' in *The National Interest*, 16 (1989).

Gaddis, John Lewis, *We Now Know: Rethinking Cold War History* (Oxford: Clarendon Press, 1997).

Garthoff, Raymond L., *Reflections on the Cuban Missile Crisis* (rev. ed., Washington: Brookings Institute, 1989).

Garthoff, Raymond L., *Détente and Confrontation: Soviet–American Relations from Nixon to Reagan* (Washington: Brookings Institute, 1985).

Gati, Charles (ed.), *The International Politics of Eastern Europe* (New York: Praeger, 1976).

Gelman, Harry, *The Brezhnev Politburo and the Decline of Détente* (New York: Cornell University Press, 1984).

Goldgeier, James M., *Leadership Style and Soviet Foreign Policy* (Baltimore: John Hopkins University Press, 1994).

Gooding, John, *Rulers and Subjects: Government and People in Russia 1801–1991* (London: Edward Arnold, 1996).

Goodman, Elliot R., *The Soviet Design for a World State* (New York: Columbia University Press, 1960).

Gorodetsky, Gabriel (ed.), *Soviet Foreign Policy 1917–1991: A Retrospective* (London: Frank Cass, 1994).

Gorbachev, Mikhail, *Perestroika: New Thinking for Our Country and the World* (New York: Harper & Row, 1987).

Gorbachev, Mikhail, *Memoirs* (New York: Doubleday, 1996).

Gromyko, A. A., and Ponomarev, B. N. (eds), *Soviet Foreign Policy, 1917–1980*. 2 vols. (4th edn, Moscow: Progress Publishers, 1981).

Haslam, Jonathan, *The Soviet Union and the Struggle for Collective Security in Europe 1933–39* (New York: St Martin's Press, 1984).

Hoffman, Erik P., and Fleron, Frederick J. (eds), *The Conduct of Soviet Foreign Policy* (Chicago: Aldine-Atherton, 1980).

Holloway, David, *The Soviet Union and the Arms Race* (New Haven: Yale University Press, 1983).

Holloway, David, *Stalin and the Bomb: The Soviet Union and Atomic Energy 1939–1956* (New Haven: Yale University Press, 1994).

Hosking, Geoffrey, *A History of the Soviet Union* (London: Fontana/Collins, 1985).

Horelick, Arnold L., and Ruch, Myron, *Strategic Power and Soviet Foreign Policy*, (Chicago: University of Chicago Press, 1966).

Hough, Jerry, and Fainsod, Merle, *How the Soviet Union is Governed* (Cambridge, Mass.: Harvard University Press, 1979).

Hough Jerry, *The Struggle for the Third World: Soviet Debates and American Options* (Washington: Brookings Institute, 1986).

Hough, Jerry, 'The Brezhnev Era', in *Problems of Communism,* 25, March-April, 1976.

Jukes, Geoffrey, *The Soviet Union in Asia* (Berkeley, Calif.: University of California Press, 1973).

Kaplan, Stephan S., *The Diplomacy of Power* (Washington Brookings Institute, 1981).

Kennan, George F., *Memoirs* (Boston: Little, Brown, 1967).

Kennan, George F., *Russia and the West Under Lenin and Stalin* (Boston: Little, Brown, 1961).

Kennedy-Pipe, Caroline, *Stalin's Cold War: Soviet Strategies in Europe 1943–1956* (Manchester: Manchester University Press, 1995).

Khrushchev, Nikita, *Khrushchev Remembers*, with an introduction, commentary and notes by Edward Crankshaw, transl. and ed. by Strobe Talbott (Boston: Little, Brown, 1970).

Khrushchev, Nikita, *Khrushchev Remembers: The Last Testament*, transl. and ed. by Strobe Talbott, with a foreword by Edward Crankshaw (Boston: Little, Brown, 1974).

Kissinger, Henry, *White House Years* (Boston: Little, Brown, 1979).

Kissinger, Henry, *Years of Upheaval* (Boston: Little, Brown, 1982).

Knight, Amy, *Beria: Stalin's First Lieutenant* (Princeton, NJ: Princeton, 1993).

Kull, Steven, *Burying Lenin: The Revolution in Soviet Ideology and Foreign Policy* (Boulder, Colo.: Westview, 1992).

Large, J. A., 'The Origins of Soviet Collective Security Policy, 1930–1932', in *Soviet Studies* (April, 1978).

Laquer, Walter A., *Struggle for the Middle East: The Soviet Union and the Middle East 1958–1968* (Baltimore: Penguin, 1972).

Lebedev, Nikolai, *The USSR in World Politics* (Moscow: Progress Publishers, 1980).

Lebow, Richard Ned, and Stein, Janice Gross, *We All Lost the Cold War* (Princeton: Princeton University Press, 1994).

Lenin, V. I., 'Imperialism, the Highest State of Capitalism', in Robert C. Tucker, (ed.), *The Lenin Anthology* (New York: W. W. Norton, 1975).

Levesque, Jacques, *The USSR and the Cuban Revolution: Soviet Ideology and Strategic Perspectives, 1959–1977* (New York: Praeger, 1978).

Lih, Lars H., Naumov, Oleg V. and Khlevniuk, Oleg V. (eds), *Stalin's letters to Molotov, 1925–1936* (New Haven: Yale University Press, 1995).

Loth, Wilfried, *The Division of the World: 1941–1945* (London: Routledge, 1988).

Lynch, Allen, *The Soviet Study of International Relations* (Cambridge: Cambridge University Press, 1987).

Mackintosh, J. M., *Strategy and Tactics of Soviet Foreign Policy* (New York: Oxford University Press, 1963).

Mastny, Vojtech, *Russia's Road to the Cold War: Diplomacy. Warfare and the Politics of Communism, 1941–1945* (New York: Columbia University Press, 1979).

Mastny, Vojtech, *The Cold War and Soviet Insecurity: The Stalin Years* (Oxford: Oxford University Press, 1996).

McCauley, Martin (ed.), *The Soviet Union After Brezhnev* (London: Heinemann, 1983).

McGwire, Michael, *Perestroika and Soviet National Security* (Washington: Brookings Institute, 1991).

Medvedev, Roy A., and Zhores, A., *Khrushchev: The Years in Power* (New York: Columbia University Press, 1976).

Medvedev, Roy A., *All Stalin's Men* (New York: Garden City, 1985).

Mee, Charles L., Jr., *Meeting at Postdam* (New York: Dell, 1975).

Meyer, Alfred G., *Leninism* (Cambridge, Mass.: Harvard University Press, 1957).

Mitchell, R. Judson, *Ideology of a Superpower: Contemporary Soviet Doctrine on International Relations* (Stanford, Calif.: Hoover Institution Press, 1982).

Mosely, Philip E., *The Kremlin and World Politics, Studies in Soviet Policy and Action* (New York: Vintage Books, 1960).

Naimark, Norman N., *The Russians in Germany: A History of the Soviet Zone of Occupation, 1945–1949* (Cambridge, Mass.; Harvard University Press, 1995).

Parrish, Scott, D. and Narinsky, Mikhail M., 'New Evidence on the Soviet Rejection of the Marshall Plan, 1947; Two Reports,' Working Paper no. 9; *Cold War International History Project* (Washington, DC: Woodrow Wilson International Center for Scholars, 1994).

Paterson, Thomas G., *Soviet–American Confrontation: Postwar Reconstruction and the Origins of the Cold War* (Baltimore: Johns Hopkins University Press, 1973).

Raack, R. C., *Stalin's Drive to the West, 1938–1945: The Origins of the Cold War* (Stanford; Stanford University Press, 1995).

Ra'anan, Gabriel, *International Policy Formation in the USSR: Factional Debates during the Zhdanovschina* (Hamden, Conn.: Archon Books, 1983).

Remington, Robin Allison (ed.) *Winter in Prague: Documents on Czechoslovak Communism in Crisis* (Cambridge, Mass.: MIT Press, 1969).

Roberts, Geoffrey, *The Soviet Union and the Origins of the Second World War, Russo–German Relations and the Road to War, 1933–1941* (London; Macmillan, 1995).

Roberts, Geoffrey, 'Moscow and the Marshall Plan: Politics, Ideology and the Onset of the Cold War, 1947', in *Europe-Asia Studies*, 46 (1994).

Rosser, Richard F., *An Introduction to Soviet Foreign Policy* (Englewood Cliffs, NJ: Prentice-Hall, 1969).

Rubenstein, Alvin Z. (ed.), *Soviet and Chinese Influence in the Third World* (New York: Praeger, 1975).

Rubenstein, Alvin Z., *Moscow's Third World Strategy* (Princeton, NJ; Princeton University Press, 1988).

Saikal, Amin, and Maley, William (eds), *The Soviet Withdrawal from Afghanistan* (Cambridge: Cambridge University Press, 1989).

Schwartz, Morton, *Soviet Perceptions of the United States* (Berkeley, California: University of Calif Press, 1978).

Schwartz, Morton, *The Foreign Policy of the U.S.S.R.: Domestic Factors* (Encino, Calif: Dickenson, 1975).

Service, Robert, *A History of Twentieth-Century Russia* (London: Allen Lane, 1997).

Sheinis, Zinovy, *Maxim Litvinov* (Moscow: Progress Publishers, 1990).

Shulman, Marshall D., *Stalin's Foreign Policy Reappraised* (New York: Atheneum, 1965).

Sokolovsky, V. D., *Soviet Military Strategy*, ed. Harriet Fast Scott (New York: Crane Russak, 1975).

Stalin, Joseph, *Economic Problems of Socialism in the U.S.S.R.* (New York: International Publishers, 1952).

Tatu, Michel, *Power in the Kremlin: From Khrushchev to Kosygin* (New York: Viking, 1967).

Taubman, William, *Stalin's American Policy; From Entente to Détente to Cold War* (New York: Norton, 1982).

Taylor, A. J. P., *The Origins of the Second World War* (New York: Atheneum, 1961).

Thompson, William J., *Khrushchev: A Political Life* (New York: St Martin's Press, 1995).

Tucker, Robert C., *The Soviet Political Mind: Stalinism and Post-Stalin Change* (New York: Norton, 1971).

Ulam, Adam B., *Dangerous Relations: The Soviet Union in World Politics, 1970–1982* (Oxford: Oxford University Press, 1983).

Ulam, Adam B., *Expansion and Coexistence: Soviet Foreign Policy 1917–1973* (New York: Praeger, 1974).

Ulam, Adam B., *The Communists: The Story of Power and Lost Illusions, 1948–1991* (New York: Scribners, 1992).

Valenta, Jiri, *Soviet Intervention in Czechoslovakia, 1968* (Baltimore: John Hopkins Press, 1979).

Volkogonov, Dmitri, *Stalin: Triumph and Tragedy*, ed. and trans. by Harold Shukman (New York: Weidenfeld & Nicolson, 1991).

Westad, Odd Arne, 'Concerning the Situtaion in "A" New Russian Evidence on the Soviet Intervention in Afghanistan', in *Cold War International History Project Bulletin* (Washington, DC: Woodrow Wilson International Center for Scholars).

Wolfe, Bertram D., *Marxism: One Hundred Years in the Life of a Doctrine* (New York: Dial Press, 1965).

Wolfe, Thomas W., *Soviet Power and Europe 1945–1970* (Baltimore: John Hopkins University Press, 1970).

Zimmerman, William, *Soviet Perspectives of International Relations 1956–1967* (New York: Columbia University Press, 1969).

Zubok, Vladislav, and Peshakov, Constantine, *Inside the Kremlin's Cold War: From Stalin to Khrushchev* (Cambridge, Mass.: Harvard University Press, 1996).

Index